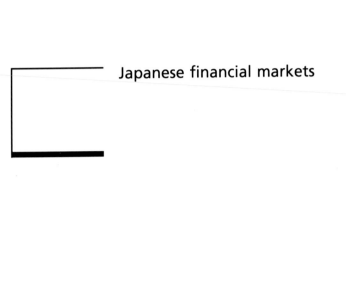

Japanese financial markets

Japanese financial markets

Edited by
Shigenobu Hayakawa

GRESHAM
BOOKS

WOODHEAD
PUBLISHING
LIMITED
IN ASSOCIATION WITH
THE CHARTERED
INSTITUTE OF
BANKERS

Published by Gresham Books, an imprint of Woodhead Publishing Ltd, Abington Hall, Abington, Cambridge CB1 6AH, England

First published 1996

British Library Cataloguing in Publication Data
A catalogue record for this book is available from the British Library.

ISBN 1 85573 178 9

Designed by Andrew Jones (text) and The ColourStudio (jacket).
Typeset by Best-set Typesetter Ltd, Hong Kong.
Printed by St Edmundsbury Press, Suffolk, England.

Contents

Contents

Foreword

Japanese financial markets affect us all. If we are domestic investors, we need to know what Japanese financial flows into the West signify. If we invest there in what currently is a depressed environment, we need to know the market structure and the market outlook. If we are bankers, we need to know about the recycling of the still huge Japanese balance of payments surpluses, about the future of the yen and about the competition (or not) from Japanese banks. Even if we are only interested in local matters, the role of the Japanese in helping cover the UK public sector borrowing requirement has a significant impact on government finances and, indirectly, UK tax levels.

The Japanese economy has been in serious difficulty for several years, as has its financial sector. Yet it is not easy to measure the resilience of the Japanese nation to a number of pressures, particularly *endaka* – the strong yen, the constant trade pressure from Japan's Western partners, the ageing of its population or the intense competition from South East Asia. Even harder to evaluate right now is Japan's over-regulated and over-extended financial sector. That over-regulation and over-extension might have been acceptable in the boom days, but now reveal severe weaknesses, the magnitude of which has yet to be fully disclosed. Compounding the problem, the Japanese financial system is also undergoing a long but steady phase of liberalisation and deregulation. The outcome could well be a more modern, more efficient and more competitive financial sector. The immediate impact of liberalisation, however, could be to weaken further some of its players and worry further the rest of us.

There is not much in-depth analysis in English of the changes taking place in the Japanese financial system. While we can read newspaper articles every day on Japan's current problems of failing credit unions and regional banks, it is not easy to grasp the details of change and the significance for each participant in the financial system.

I tried to write about this myself 20 years ago, as the Japanese financial system entered its early stages of liberalisation. I was more bullish then than now. In 1987 a major work by Yoshio Suzuki of the Bank of Japan was published, and the Ministry of Finance sponsored a collection of articles on the Japanese financial system in 1991. However, the financial system has moved on significantly since those books appeared and has recently deteriorated in many respects. It is important for all of us to know Japan's present financial sector make-up, pressures and outlook. This volume concentrates on the elements of change and strain in the last decade. Its structure is simple, but useful: a review of the historical development and contemporary changes; an in-depth analysis of the players; a description of the changing markets; and, perhaps most importantly of all, a prediction of the effect of the reforms and the outlook for the markets until 2000. Various authors have written on their particular specialities. Virtually all of them come from Nomura Research Institute, whose role, as perhaps the leading think-tank in Japan on financial matters, is to disseminate such findings to all users of the system. The structure of this volume means one can dip in to any particular topic at will and expect to find a detailed, up-to-date and useful portrayal of what is going on in that key country and I recommend it to anyone interested in understanding the dramatic changes in today's financial markets in Japan.

Dr A R Prindl
Vice-President
Chartered Institute of Bankers

Preface

During the past 10 years, the financial and capital markets of Japan have undergone a sea change. The report of the Japan–US Yen/Dollar Committee released in May 1984 marked a symbolic start of changes to come. Put simply, it led to a phased opening and internationalisation of the domestic market which had been isolated from foreign influences by blocking cross-border money flow.

The past 10 years were also a period of formation and bursting of what was later commonly called the 'economic bubble'. Fuelled by super-low interest rates, prices of real estate and stocks soared far above their fundamental values. Lured by huge trade surpluses which Japan had piled up year after year, capital transactions converged on the Tokyo market, propelling it to the position of an international money centre; in size, neck and neck with New York and London. Come 1990, however, stock prices collapsed, and the Tokyo market fell out of favour with investors on account of banking and brokerage irregularities that came to light – with the result that participants are defecting from the Tokyo market in droves. Responding to such debilitating developments, the government has enacted a series of financial reform laws, under which the regulatory wall that had separated investment banking from commercial banking was torn down to allow reciprocal entry into one another's market through 100 per cent owned subsidiaries.

The dust has not settled, and there are many problems yet to address. But we felt that a review of what Japan has done during the past 10 years to internationalise its financial and capital markets would go a long way towards improving the understanding of the world's financial communities about where Japan stands now and where it will go in coming years. Hence this book.

The book is divided into four parts. Part I surveys changes that have occurred in the framework of Japan's financial system since the end of World War II, and puts the late 1980s, the period of our focus in this book, in a historical perspective. Part II describes the behaviour of its market participants exhibited mainly since the second half of the 1980s. Part III analyses different sectors of the market, and finally, Part IV reviews the regulatory reform efforts the government has made in recent years and outlines the challenges confronting the Japanese financial markets. In analysing different sectors of the market, we have employed the quantitative approach to help the reader understand the dynamics of the markets.

Each chapter was written by senior staffers who have been in close contact with, and have long specialised in, the particular sector. Cross references are provided to help the reader locate relevant issues in other chapters.

We appreciate the tremendous effort made by Mr Tohru Mori, our translator of the manuscripts written in Japanese. We dedicate this book to the market participants who have helped us improve our market analyses by providing us with their enlightened criticisms. If this book helps readers deepen their understanding of the Japanese market, encourages their active participation in the market, and helps them achieve their investment objectives, we could not be happier.

Shigenobu Hayakawa
Managing Director
Nomura Research Institute

PART

I

Overview

1

Historical development of the Japanese financial system

This chapter surveys the basic framework of the financial system which Japan has developed since World War II, and changes that have occurred therein, to help the reader understand Japan's financial and capital markets in and since the 1980s. Historical analysis of the changes in money flow patterns will be found in the next chapter.

The basic framework of Japan's financial system

THE FUND ALLOCATION SYSTEM UNDER 'DEVELOPMENTALISM'[1]

While the basic policy orientation in post-war Japan was towards a market economy, Japan employed many policy measures inspired by a centrally planned economy for rehabilitation. (More recently, many economists see a continuity between the style of post-war economic management and the wartime national mobilisation policy.) After the war, the government sought to protect the domestic market and allocate resources preferentially to strategic industries. A case in point is the so-called *Keisha Seisan Hoshiki* (the Priority Production System). Under this system, imported oil was allocated preferentially

1 The theory of developmentalism is a concept proposed by Yasusuke Murakami in his book *An anti-classical political-economic analysis*, Tokyo, 1992, which argues that when the production function has a characteristic of decreasing cost, there is no 'equilibrium' under the perfect competition, and that government intervention becomes theoretically necessary.

*Shielding of the movement of domestic funds from foreign funds (the Foreign Investment Law and the Foreign Exchange Control Law)

Public channel through government run intermediaries	Private channel * Artificial low interest policy * Strict regulation of players * Compartmentalisation of financial services * Regulation of price and non-price competition	
* Policy-dictated allocation of funds * Low interest loans through government run financial institutions (the Development Bank, etc.) * Tax incentives	The banking market * Domination of indirect financing * Toleration of overloan and overborrowing * Tax incentives for saving through deposits	The securities market * Marginal role * Separation of the new issue and trading markets * Over protection of investors (over use of uniform rules and elimination of risks)

Underlying preconditions:

1. Perception as a small country (assuming that the economic behaviour of Japan does not affect the economies of other countries)
2. Cold war (which created an international consensus sympathetic to the protectionist measures taken by Japan)
3. Rehabilitation of the war-torn economy (a national consensus supporting the government's policy objectives)

1.1 The framework of Japan's post-war financial system (source: Nomura Research Institute).

to steel mills, and by preferentially allocating steel mill products to coal mines, the government sought to secure the supply of low cost coal. As means for achieving these goals, the government employed import quotas and price adjustment subsidies.

The framework of the financial system was also tailored to achieve this objective. That is to say, policy-dictated allocation of funds took precedence over a market-driven one. The system was built on four building blocks outlined below (see also Fig. 1.1).

Domestic financial markets shielded from foreign competition

By virtue of the foreign exchange control policy of the Supreme Command of Allied Powers (SCAP) and the Foreign Exchange and Foreign Trade Control Law of 1949, the movement of funds (international capital and current transactions) was controlled, and the financial markets of Japan were, in effect, cut off from those of other countries. Under the law, non-residents' investments, in Japanese equities had to be cleared in advance with the Bank of Japan, and their proceeds were not allowed to be repatriated. In addition, non-residents' holdings of shares of companies in many industry groups were restricted below certain percentages. It is true that Japan had borrowed funds selectively from international agencies such as the World Bank, but the bulk of investment required for the rehabilitation of the war-torn economy and the rapid growth that followed was financed by domestic savings (thanks to the preferential tax treatment given to savers by the government).

Allocation of funds through public financial institutions

In an effort to make up the acute shortage of commercial credits which had resulted, in part, from heavy losses of both overseas and domestic assets of private banking institutions, the government allocated investment funds and working capital to private firms in special loans made from Treasury funds and credits extended by the Rehabilitation Finance Corporation. When the economy began to grow rapidly, loans from public agencies continued to carry heavy weight. During the 10 years to 1975, these loans to private industry accounted for 13 per cent of the funds supplied through the broadly defined financial markets, and their share continued to grow thereafter (Table 1.1). More specifically, Treasury investments and loans financed with postal savings were channelled to the financial markets in the form of low interest loans given by, for example, Japan Development Bank and Housing Finance Corporation. Moreover, tax incentives, such as preferential tax treatment of capital investment, were offered to spur business spending on new plant and equipment.

Artificially low interest policy

In the area of private finance, also, an artificially low interest policy was adopted, under which funds were made available to private firms as well as to the government at an interest rate below market-cleared level. The government promulgated an Interim Interest Adjustment Law in 1947 which set a ceiling on the deposit rates 'for the time being'. The adjustment of deposit rates in relationship with the official discount rate then prevailing was determined through some Councils and a Policy Committee at the Bank of Japan. As the infrastructure of the capital markets (such as the means of infor-

Table 1.1 Brokering of funds in the broadly defined financial markets

Fund supplier	Channel of supply	1965–74 Average		1975–84 Average		1985–9 Average		1990–3 Average	
		¥10 bn	%	¥10 bn	%	¥10 bn	%	¥10 bn	%
To domestic non-financial sectors	Domestic financial institutions	17,180	84.4	46,800	79.9	81,630	66.3	63,330	82.1
	Loans	14,280	70.2	32,000	54.6	55,480	45.1	47,110	61.1
	Financing through private institutions	11,740	57.7	21,590	36.9	46,140	37.5	30,080	39.0
	Financing through public institutions	2,540	12.5	10,420	17.8	9,340	7.6	17,040	22.1
	Securities	2,900	14.3	14,800	25.3	22,720	18.5	16,560	21.5
	Commercial paper (CP)	–	–	–	–	3,430	2.8	−350	−0.5
	Domestic securities market	1,000	4.9	3,920	6.7	−1,200	−1.0	−1,770	−2.3
	Individuals	520	2.6	2,200	3.8	−850	−0.7	−1,810	−2.4
	Business corporations	430	2.1	1,330	2.3	1,620	1.3	−270	−0.3
	Public entities	40	0.2	320	0.5	−2,020	−1.6	−180	−0.2
	Investment by foreigners	560	2.8	1,460	2.5	5,320	4.3	6,430	8.3
	Foreigners' investment in Japanese securities	90	0.4	1,740	3.0	3,480	2.8	5,020	6.5
	Others	460	2.3	−280	−0.5	1,840	1.5	1,410	1.8
	Subtotal	18,740	92.1	52,180	89.1	85,750	69.7	67,980	88.2
To the foreign sector	Domestic financial institutions	580	2.9	3,870	6.6	26,960	21.9	3,990	5.2
	Japanese investment in foreign securities	60	0.3	1,150	2.0	9,060	7.4	4,160	5.4
	Others	520	2.6	2,710	4.6	17,900	14.5	−180	−0.2
	Others	610	3.0	2,220	3.8	8,640	7.0	4,990	6.5
	Japanese investment in foreign securities	40	0.2	770	1.3	5,130	4.2	2,270	2.9
	Japanese direct investment in other countries	180	0.9	740	1.3	2,490	2.0	3,130	4.1
	Others	380	1.9	710	1.2	1,020	0.8	−400	−0.5
	Changes in foreign currency reserves	420	2.1	300	0.5	1,720	1.4	130	0.2
	Subtotal	1,610	7.9	6,390	10.9	37,320	30.3	9,110	11.8
Total		20,350	100.0	58,570	100.0	123,070	100.0	77,090	100.0

Source: Bank of Japan, Flow-of-Funds Accounts.

mation dissemination) was still inadequate, funds flowed mainly in the form of negotiated loans from banks and insurance companies. (This is often referred to as 'the domination of indirect financing'.) And the total amount a bank could lend during a particular period was capped by the Bank of Japan. Essentially, loans were rationed. As shown in Table 1.1, 70 per cent of the funds supplied during the

10 years to 1975 were accounted for by loans (including those made by publicly run financial institutions). In the case of external funds raised during the same 10 year period by companies listed on the First Section of the Tokyo Stock Exchange (TSE), borrowings from banking institutions and insurance companies accounted for 79 per cent (7 per cent from bond offerings and 14 per cent from equity offerings).

With the backing of the Bank of Japan, city (large commercial) banks have built 'overloan' portfolios (a practice of making commercial loans in excess of their deposits and equity capital by financing them with funds borrowed from the Bank of Japan) to meet vigorous business demand for loans.

At the same time, the government also provided tax incentives – the tax-exempt small amount savings system known as *maruyu* and deduction of insurance premiums from taxable income – to back up this policy.

Stringent regulation of the financial markets

An element that defined the framework of private financial transactions was the regulation of financial intermediaries. Its features may be summed up into the following points.

Compartmentalisation of financial services
The regulatory agency (predominantly the Ministry of Finance (MOF)) compartmentalised financial services into several groups according to the kinds of services financial institutions provided, adopted a licensing system and required them to engage exclusively in the area of financial service specified in the licence. (The licensing system for securities companies was adopted in April 1968 in the wake of the securities market crisis of 1965, during which leading securities companies had to be bailed out with special loans from the Bank of Japan.) On top of the basic compartmentalisation of financial institutions into three areas, i.e. banking, securities, and insurance sectors, the banking sector was further subdivided in terms of long and short term credits banks extended – long term credit banks, commercial banks providing short term working capital, and trust services (loan trusts which guarantee the principal and other trust services).

The compartmentalisation of financial services discouraged disintermediation of funds from one group to another. Any attempt by a group of institutions to lure deposits from another group by offering a higher yield often triggered a bureaucratic turf battle, often leading to infighting between their respective regulatory agencies (various bureaux within MOF).

Restriction of entry into others' markets
Each business-specific law allows, at least in theory, a financial service company belonging to one financial service group to enter the markets of other groups. In practice, however, the regulatory agencies did not (until very recently) allow such entry and have sought to consolidate the existing participants in a given market into a smaller number (Table 1.2). As a result, the regulatory agencies have consistently denied the entry of new participants in any of those compartmentalised markets since the war. That explains the fact that the number of financial intermediaries has not increased through mergers.

Restriction of price and non-price competition
Price competition among the participants in one and the same market has in effect been barred by regulating deposit rates, stock brokerage commissions, and insurance premium rates. In short, one and the same kind of financial product or service is offered at the same price or fee.

Non-price competition also was frowned upon by the regulators as demonstrated by the regulation of branching and advertising or by the practice of financial service institutions offering one and the same financial product or service at the same time. Because of the lack of competitive tools, market shares of different players have tended to remain unchanged, and the lack of competition has offered no incentives for innovative efforts.

This 'policy over market' approach worked effectively for the recovery of the Japanese economy. But, at this point, we need to clarify the underlying preconditions for this approach to work.

The first one is that Japan is a small country, that is to say, the economic behaviour of Japan has no impact on – or does not become a disruptive factor for – the world economy or international financial systems. Given the fact that Japan lost about one-third of its wealth on account of the war, this precondition seems valid.

The second precondition is that there was an international consensus among Western countries, particularly the United States, which was sympathetic to the approach taken by Japan after the war

Table 1.2 Changes in the number of financial institutions

	All banks	Commercial banks	Regional banks	Trust banks	Long term credit banks	Life insurance companies	Property & casualty insurance companies	Securities companies
1945	70	NA	NA	NA	1	21	16	531
1950	70	13	50	6	1	20	20	936
1955	83	13	62	6	2	20	20	700
1960	87	13	64	7	3	20	20	552
1965	87	13	64	7	3	20	20	484
1970	86	15	61	7	3	20	21	271
1975	86	13	63	7	3	21	22	258
1980	86	13	63	7	3	21	22	251
1985	87	13	64	7	3	23	23	221
1990	87	13	64	7	3	26	25	220
1994	85	11	64	7	3	27	25	212

Note: Domestic institutions only. The second-tier regional banks (former mutual banks) are not included.
Source: Compiled by Nomura Research Institute on the basis of data drawn from the annual reports of the various bureaux of the Ministry of Finance.

in which it focused its efforts on the rehabilitation of the economy by closing its markets to foreign competition. Obviously, the cold war between the United States and the Soviet Union had a hand in reinforcing such consensus.

The third precondition is that within Japan, also, there developed a consensus on giving top priority to achieving an early rehabilitation of the war-torn economy and on the means employed to achieve it. Although the loss of income caused by lower deposit rates was partly alleviated by tax concessions, the artificially low deposit rates in effect transferred wealth from lenders (households) to borrowers (firms), but few people complained about it. Perhaps there was a tacit understanding on the part of the people that the loss of interest income could eventually be compensated for by benefits to be derived from a larger economic pie.

THE LIMITED ROLE OF THE SECURITIES MARKET

The basic framework of Japan's Securities and Exchange Law of 1948 is based, in the main, on those of the Securities Act of 1933 and the Securities Exchange Act of 1934 of the United States. Therefore, the components of the Japanese securities market – the creation of an enforcement agency and self-regulation bodies, and the enforcement of disclosure – are similar to those in the US market. For example, a Securities and Exchange Commission was created in 1948 (later absorbed into the Ministry of Finance in 1952) on the model of the US SEC. However, the way the Securities and Exchange Law was administered was quite different from that in the United States. The following three features stand out.

Limited choice of vehicles for financing

As bank loans were available at rates below market-cleared ones, the securities market was tapped only in exceptional cases. Particularly, the eligibility standards and issuing terms for corporate bonds were set at a prohibitively stringent level by the regulators, so that except for utility bonds and telegraph and telephone bonds, the new issue market of bonds to all intents and purposes remained closed. Public offering of equity shares was typically used for expanding debt capacity or as a substitute for loans during the tight money periods. Thus, the use of the securities market was limited to emergency financing.

Meanwhile, securities failed to serve as a major vehicle for forming personal assets by the investing public.

Separation of the new issue market and the trading market

The secondary market for securities was reopened soon after the war, but the prices formed in the market were not directly reflected on the issuing terms of new securities. What is more, the volume of bonds or equities to be offered on the new issue market was determined by the regulatory agency or market intermediaries.

Following the dismemberment of *zaibatsu* (great industrial or financial combinations) by order of the occupation authorities, and thanks to a campaign for 'the democratisation of securities owner-ship', individual ownership of shares increased rather rapidly, and the trading market served as a marketplace for cashing their shareholdings. However, new shares were allocated to existing shareholders at par value through rights offerings; thus their issuing terms had nothing to do with their market prices.

In the case of bonds, the new Nippon Telegraph & Telephone (NTT) bonds, the first debt securities traded on the market after the war, were allocated compulsorily to new subscribers for a telephone on terms dictated by the government run telephone company. Therefore, the interest rate carried by such NTT bonds or their maturity had no link with the prevailing market conditions.

The same separation was seen in the government bond market. New issues were started in 1966. But underwriting institutions (mainly banks) were not allowed to resell them on the market during the early years. Therefore, there was no secondary market for the government bond in those years. As an alternative, the Bank of Japan bought through open market operations those bonds which had been outstanding for more than one year at an artificially set high price (called the 'exchange-traded price').

Overprotection of investors

Article 1 of the Securities and Exchange Law of 1948 set forth its objective 'to contribute to the proper management of the economy and the protection of investors'. As a tool for achieving the objective of protecting the investors, the law mandates disclosure of corporate information of the issuer as is the case with the US securities laws, but it assumes that the investor does not have the knowledge or know-how necessary for making securities investment, and that the investor is not adequately equipped to make use of the information thus disclosed. This assumption was applied to institutional investors, if in lesser degree, as well as to individual investors. Specific measures taken in line with this assumption include the following.

Circumvention of risks

In almost any country, the securities market restricts the access to capital markets by imposing various regulations such as listing criteria, etc. But in the case of the Japanese securities market, its criteria of selection are more stringent than its equivalents in other countries and cover relatively wider-ranging areas. The Japanese securities market has followed a policy of not admitting securities which are suspected of having high risks or being involved in a highly complex structure. As the Securities and Exchange Law defined securities not in terms of their attributes but listed specific categories of securities, there was little room to debut new classes of securities. Even more prohibitive is the new issue market for corporate bonds. On account of the additional debt restriction covenant,[2] the eligibility criteria (credit rating and financial ratio) for issuing unsecured straight bonds, and the trustee system,[3] few would-be issuers were able to satisfy these criteria. In addition, the practice of buying out all defaulted bonds by the trustee bank has been established.

Overuse of uniform rules

The numerical standards have often been applied by the regulatory agency or self-regulation organisations to matters which should have been left to the discretion of issuers, investors or securities companies. Cases in point are the rule for reverting to shareholders the premiums resulting from a public offering of new shares at market price, the ceilings imposed on the ratios of different asset classes which life insurance companies and other institutional investors can

2 An agreement entered into between the issuer of unsecured bonds, on the one hand, and the trustee bank and the underwriting securities company, under which the issuer undertakes not to incur an additional debt beyond a certain agreed-upon limit.

3 A system under which the trustee bank agrees to accept on behalf of the issuer subscriptions to the bonds and to manage the collateral offered by the bonds' issuer on behalf of the bondholders. Despite the obvious conflict of interest inherent in these two kinds of services, a bank that has a close business relationship with the issuer (main bank) customarily accepts such trusteeship.

hold, and the eligibility criteria for issuing straight bonds mentioned above.

Regulation of securities companies
The government sought to protect investors by regulating the activities of securities companies down to their trivial details. Many of the circular notices and oral guidance (administrative guidance or directives given verbally), and the self-regulation rules (the fair practice rule) inspired by regulators created overregulation.

Changes in the system under the pressure of the two *kokusai-ka*

The basic structure of Japan's post-war financial system outlined in the foregoing has begun to change since around 1970, largely triggered by the pressure of the two *kokusai-ka*. One is the impact of the growing government bond (*kokusai* in Japanese) market, and the other is that of the internationalisation (*kokusaika*) of the Japanese economy. These changes may be characterised as a process of the market mechanism, rather than policies, playing a more important role in the financial markets of Japan.

ISSUANCE OF NEW SHARES AT MARKET PRICE, AND CHANGES IN THE EVALUATION OF JAPANESE STOCKS BY FOREIGN INVESTORS

By shifting its status to that designated by Article 8 of the IMF Charter in 1964 and by joining the Organisation for Economic Co-operation and Development (OECD) in the same year, Japan committed itself to the liberalisation of international capital transactions, and took liberalisation measures in five stages starting from 1967. Although these measures were taken with direct investment in mind, they also occasioned gradual increases in non-residents' investment in Japanese securities. In April 1963, the ban on the repatriation of proceeds of securities was lifted, although it still required government permits. Subsequently, growth in the total value of foreign investment in Japanese securities slowed down owing to the introduction of interest equalisation taxes by the United States and a stock market adjustment occurred in Japan. Around 1967, however, foreign investment in Japanese securities began to pick up again. Playing the

13

leading role in this phase of the rising market were Japanese stock funds run by European investment trusts. In the second half of the 1960s, the number of Japanese ADRs (American depository receipts) listed on the New York Stock Exchange, and debt offerings on the Euro market by Japanese companies after the introduction of the interest equalisation taxes in the United States have turned upwards. As residents' investment in foreign securities still remained under strict control, there was not much freedom of movement of funds, and although the government enacted a Law Concerning Foreign Securities Firms in 1971, only six foreign firms got the necessary licence during the following 10 years.

This gradual shift nevertheless had big impacts in the following three areas.

First, the issuance of ADRs by Japanese firms was instrumental in establishing the practice of issuing shares at market price in Japan. During the initial months, the issuance of new shares at market price stirred up a big controversy between investors and issuers, but it started in earnest early in 1970. This has generated pressure to reflect the market price formed on the secondary market in the issuing terms of new shares. However, it is to be noted that issuers still cling to the decade-old practice of computing dividends on the basis of par value.

Second, there was an impact on the method of evaluating stocks. More specifically, the yardstick used for evaluating a stock was changed from dividend yields to price–earnings ratio (PER). As shown in Fig. 1.2, the average PER of the First Section stocks began to rise rapidly, from around 10 at the end of 1972 to 28-plus at the end of 1973. Except for a brief drop-off in 1974 in the wake of the first oil crisis, the average PER has consistently remained above 20. Meanwhile, dividend yields dropped from the 4 per cent area to mid-2 per cent during the same period. This development was locally dubbed a 'PER revolution'.

Third, as a means of shielding themselves from hostile takeovers by foreign investors, a growing number of listed firms have worked out arrangements of cross-shareholding with friendly companies.

MASSIVE GOVERNMENT DEBT OFFERINGS AND THE BIRTH OF A BOND TRADING MARKET

Under mounting political pressure to reflate the economy from an oil crisis-induced recession and international pressure brought to bear on Japan at the summit meetings of the seven richest countries to

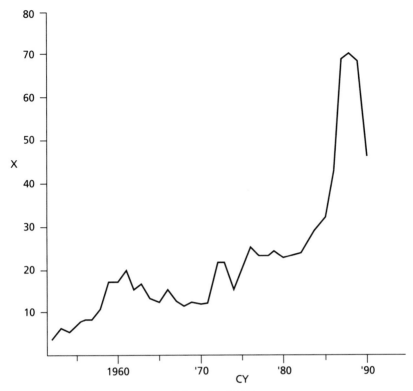

1.2 Changes in the average PER of the Nikkel 225 stocks.

play the role of a locomotive in pulling the world economy out of recession, Japan began to issue deficit-covering bonds in 1975, which led to a dramatic increase in its debt offerings (Fig. 1.3). Under such circumstances, the practice of issuing artificially low interest government bonds and recycling them through open market operations could no longer withstand the tremendous pressure that had been building since the massive government bond offerings. Already in the second half of the 1960s, short term rates negotiated through *gensaki* deals (repurchase agreements, or repos) had inched closer to the market rates, seriously eroding the fund positions of banking institutions and saddling them with huge evaluation losses. And this created growing pressure to deregulate the bond trading market. Under such pressure, the ban on reselling government bonds by their underwriting banks during the first year of their acquisition was lifted in 1977. (But they had to wait until 1987 before they could freely resell government bonds immediately after their acquisition.) Initially, the Ministry of Finance continued to issue government

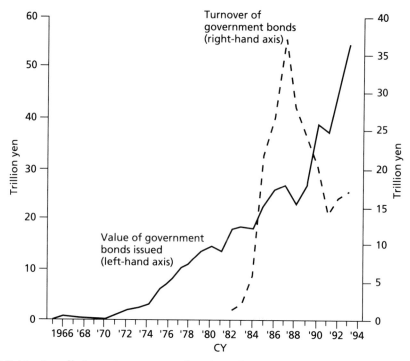

1.3 Massive offerings of government bonds, and turnover.
Note: Turnover includes bonds traded over the counter and stock exchanges (but excludes those involved in *gensaki* deals).

bonds at low coupon rates and used the funds drawn from the Trust Fund Bureau (of the Finance Ministry) to support the prices of government bonds. However, as the US Federal Reserve Board changed its monetary policy, interest rates became increasingly volatile and their effect rippled through the Japanese market, eventually making it impossible for the Finance Ministry to ignore interest rates formed on the bond trading market. In 1981, the Banking Law Amendment enabled banks to engage in government bond trading.

Maturities and issuing methods were also diversified. In 1977, the Ministry of Finance issued five year discount notes, and the following year it began to issue so-called 'medium term government bonds' (government notes) which matured in two, three, or four years. These government notes were auctioned off at prices that reflected market prices then prevailing.

Such pressure for normalising government bond prices forced the Finance Ministry to shelve the artificial low interest policy. This in turn demolished the rigid seniority based interest rate structure, under which interest rates were determined in the order of priority for bank debentures, government-guaranteed bonds, publicly offered municipal bonds, and industrial bonds. And the emergence of short maturity debts touched off a ground swell which precipitated the movement towards the liberalisation of deposit rates (see Chapter 2).

The Japanese financial markets after the Japan–US Yen/Dollar Committee

The changes in Japan's financial system reviewed in the preceding section have accelerated since 1984. The main engine that set the changes in motion was the Japan–US Yen/Dollar Committee ('the Committee'), a forum of currency specialists from both countries created pursuant to an agreement reached between President Ronald Reagan on a visit to Japan and his Japanese counterpart for the purpose of hammering out measures designed to remedy the situation caused by a weakened yen and a super-strong dollar. Changes that have since occurred may be summarised as follows.

INTERNATIONALISATION GAINS MOMENTUM IN EARNEST

Following the amendment of the Foreign Exchange and Foreign Trade Control Law (hence Foreign Exchange Control Law) in 1979, international movement of funds was liberalised in principle (see Chapter 2). And on the recommendations of the Committee, internationalisation of Japan's currency market gained momentum in earnest. Summing up the developments that occurred in the ensuing months, the International Finance Bureau of the Ministry of Finance states in its annual report (No. 9, 1985).

> *Up to now, liberalisation measures have been geared to changes occurring in the nation's financial and capital markets and have been taken as necessity arose. In contrast, however, the report of the Japan–US Yen/Dollar Committee proposed a large variety of measures to be taken by Japan which were accompanied by specific schedules for their implementation. In this respect, it deserves recognition as an epochal document.*

In fact, many of the measures controlling the international movement of funds, for example, the ban on converting dollar funds raised on the Euro market into yen funds, and the restriction, in principle, against purchasing foreign currency futures for speculation purposes, have been removed step by step pursuant to the recommendations of the Committee (Table 1.3).

The impact of internationalisation of the Japanese market was not confined to the liberalisation of international capital transactions. By combining with the foreign pressure that came from the Committee, it – together with the pressure generated by the massive offerings of government bonds noted earlier – compelled the Japanese government to commit itself to a specific schedule for liberalising deposit rates which constitute the backbone of the domestic financial system. The same is true of the introduction of financial derivatives. However, the incremental approach continues to this day. As shown in Table 1.4 at the end of this chapter, deregulation is being implemented bit by bit.

THE ECONOMIC BUBBLE AND THE MEANING OF ITS BURSTING

If the economic bubble is defined as a process in which a price has strayed from the fundamental value of an asset, economic bubbles have occurred at various stages of economic development of all countries. It is not a result of liberalisation or internationalisation of an economy. One does not have to be reminded of the collapse of 'tulipmania' that occurred in The Netherlands in the eighteenth century and left economic scars for decades. In Japan, also, speculative frenzy occurred on more than one occasion. During the years from late in the Edo period (1603–1867) to the early years of the Meiji period (1868–1912), extraordinary booms of speculation in rabbit and *Rhodea japonica* developed a number of times.

An abnormal expansion of money supply, even larger than that which occurred in the wake of the first oil crisis of 1973, developed during the bubble years that ended at the end of the 1980s (Fig. 1.4).

If there is any lesson to be learned from the developments that have led to the recent economic bubble and its bursting, it is the yawning gap between the assumptions on the basis of which Japan had built its financial system after the war and the market reality. And this phenomenon was aptly diagnosed as 'an institutional fatigue'.

The preconditions underlying Japan's financial system have gone through a sea change. Japan has amassed the world's largest net credits outstanding outside the country and boasts the second largest

Table 1.3 Agenda of the Yen/Dollar Committee

Items	Date implemented	Items	Date implemented
– The ban on issuing Euro-yen bonds by residents is lifted.	4/84	– The advisability of opening a Treasury bill market is considered.	
– Regulation of issuing Euro-yen bonds by non-residents is eased.	4/86	– The market for yen-denominated bank acceptance is opened.	6/85
– Issuing Euro-yen CP is authorised.	4/85	– The advisability of establishing a Tokyo offshore market is considered.	12/86
– Short term impact loans in Euro-yen are liberalised.	6/84	– The advisability of opening a financial futures market is considered.	12/85
– Lead managership of underwriting debt issues of Japanese firms is opened to foreign firms.	12/84	– The regulation banning, in principle, speculative currency transactions is abolished.	4/84
– Taxes on Euro-yen bonds are revised.	4/85	– The regulation banning foreign currency funds raised in the Euro market or Tokyo's offshore market into yen funds is abolished.	6/84
– The advisability of authorising long and medium term loans in Euro-yen is considered.	4/85	– Foreign banks are authorised to provide trust services in Japan.	10/85
– The minimum issuing unit of CP is lowered.	4/85	– The membership of foreign securities firms into the Tokyo Stock Exchange is considered.	11/85
– Issuing floating rate financial instruments is authorised.	3/85	– The advisability of creating bond credit rating agencies is considered.	7/87
– Interest rates on large denomination deposits are liberalised.	10/85	– Issuing terms of corporate bonds are liberalised.	2/87
– Interest rates on small amount deposits are liberalised.	6/89		
– The long and short term prime rate system is revised.	1/89		

Source: Nomura Research Institute.

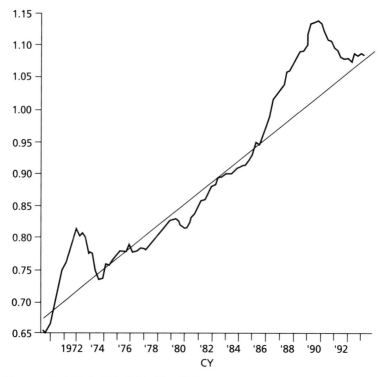

1.4 Changes in (M2 + CD) divided by GDP.

gross national product after the United States. Japan simply can no longer assume that it is a small country. Of late, regulation of its domestic market has often produced disruptive effects on the world markets. The end of the cold war has rendered old international priorities meaningless. Because of these far-reaching changes, financial frictions with other countries continue unabated. What is worse, there are reasons to believe that the domestic consensus which once backed the old policies has vanished.

Under such circumstances, the economic and financial systems of Japan have become more interdependent with those of other countries, and the institutional framework Japan has built over the decades is growing rapidly irrelevant to the changing world.

In the securities market, the force of changes that occurred in the second half of the 1970s and accelerated in the 1980s has eased the limitation of means of financing and has lowered the wall separating the new issue market and the secondary market. In the process, there has developed a link between the two markets, if in a limited degree, helping equity and equity-linked financing (convertible bonds and bonds with equity warrants) to take hold as an important vehicle for financing since the first oil crisis of 1973, and particularly in the 1980s. And thanks in part to a sharp increase in government bonds, financing through securities offerings has taken on a growing weight in financial transactions.

However, the overemphasis on the protection of investors has not changed. Allocation of resources was made not by the collective preference of investors but by the dictate of government-imposed uniform rules.

Such irrationality notwithstanding, the regulatory agencies managed to maintain the consistency of their policies until the speculative bubble burst at the end of the 1980s, because they had strictly limited the accessibility of the stock market and the investing public believed the myth of ever rising stock prices. For example, cross-shareholding between a financial institution (a bank or an insurance company) and a business corporation no longer made any economic sense and was incompatible with issuing new shares at market price particularly after banks, which had been allocating new shares at par value to their shareholders through rights offerings, began to issue new shares at market value in order to meet the primary capital ratio imposed by the Bank for International Settlements (BIS) (this in itself is a manifestation of the internationalisation of their operation). Now the cost of carrying one another's shares under a cross-shareholding arrangement became prohibitively high for both parties. But they were able to carry them, because stock prices continued to rise to such a height that they had – or expected to have – hidden (unrealised) capital gains to justify their carrying cost. But since 1990, when the stock market began to go down, this has no longer held.

Table 1.4 Current state of liberalisation of the financial and capital markets (as at 31 May 1994)

Deposit	Certificates of deposit (CD)	May 1979	CD is introduced with a minimum issuing unit of ¥500m.
		Jan. 1984	The issuing unit of CD is lowered to ¥300m.
		Apr. 1985	The issuing unit of CD is lowered to ¥100m, and the minimum period of deposit is reduced to one month.
		Jun. 1985	Securities companies start handling CDs.
		Apr. 1986	The maximum period of deposit is extended to one year.
		Oct. 1986	The ceiling on the amount of CDs a bank can issue is abolished.

Table 1.4 *Continued*

	Apr. 1988	The issuing unit is lowered to ¥50m, the minimum period of deposit is reduced to two weeks, and the maximum period of deposit is extended to five years.
Time deposits whose interest rates are deregulated	Oct. 1985	The minimum unit of deposit is set at ¥1 bn. Interest rates on large denomination time deposits with a maturity from three months to two years are deregulated.
	Apr. 1986	The minimum unit of deposit is lowered to ¥500m.
	Sept. 1986	It is further lowered to ¥300m.
	Apr. 1987	It is further lowered to ¥100m.
	Oct. 1987	The minimum period of deposit is shortened to one month.
	Apr. 1988	The minimum unit of deposit is lowered to ¥50m.
	Nov. 1988	It is further lowered to ¥30m.
	Apr. 1989	It is further lowered to ¥20m.
	Oct. 1989	It is further lowered to ¥10m.
	Nov. 1991	A super time deposit with a minimum unit of deposit of ¥3m is introduced.
	Jun. 1993	With the abolition of the minimum unit of deposit, interest rates on time deposits are completely liberalised.
	Oct. 1993	Banks start accepting medium term (four year) time deposits.
Money market certificates (MMC)	Mar. 1985	Banks launch MMCs with a minimum unit of deposit of ¥50m, maturing in one to six months.
	Apr. 1986	The maximum period of deposit is extended to one year.
	Sept. 1986	The minimum unit of deposit is lowered to ¥30m.
	Apr. 1987	It is lowered to ¥20m, and the maximum period of deposit is extended to two years.
	Sept. 1987	It is further lowered to ¥10m.
	Jun. 1989	It is further lowered to ¥3m, and small denomination MMCs with maturities of six months and one year are launched.
	Oct. 1989	Small denomination MMCs with a maturity of three months, two or three years are launched. Following the lowering of the minimum unit of time deposit with deregulated interest rates, MMCs with a minimum deposit unit of ¥10m or more are absorbed into deregulated MMCs with a minimum deposit unit of ¥10m or more.

Table 1.4 *Continued*

		Nov. 1989	A floor of interest rates for small denomination MMCs is set.
		Apr. 1990	The minimum unit of deposit for small denomination MMCs is lowered to ¥1m.
		Nov. 1990	The formula for setting interest rates is changed into one that is pegged to the base rates of large denomination time deposits. Interest rates for those with a face value of less than ¥3m and for those with a face value of ¥3m or more are differentiated. In addition, small denomination MMCs are divided into small and medium denomination MMCs.
		Apr. 1991	The minimum unit of deposit of small denomination MMCs is lowered to ¥0.5m.
		Nov. 1991	Following the introduction of super time deposits (with the minimum deposit unit of ¥3m), medium denomination MMCs are absorbed into the super time deposits.
		Jun. 1992	The minimum unit of deposit of small denomination MMCs is abolished.
		Jun. 1993	Following the liberalisation of interest rates on time deposits, issuance of new MMCs is abolished.
	Savings deposit	Jun. 1992	Two kinds of the new type of savings deposit are introduced: one with a minimum outstanding balance of ¥400,000 and the other with a minimum outstanding balance of ¥200,000.
		Oct. 1993	Their minimum outstanding balances are lowered to ¥300,000 and ¥100,000, respectively. At the same time, the service of switching these accounts with passbook accounts is started.
	Floating rate deposit	Oct. 1993	A floating rate deposit account is introduced.
Money market and foreign exchange	Yen-denominated bank acceptance (BA)	Jun. 1985	The yen-denominated bank acceptance market is launched.
		Aug. 1986	Securities companies start trading in yen-denominated bank acceptance certificates.
		May 1987	The minimum unit of trading of BA certificates is lowered from ¥100m to ¥50m, and their maximum maturity is extended to six months to one year.

Table 1.4 *Continued*

Foreign exchange market	Apr. 1984	The ban on speculative trading in currency futures is lifted, in principle.
	Jun. 1984	The ban on converting dollar funds raised on the Eurodollar market or the Tokyo offshore market into yen funds is lifted.
	Feb. 1985	Direct dealing between yen and dollar starts.
Offshore market	Dec. 1986	Japan's offshore market is launched.
	Apr. 1989	Regulation of day-to-day surplus or deficit of yen–dollar transactions is eased, and the procedure for identifying non-residents is simplified.
	Apr. 1992	A measure exempting foreign corporations from taxation on their currency transactions is implemented.
Call money and *gensaki* (repos)	Apr. 1979	Call rates are liberalised (current quotations are abolished).
	Apr. 1980	The ban on selling *gensaki* by commercial banks is lifted.
	Nov. 1980	Securities companies are authorised to take in call money.
	Apr. 1981	Commercial banks release call money, and the ban on buying *gensaki* by commercial banks is lifted.
	Jul. 1985	The system of making unsecured call loans is launched.
	Sept. 1985	Two to three week unsecured call loans are launched.
	Aug. 1986	Weekend unsecured call loans are launched.
	Jul. 1987	Two to six day unsecured call loans are launched.
	Nov. 1988	One to six month unsecured call loans are launched.
	Apr. 1989	The period of unsecured call loan contracts is extended up to one year.
	Nov. 1990	The system of making secured call loans is changed to the offered and bid system.
	Nov. 1991	Call brokers start brokering unsecured postdated call loans (spot call loans).
	Mar. 1993	The variety of call loans for postdated transactions is widened (from one week to one year contracts).
Treasury bills (TB) (financial bills (FB))	Feb. 1986	Public sale of TBs starts.
	Aug. 1987	The minimum unit of trading is lowered from ¥100m to ¥50m. A formula of refunding withholding tax to sovereign entities at the time of acquisition of TBs is introduced.

Table 1.4 *Continued*

		Sept. 1989	A three month TB is introduced, in addition to six month TBs.
		Apr. 1990	The minimum unit of trading is lowered to ¥10m.
		Apr. 1992	Foreign corporations are exempted from withholding tax.
		Jun. 1992	Japan Mutual Securities starts publishing information concerning TB trading.
	Commercial paper (CP)	Nov. 1987	The ban on issuing domestic CP is lifted.
		Jan. 1988	The ban on issuing *samurai* (yen-denominated) CP by non-residents is lifted.
		Dec. 1988	The method of issuing domestic CP is revised. (Among other things, the eligibility of business corporations for issuing CP is expanded by introducing credit rating system, and the minimum maturity is shortened from one month of two weeks.) At the same time, the system of issuing *samurai* CP is revised, and the ban on issuing *shogun* (foreign currency-denominated) CP by non-residents is lifted.
		Feb. 1990	The method of issuing domestic CP is revised (the eligibility standards for issuing corporations are expanded). The ban on issuing CP by securities companies is lifted, and at the same time, the system of issuing *samurai* CP is also revised.
		Apr. 1991	The method of issuing domestic CP is revised (replacing the old eligibility standards with credit ratings). At the same time, a similar revision of the method of issuing *samurai* CP is also revised.
		Apr. 1993	With the amendment of the Securities and Exchange Law, CP is officially designated as a security.
		Jun. 1993	The ban on issuing CP by non-banks is lifted.
Capital markets	Government bonds	Jun. 1985	Banks start dealing in the full range of public bonds.
		Feb. 1986	The system of auctioning off TBs starts.
		Apr. 1986	The period during which underwriting banks are barred from reselling government bonds they underwrote is shortened to about 10 days.
		Aug. 1987	The period referred to above is, in effect, abolished.

25

Table 1.4 *Continued*

	Sept. 1987	The system of offering 20 year government coupon bonds through public auction starts.
	Oct. 1987	Requirements imposed on foreign banks to participate in government bond underwriting syndicates (requiring a certain number of years after the opening of their branches in Japan) are lifted.
	Nov. 1987	The system requiring bidders on 10 year government bonds to commit themselves to a certain amount is introduced.
	Oct. 1988	Shares of foreign banking institutions in underwriting government bonds are raised.
	Apr. 1989	The system of inviting price bids on 40% of the monthly offering of 10 year government coupon bonds is introduced.
		Four foreign securities companies are appointed as managers of government bond underwriting syndicates.
	Oct. 1990	The portion of 10 year government coupon bonds subject to competitive price bidding is increased to 60%.
	Apr. 1993	The schedule for auctioning government bonds is shortened.
Domestic corporate bonds and bank debentures	Jan. 1985	Issuing unsecured straight bonds starts.
	Jun. 1985	The eligibility standards for issuing unsecured convertible bonds are eased.
	Feb. 1987	The eligibility standards for issuing unsecured straight bonds are further eased.
	Apr. 1987	A proposal system for determining issuing terms of NT&T bonds is introduced.
		The ban on issuing domestic convertible bonds by banks is lifted.
	Jul. 1987	A credit rating standard is introduced into the eligibility standards for issuing unsecured straight bonds and the additional debt restriction covenant.
	Apr. 1988	The proposal system is introduced for all issues of industrial bonds.
	Oct. 1988	The system of shelf registration is introduced.
	Nov. 1988	The credit rating system is incorporated into the eligibility standards for issuing publicly offered corporate bonds, to be

Table 1.4 *Continued*

	used along with the numerical standards. The net asset standards required of issuers of unsecured corporate bonds are eased.
Nov. 1990	The eligibility standards for issuing straight bonds, convertible and warrant bonds are unified into a single standard based on credit rating. The standards for credit rating unsecured bonds and the additional debt restriction covenant are revised.
Apr. 1991	The regulation setting a limit on the amount of corporate bonds that can be issued is eased.
Nov. 1991	Banks start issuing two year debentures, and the Bank of Tokyo starts issuing five year debentures.
Dec. 1991	Business firms issue straight bonds which are sold at a fixed price.
Jan. 1992	Business firms issue convertible four year discount notes.
Mar. 1992	The method of selling corporate bonds at a uniform price is introduced.
Jul. 1992	The requirements for filing shelf registrations are eased. Business firms issue convertible bonds based on the book building system.
Nov. 1992	The bond market introduces a bond issuing method by which issuing terms are determined on the basis of a prior survey of investor demand.
Mar. 1993	Part of the Three Bureau guidance (that locally incorporated foreign subsidiaries of securities companies should be given the lead managership of underwriting foreign bonds issued by Japanese firms abroad) is abolished.
Apr. 1993	The eligibility standards for issuing unsecured corporate bonds and the additional debt restriction covenant are eased.
Jun. 1993	Business firms start issuing straight bonds with the guarantee of their parent companies.
Jul. 1993	Business firms issue two year convertible bonds. Procedures for issuing foreign bonds by residents under a bond issuing programme are simplified.
Aug. 1993	Business firms issue three year convertible bonds.
Sept. 1993	The ban on issuing floating rate notes and five year coupon notes is lifted.

Table 1.4 *Continued*

	Nov. 1993	Business firms issue five year notes and 20 year straight bonds.
	Dec. 1993	The eligibility standards for issuing foreign bonds are eased.
	Jan. 1994	Business firms issue five year convertible bonds.
	Mar. 1994	Business firms issue straight bonds based on the book building system and dual currency bonds.
Domestic bonds issued by non-residents	Apr. 1986	The rules for issuing yen-denominated bonds by non-residents are integrated into the credit rating system.
	Oct. 1986	Maturities of yen-denominated bonds issued by non-residents are extended, and a rule mandating a wholesale redemption at maturity is adopted.
	Nov. 1986	The requirements for issuing yen-denominated bonds by non-residents, and the additional debt restriction covenant, are eased.
	May 1989	The ban on issuing foreign currency-denominated convertible bonds in Japan by non-residents is lifted.
	Jul. 1989	The ceiling imposed on domestic bonds issued by non-residents and on maturity is lifted.
	Sept. 1989	The system of authorising each issue of yen-denominated notes issued by foreign issuers with a maturity of less than four years is abolished.
	Aug. 1992	The eligibility standards for issuing yen-denominated bonds by foreign issuers are eased.
	Feb. 1993	Foreign firms issue 20 year yen-denominated bonds.
	Dec. 1993	The eligibility standards for issuing domestic bonds by non-residents are eased.
Privately placed industrial bonds	Apr. 1987	With the adoption of a rule for privately placing large amount corporate bonds, the rule of no return is abolished.
	Apr. 1993	The ceiling on annual amounts of bonds and issuing lot is raised, and the regulation of resale of privately placed bonds is eased.
Bond trading market	Sept. 1986	Banks and securities companies start publishing quotations of debt issues.
	May 1987	Short selling of bonds by banks and securities companies is authorised.
	May 1989	The market for lending bonds is launched.

Table 1.4 *Continued*

	Sept. 1990	The Tokyo Stock Exchange starts publishing real time quotations of foreign currency-denominated warrants.
	Jan. 1991	Securities companies start providing market-making service for domestic straight bonds.
	Apr. 1991	The formula of publishing standard quotations of bonds traded over the counter is changed.
Futures and options	Oct. 1985	The market for 10 year government coupon bonds is launched.
	May 1987	Overseas financial futures trading by financial institutions (banks, securities companies, investment trusts, life insurance companies, etc) for their own account is liberalised.
	Jun. 1987	The Osaka Securities Exchange starts trading in a package of 50 stock futures.
	Mar. 1988	Overseas stock options trading by financial institutions (banks, securities companies, investment trusts, life insurance companies, etc) is liberalised.
	May 1988	The Financial Futures Trading Law is promulgated, and an amendment to the Securities and Exchange Law authorising securities futures trading passes through Parliament.
	Jul. 1988	Trading in 20 year government coupon bond futures starts.
	Sept. 1988	The TSE and the OSE start trading in stock index futures.
	Apr. 1989	The Tokyo International Financial Futures Exchange (TIFFE) is launched. The ban on trading in OTC bond options is lifted.
	Jun. 1989	The TIFFE starts trading in interest and foreign exchange futures. Investors at large begin participating in foreign financial futures trading. The OSE starts trading in stock index options.
	Oct. 1989	The Nagoya Stock Exchange starts trading in Options 25. The TSE starts trading in stock index options.
	Dec. 1989	The TSE starts trading in Treasury bond futures.
	May 1990	The TSE starts trading in government bond futures.

Table 1.4 *Continued*

		Oct. 1990	The system of market-making on dollar based short term interest rate futures and currency futures is introduced.
		Mar. 1991	The TIFFE starts trading in currency (dollar and yen) futures.
		Jul. 1991	The TIFFE starts trading in yen based short term interest rate future options.
		Oct. 1991	The system of market-making on dollar based short term interest rate futures, and currency futures is introduced.
		Jun. 1992	The OSE toughens the requirements for disclosure of information concerning futures and options trading.
		Jul. 1992	The TSE lists one year yen futures.
		Apr. 1993	The standards for starting stock index options trading are eased.
		Feb. 1994	The OSE lists Nikkei 300 futures and options.
	Securitisation of credits	Dec. 1973	Housing Loan Company starts handling housing loan credit-backed trusts.
		Sept. 1974	Financial institutions start handling mortgage-backed securities.
		Dec. 1987	The Law for Regulating Mortgage-Backed Securities passes through Parliament.
		May 1988	The marketability of mortgage-backed investment trusts improves.
		Jun. 1988	Housing Loan Company starts handling housing loan credit-backed trusts following improvement in their marketability.
		Nov. 1988	Financial institutions start handling housing loan credit-backed trusts.
		Jul. 1989	Liquidation of credits given to local public bodies starts.
		Mar. 1990	Liquidation of general loan credits starts.
		Nov. 1991	Regulation of liquidation of general loan credits is eased.
		Jun. 1992	The Law Concerning the Regulation of Transfer of Lease Credits is promulgated.
		Dec. 1992	The ban on liquidating general loan credits in the form of investment trusts is lifted.
		Jan. 1993	Co-operative Credit Purchasing Company is founded.
		Apr. 1994	The ban on liquidating loan credits to local public bodies in the form of investment trusts is lifted.
Euro market	Lending	Jun. 1983	Short term Euro-yen loans to non-residents are liberalised.

Table 1.4 *Continued*

	Jun. 1984	Short term Euro-yen loans to residents are liberalised.
	Apr. 1985	Long and medium term loans to non-residents are liberalised.
	May 1989	Long and medium term loans to residents are liberalised.
Certificates of deposit (CD)	Dec. 1984	Issuing short term (less than six months) Euro-yen CDs is liberalised.
	Jul. 1985	Issuing long and medium term (up to one year) Euro-yen CDs is liberalised.
	Apr. 1988	The maximum maturity of Euro-yen CDs is extended to two years.
Commercial paper (CP)	Nov. 1987	Issuing Euro-yen CP by non-residents is liberalised.
	Dec. 1988	The rule for issuing CP is revised.
Eurobonds	Apr. 1985	The withholding tax on interest income of non-residents from Euro-yen bonds issued by residents is abolished. The eligibility standards for issuing Euro-yen bonds by non-residents are eased.
	Jun. 1985	The ban on issuing dual currency bonds is lifted.
	Jul. 1985	The eligibility standards for issuing Euro-yen bonds by residents are eased.
	Oct. 1985	The eligibility standards for issuing Euro-yen bonds by residents are further eased.
	Apr. 1986	The eligibility standards for issuing Euro-yen bonds by non-residents are abolished in favour of the credit rating system. Financial products are diversified by allowing the issuing of floating rate notes. The regulation banning the resale of Euro-yen bonds during the initial 180 days is eased.
	Jun. 1986	The ban on issuing Euro-yen bonds by foreign banks is lifted.
	Feb. 1987	The eligibility standards for issuing Euro-yen bonds are further eased.
	Jun. 1987	The ban on issuing four year notes is lifted completely.
	Jul. 1987	The credit rating system is integrated into the eligibility standards for issuing Euro-yen bonds by residents.
	Jun. 1989	The regulation limiting the maturity of Euro-yen bonds issued by non-residents is lifted.
	Jul. 1989	The eligibility standards for issuing Euro-yen bonds by residents are further eased.

Table 1.4 *Continued*

		Aug. 1992	The eligibility standards for issuing Euro-yen bonds by residents are further eased.
		Jul. 1993	The eligibility standards for issuing Euro-yen bonds by non-residents are further eased.
		Dec. 1993	The regulation restricting the resale of Euro-yen bonds issued by non-residents is lifted.
Futures and options		Jul. 1991	Trading in Euro-yen interest rate futures options starts.

PART II The players

2 Private investors and the investment–savings balance

Shifting investment–savings balance and changes in the financial and capital markets

1970–4: SHAKEN BY EXTERNAL FORCES

Table 2.1 sums up the characteristics of the Japanese economy in each of the five year periods since 1970. In 1970–4, the yen appreciated dramatically against the dollar following the flotation of the yen – registering a 25 per cent jump in three years from ¥358 to the dollar in April 1970 to ¥265.5 in April 1974. In an effort to mitigate the deflationary impact of the stronger yen, the monetary authorities implemented a low interest rate policy during the period. Meanwhile, the government of Prime Minister Kakuei Tanaka (1972–4) sharply increased its fiscal spending under the slogan of 'Redevelopment of the Japanese Archipelago'. As a result, the financial and capital markets of Japan were inundated with surplus cash, which sharply lifted the prices of stocks and land, a phenomenon now euphemistically dubbed 'the first bubble economy'. In the process, general trading companies (which went on a stock investment frenzy) and property developers (who went on an acquisition binge) came under scathing criticism for their speculative activities.

As the Bank of Japan tightened its credit policy to tame the inflation ignited by the first oil crisis in the autumn of 1973, the economic bubble burst. However, consumer prices soared 20 per cent in 1974 over the previous year, largely due to the increase in the crude oil price and rapid growth in money supply. The central bank had to keep its tight money policy for an extended period, and real gross national product (GNP) recorded a negative growth in 1975 for

Table 2.1 Changes in the Japanese financial markets

	1970–4	1975–9	1980–4	1985–9	1990–4
Historical background	The first oil crisis 'Redevelopment of the Japanese Archipelago'	'Locomotive Japan'	The second oil crisis The government budget restructuring	The bubble economy (The sharp rise of land and stock prices) 'Young Creditor Japan'	The end of the bubble economy Deregulation of the market
Investment–Savings (I–S) balance	Corporate sector 65%	Public sector 73%	Public sector 60%	Corporate sector 44% Overseas sector 37%	Corporate sector 59% Overseas sector 28%
Economy	Overliquidity	Energy savings Retrenchment	Information revolution	The rapid expansion of overseas investment	Corporate restructuring
Japan–US bilateral talks	Textile	Steel	Automobiles	Semiconductor	Introduction of numerical goals
Financial market and foreign exchange	Floating exchange rate	Rapid expansion of government bond and *samurai* bond issuance	The reform of Foreign Exchange Law Japan–US Yen/Dollar Committee	The rapid expansion of equity finance The rapid expansion of real estate/non-bank loans	Instability of financial system, crash of stock market, establishment of securities subsidiaries by banks

Notes: **1** The I–S balance shows how much of personal savings is used to make up fund shortages in different sectors.
2 The I–S balance for FY 1993/4 is an estimate made by the Nomura Research Institute.

the first time since the war. To be sure, prices subsided but at the price of recession.

During the rapid growth period up to the first oil crisis, businesses invested heavily in new plant and equipment, creating a large shortage of funds year after year. And personal savings were tapped mainly through banking institutions to meet such shortage of funds. Indeed, the shortage of funds in the corporate sector in each of the 10 years from fiscal 1965 to 1974 averaged at 7 per cent of gross national product, and 80 per cent of personal savings were absorbed into the corporate sector through the banks.

1975–9: DEVELOPMENT OF THE GOVERNMENT BOND MARKET

The years 1975 to 1979 were marked by massive issuing of government bonds, as mentioned in Chapter 1. In an effort to jump-start the stalled economy, the government had sharply boosted its deficit spending since 1975 – to such an extent, in fact, that funds raised through debt offerings accounted for 40 per cent of the original budget revenue for fiscal 1979 (ended in March 1980). And this changed the investment–savings balance. The aftermath of the first oil crisis and the prolonged recession that followed brought profound changes in the industrial structure. Retrenchment became a catchword among corporate managers, and business spending on new plant and equipment slumped for an extended period, easing the shortage of funds. Meanwhile, massive issuing of government bonds to buoy the economy, by combining with an increase in municipal bond offerings, continued. As a result, the public sector sopped up 73 per cent of personal savings.

The massive offering of government and other public bonds had big impacts on the financial and capital markets. One of them was the pressure for liberalising interest rates.

Deposit rates had been fixed at a low level under the artificially low interest rate policy during the rapid growth period from 1961 to 1970. As the years rolled on into the 1970s, however, the government began to change deposit rates in step with changes occurring in the yen rate. Coming as it did at such a critical juncture, the government began to issue bonds on a massive scale, which generated mounting pressure to liberalise interest rates.

Until then, the bulk of government bonds were allocated to member banks of underwriting syndicates at a low interest rate on condition that they did not resell the government bonds to others. However, as the amount of bonds the government issued each year increased from ¥1 trillion to ¥2 trillion to ¥8 trillion to ¥9 trillion, underwriting syndicate members had to liquidate them. However, if they sold at a market rate the government bonds which carried a low coupon, they stood to suffer a huge capital loss. Therefore, syndicate members pressed the government to raise the coupon rates to a level matching the market rate. Because of such pressure, the coupon rates of government bonds were raised at a rapid pace to market rates during fiscal 1975 to 1979.

The massive offering of government bonds also had the effect of liberalising short term rates. As the trading volume of bonds increased sharply, securities companies needed extra funds to finance their bond inventories, but they were not allowed to raise funds on the interbank market. To get around this hurdle, securities companies sold their bond holdings to companies with excess short term cash on condition that they would repurchase the bonds at an agreed-upon price, and used the proceeds to finance their inventories. A market for *gensaki* (repurchase agreements, or repos, for short) has thus emerged. Although *gensaki* deals take the form of the sale and repurchase of bonds, it is actually a short term money market vehicle that carries a deregulated interest rate. Because of the attractiveness of the interest rate it carries, a considerable portion of excess cash business firms had on hand flowed to the *gensaki* market in fiscal 1975 through fiscal 1979. With the aim to lure these surplus funds idling at corporate treasuries, banks started issuing in April 1979 certificates of deposit (CD) in units of ¥500 million carrying deregulated interest rates.

Then, under the foreign pressure brought to bear on Japan by the Japan–US Yen/Dollar Committee and financial friction between the two countries in the 1980s, Japan lowered step by step the size of time deposit for which interest rates were deregulated until the whole gamut of interest rates was liberalised in 1994 with the deregulation of deposit rates on passbook accounts (see Table 1.4).

1980–4: INTERNATIONALISATION

Developments that distinguished the years 1980 to 1984 from other periods were a surge in the international movement of capital triggered by the 1979 amendment of the Foreign Exchange Control Law and the efforts by the government of Prime Minister Yasuhiro Nakasone (1982–7) to rehabilitate the worsening situation of government finance.

In order to help the economy climb out of the recession after the first oil crisis of 1973, the government of Prime Minister Takeo Fukuda (1976–8) had issued large amounts of government bonds for several years running and exacerbated the fiscal balance in the process. To decrease the issuance of government bonds, the government's Tax Council proposed a general consumption tax, but it ran into a wall of voter resistance and the ruling Liberal Democratic Party (LDP) suffered a setback in the October 1979 general elections. With the hope of increasing its revenues thus dashed, the LDP government sought to rehabilitate its finances by cutting down on its spending in the first half of the 1980s. In March 1981 the government appointed a task force named the 'Provisional Administration Research Committee'. This committee examined the causes of the ballooned budget deficits and took a searching look at the whole gamut of administration, including the inefficiency of government run enterprises (such as Japan National Railways which had piled up colossal debts) and government regulation of the market which inhibited the freedom of business activities and competition.

The government's efforts to improve its finances made little progress in the first half of the 1980s due to a weak economy. In the United States, meanwhile, the Federal Reserve Board implemented a tight monetary policy which pushed up interest rates to a high level by historic standards, and the dollar continued on a high plateau. There was little room for the Bank of Japan to cut interest rates to stimulate the domestic economy. Thus, the government had to curb its spending continuously, and, as a result, the economy remained in the doldrums. As a result, it was extremely difficult for the government to cut down on its debt offering. Under such circumstances, the public sector still soaked up 60 per cent of personal savings.

It was in the second half of the 1980s when private capital spending, triggered by a hefty increase in exports, turned sharply upwards that the government was able to make significant headway in its effort to rehabilitate its finances.

While the public sector absorbed a huge amount of personal savings during 1975 and 1984, it is also notable that the yen-denominated foreign bond (*samurai*) market was developed. Following the switchover to a floating rate system, the international movement of funds was liberalised in measured steps (as explained in Chapter 1). And the offering of yen-denominated foreign bonds on the Tokyo market by the Asian Development Bank in 1971, the first since the war, opened the gates to the international movement of capital. Then the volume of yen-denominated bonds increased from ¥300 billion ($3 billion) in fiscal 1976 to ¥720 billion ($7.2 billion) in fiscal 1978. The sharp increase that occurred in government debt offerings in the second half of the 1970s may be explained by the fact that in an effort to avert the negative impacts that the current account surplus-induced rises in the yen might have on the domestic economy, the government sought to curb the growing current account surplus by stimulating domestic demand. Further, to head off rises in the yen caused by surplus dollars floating around in the foreign exchange market, the government assisted yen-denominated foreign bond markets to expand as a means of recycling the growing current account surplus. As the international movement of capital picked up, pressure mounted for an amendment of the Foreign Exchange Control Law, and finally, in December 1979, an amendment was passed and became effective in December 1980.

The liberalisation of foreign exchange control prompted not only capital outflow from Japan, but also inflow (especially in the form of securities investment). Overseas investors got interested in the Japanese economy and some of its industries which had survived two oil crises and become more competitive.

In the wake of the first oil crisis in 1973, there developed a clear polarisation of industry into two groups: the waning traditional crude materials industries and the rising electronics and precision machinery industries. As industrial machinery incorporated ever increasing varieties of electronic components after the second oil crisis of 1979, this tendency of polarisation became increasingly pronounced. The spread of electronic equipment did not stop at factory automation (such as 'mechatronics' (mechanical electronics) and industrial robots) but reached office equipment and home appliances. In fact, the spread of electronics was so pervasive that a new coinage, 'information revolution', has become an integral part of the vocabulary of ordinary people. (Taking its cue from this development, the government enacted in 1984 a law privatising Nippon Telegraph & Telephone Company (NTT) on a recommendation made by Panel Four of the Provisional Administration Research Committee in 1982 and auctioned off a tranche of shares of NTT in 1988, see Chapter 4.)

As a result of a four-fold increase in oil prices during the second oil crisis of 1979, member countries of OPEC piled up huge sums of oil money, touching off a worldwide clamour for recycling their mountainous cash. Part of their idle cash found its way into Japanese stocks – shares in steel companies which enjoyed a competitive edge on the world market, and in those of electronic and electrical machinery makers and precision machinery builders which grew rapidly riding the wave of the information revolution. A sharp increase in investment in Japanese stocks by oil exporting countries had a big impact on the Tokyo stock market, and the value of equity and equity-linked securities offerings made by Japanese companies more than doubled from ¥1.6 trillion ($16 billion) in 1979 to ¥3.7 trillion ($37 billion) in 1981. In the process, the ratio of equity capital of Japanese firms, which had fallen consistently during the rapid growth period, stopped declining thanks to the 'retrenchment drive' in the second half of the 1970s and then turned upwards on account of the equity-linked securities offerings they made in the first half of the 1980s (see Chapter 5).

The sharp increase in investment of oil money in Japanese stocks helped raise the name recognition of Japanese firms, and thanks, in part, to the amendment of the Foreign Exchange Control Law of 1979, bond offerings on foreign markets by Japanese firms also increased smartly. Coupled with a wave of investment in foreign bonds by Japanese institutional investors (during this period, the difference in interest rates between Japan and the United States rose to 5–6 per cent), a concept of 'International Financial Centre Japan' emerged.

1985–9: BUBBLE ECONOMY

The period 1985–9 is marked by the development of the second economic bubble, and the period 1990–4 by the bursting of this bubble, which was punctured by the fourth hike in the discount rate in March 1990. Since 1986, Japan has run a huge current account surplus each year, hitting $80 billion in a peak year, and the yen to dollar rate jumped from ¥245 in December 1985 to ¥120 in December 1989. With a view to defusing the deflationary pressure generated by the high yen, the Bank of Japan cut the discount rate in rapid steps, down to 2.5 per cent in February 1987.

The sharp drop in interest rates caused stock prices to pick up, which in turn facilitated offerings of equity-linked securities. The value of equity-linked offerings jumped from an annual average of ¥3 trillion ($30 billion) in the first half of the 1980s to ¥5.8 trillion ($58 billion) in 1986 to ¥14.7 trillion ($147 billion) in 1988 to ¥24.9 trillion ($249 billion) in 1989. As big firms shifted the bulk of their financing to the capital markets, growth in bank lendings continued to slow down. However, as lower interest rates helped boost the profitability of commercial property developers, loans to them picked up sharply, taking up the slack generated by the defection of big firms. In fact, loans made during this period to property developers and 'non-banks' (finance companies, leasing companies, consumer loan companies, etc) accounted for 50 per cent of the increases in loans of commercial banks, long term credit banks, and trust banks – most of which soured, adding to the bad loan burden weighing down on the banking institutions in the 1990s (see Chapter 7).

During the bubble years (1986–9), land and stock prices increased by two or three times, and this fired a speculation frenzy which spread to acquisitions of condominiums and golf course membership. During this period, banks' loans to individuals also picked up sharply. This was due to the widely shared speculation that tangible assets such as houses and condominiums would rise sharply in the years to come.

By the second half of the 1980s, Japan was still piling up an unprecedentedly large current account surplus, and the recycling of the surplus took on additional channels – international portfolio investment and direct investment. Thirty-seven per cent of personal savings was channelled to overseas markets.

As the high yen slowed the recovery in business spending on new plant and equipment, business demand for funds languished. As an outlet for their idle cash, life insurance companies and private pension funds sharply increased their investment in foreign securities of different countries. At the same time, individuals and business corporations sought to escape the prohibitively high costs of domestic property and bought overseas real estate in earnest. Meanwhile, the high yen ate deeply into the profitability of exports but the trade friction between Japan and the United States intensified. To circumvent these impediments, a growing number of Japanese firms moved their production base overseas. In the process, the outflow of long term capital from Japan more than doubled from $65 billion in 1985 to $130 billion in 1988, and this helped Japan earn the sobriquet 'Young Creditor Japan'.

1990–4: HANGOVER

The economy which had had all the trimmings of a bubble economy and was nicknamed 'Young Creditor Japan' in the second half of the 1980s abruptly found itself faced with sweeping changes on account of rises in interest rates from May 1989. The change took the form of the bursting of the bubble economy and a sharp drop in Japanese investment in foreign securities. The fourth hike in the discount rate in March 1990 triggered a stock market crash in Japan, and the securities market preoccupied itself in 1991–2 with controlling the damage done to its prestige and credibility caused by the revelations of irregularities committed by financial intermediaries (illegal loans, compensation of their favoured clients for trading losses, stock parking, etc).

As property prices continued to drop in the autumn of 1991, the problem of bad loans came to the fore, and the prices of bank stocks plummeted in the January–March quarter of 1992 – to such an extent that the Ministry of Finance was compelled to disclose the size of the bad loans of the commercial, long term credit and trust banks, a telling admission of its anxiety about the credibility of the nation's financial system. The big Japanese banks started to write off their bad loans in March 1993. They must clear these loans off their balance sheets within the next two to three years. Meanwhile, institutional investors (notably, life insurance companies and private pension funds) saw their unrealised gains in stock prices contract sharply and in some cases evaluation losses of their stock holdings. Alarmed by the sharp contraction in the unrealised gains from their stock holdings, saddled with a huge load of bad loans, and con-cerned about the slumping returns on their investment in foreign securities, institutional investors were having second thoughts about making additional investment in foreign securities. The damage sustained this time around in the wake of the bursting of the economic bubble was far more jolting than that which followed the bursting of the first economic bubble of 1972–3 – with the result that the banks and other institutional investors came under mounting pressures to nurse their financial positions back to health by the mid-1990s in the face of falling interest rates.

Corporate earnings also fell sharply. To meet the growing dom-estic demand, businesses had invested heavily in new capacity in the second half of the 1980s. However, domestic demand slumped in 1992–3, creating overcapacity on a scale far larger than the one witnessed after the first oil crisis of 1973. The surplus capacity squeezed corporate earnings. Major businesses reported decreases in earnings in March 1995 (for FY 1994) for five consecutive years, the first such experience since the war. The historically low profit-ability forced businesses to give top priority to restructuring their operation.

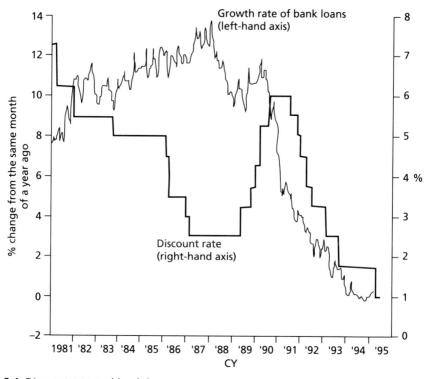

2.1 Discount rate and bank loans.
Note: Loan is offered by all banks.

Since the beginning of 1994, the Japanese government has been trying in earnest to stimulate domestic demand to stem the rising jobless rate and cut the increasing current account surplus. As shown in Fig. 2.1, the Bank of Japan has cut the discount rate a number of times since 1991 and finally reduced it to 1.00 per cent, the lowest since the start of the Meiji government in 1868. Despite the low discount rate, the rate of growth in bank lendings has fallen below the corresponding period of a year ago. This is mainly blamed on the hesitancy of the banking institutions caused by the bad loan problem. In the meantime, the balance of government bonds out-standing at the end of March 1993 swelled to ¥178 trillion ($1.78 trillion), which accounted for 38 per cent of the year's nominal gross national product. In addition, construction bonds issue (government bonds the proceeds of which are used primarily to finance public works projects) also rose to a post-war high. Increases in govern-ment spending financed by debts could further aggravate the fiscal balance, further narrowing the elbow room for fiscal policy. And pressures to recycle the current account surpluses through export of capital have been growing, but Japanese institutional investors have little capacity – or stomach – for investing in foreign securities. Therefore, the banking sector has been cutting down on its foreign borrowings to spur the recycling of the current account surpluses.

Against such a background, the coalition government of Prime Minister Morihiro Hosokawa (1993–4) championed the cause of restructuring the Japanese economy. Among other things, the Hosokawa administration advocated a reduced role for government, by slimming down bloated government intervention in the market, the creation of a competitive market environment based on informed decisions made by each market participant at its own risk and on its own responsibility (*caveat emptor*), and a vibrant economy fired by individuals' entrepreneurship. On the domestic front, his government pressed ahead with various market-opening measures in the belief that stronger foreign competition would lower domestic prices and in effect raise the real wages of the working population. In the process, there has emerged a national consensus that deregulation, competition, and narrowing the price difference between domestic and foreign goods and services are the right prescriptions for restructuring the Japanese economy. The aftermath of the first economic bubble of 1971–2 was overcome by aggressive fiscal spending undertaken by the government of Prime Minister Takeo Fukuda. Now Japan is trying to tame the after-effects of the second economic bubble of 1985–9 by pursuing economic reform based on competition and the open market, on top of the traditional expansionary policy of low interest rates and stimulative public sector expenditure.

Private investment

Table 2.2 sums up the changes that have occurred in the asset preference of individuals since 1969. Reflecting individuals' growing sensitiveness to the level of interest rates, the balance of their cash and demand deposits as a percentage of their aggregate financial assets dropped by as much as 7.4 per cent, from 16 per cent at the end of fiscal 1969 to 8.6 per cent at the end of fiscal 1992. The balance of their time deposits also declined by 3.5 per cent, from 33 per cent to 29.5 per cent during the same period.

The balance of postal time savings accounts (which are available at a nationwide network of 24,000 post offices) increased 6.9 per cent during the period, to 16.6 per cent at the end of fiscal 1992. This

Table 2.2 Individuals' asset allocation (on the basis of balance)

Fiscal year	1969		1974		1979		1984		1989		1992		(B)-(A)
	tril. yen	share (A)	tril. yen	share	tril. yen	share	tril. yen	share	tril. yen	share	tril. yen	share (B)	
		(%)		(%)		(%)		(%)		(%)		(%)	(%)
Cash and demand deposits	10.4	16.0	25.3	16.5	42.4	13.4	51.4	9.6	85.1	9.5	88.0	8.6	-7.4
Time deposits of banks	21.4	33.0	52.8	34.4	105.1	33.3	166.4	31.2	245.1	27.3	301.7	29.5	-3.5
Postal savings	6.3	9.7	19.4	12.7	51.9	16.4	94.0	17.6	134.6	15.0	170.1	16.6	6.9
Trusts	3.5	5.4	8.8	5.7	19.2	6.1	36.4	6.8	57.6	6.4	76.0	7.4	2.0
Insurance	7.9	12.2	19.0	12.4	40.9	12.9	80.0	15.0	178.4	19.9	240.5	23.5	11.3
Securities	14.1	21.8	27.3	17.8	52.1	16.5	103.2	19.3	185.9	20.7	147.2	14.4	-7.4
Government bonds	1.3	2.1	3.1	2.0	10.4	3.3	21.1	3.9	15.9	1.8	7.8	0.8	-1.3
Bank debentures	2.0	3.1	5.3	3.5	11.4	3.6	19.1	3.6	19.7	2.2	26.1	2.5	-0.6
Industrial bonds	0.1	0.2	1.0	0.7	1.7	0.5	2.2	0.4	5.2	0.6	5.8	0.6	0.4
Stocks	9.6	14.8	15.2	9.9	23.3	7.4	45.0	8.4	104.7	11.7	70.8	6.9	-7.9
Investment trust	1.0	1.6	2.7	1.8	5.3	1.7	15.8	3.0	40.4	4.5	36.8	3.6	2.0
Total including others	64.9	100.0	153.3	100.0	316.0	100.0	533.4	100.0	898.5	100.0	1023.8	100.0	
Public sector													
Public demand deposit	0.0	0.0	0.1	0.0	0.1	0.0	0.1	0.0	0.5	0.1	0.9	0.1	0.1
Postal savings	6.3	9.7	19.4	12.7	51.9	16.4	94.0	17.6	134.6	15.0	170.1	16.6	6.9
Postal insurance	2.1	3.2	5.5	3.6	13.1	4.2	25.5	4.8	46.4	5.2	65.5	6.4	3.2
Public total	8.4	13.0	25.0	16.3	65.2	20.6	119.7	22.4	181.5	20.2	236.5	23.1	10.1

Note: Stocks valued at market prices.
Source: Bank of Japan.

is largely due to the advantages of postal time savings accounts (PTSA). As of March 1993 (end of FY 1992), PTSAs offered an interest rate of 1.7 per cent for accounts with a maturity of one year or longer, 1.75 per cent for those with a maturity of 1.5 years or longer, 1.85 per cent for those with a maturity of two years or longer, 1.9 per cent for those with a maturity of 2.5 years or longer, and 2.1 per cent for those with a maturity of three years or longer (up to 10 years). This system enables depositors to get the interest rate of the term that they actually hold with no penalty. As of March 1993, indicated interest rates on the time deposits of commercial banks – 1.8 per cent for one year accounts and 2.2 per cent for three year accounts – were slightly higher than those of the PTSA. In the case of bank time deposits, however, withdrawal before maturity forfeits the privilege of guaranteed interest rates. Although the PTSA offers slightly lower interest rates, it is far more liquid and beneficial than bank time deposits because of the no penalty feature. Moreover, interest on a PTSA compounds twice a year. Accordingly, for ¥100 deposited in a PTSA with a maturity of five years, the total amount including interest five years later will be $¥100 \times (1 + 2.1/200)^{10}$.

The interest rate on a PTSA with a maturity of three years or longer has been raised to 8 per cent twice during the past 25 years in step with rises in market rates. As a PTSA offers maturities up to 10 years, any person depositing ¥100 in a PTSA with a maturity of 10 years stands to earn $¥100 \times (1 + 8/200)^{20}$ in compound interest. This means, in effect, the advent of a 10 year discount bond carrying a compound interest rate of 8 per cent without penalty for a premature withdrawal. And this has triggered a massive disintermediation of funds to postal savings. Because of the higher liquidity they offer, PTSAs have been very attractive to individuals in times of high interest rates, and their share of personal financial assets has risen sharply during the past 20 years. Concerned about the growing dominance of postal savings in the deposit market, the regulatory agency has sought to stem the disintermediation of funds by downgrading the attractiveness of PTSAs.

The bulk of trust accounts are loan trusts (with a maturity of five years) which are sold to individuals by trust banks, and they carry an interest rate pegged to long term prime rates. Under the normal yield curve which was the case most of the time during fiscal 1969 and fiscal 1992, their market share rose steadily.

The product which has made the largest gains in the individual financial asset market since 1970 has been life insurance. Its share increased by 11 per cent from 12.2 per cent at the end of fiscal 1969 to 23.5 per cent at the end of FY 1992. The insured amount tends to increase consistently in step with increases in the nominal income of the insured, although the rate of the insured population has risen to a level comparable with those of other industrial nations, Japan's high economic growth rate encouraged insured amounts to increase, and the share of life insurance in personal financial assets rose sharply. In addition, a sharp increase in single premium endowment insurance (which is designed to boost the savings element at the expense of the insurance element) introduced in the 1980s further raised the share of life insurance. Moreover, postal insurance policies (included in the insurance statistics) offered over the counter at the nation's 24,000 post offices claimed 6.4 per cent of personal financial assets and accounted for 27 per cent of the nation's life insurance policies in force at the end of fiscal 1992. The share of public sector financial products (postal savings plus postal life insurance) in personal financial assets almost doubled during the 23 year period, from 13 per cent at the end of fiscal 1969 to 23.1 per cent at the end of fiscal 1992. Ironically, the deregulation of deposit rates effected in the 1980s boosted the market share of government-related financial institutions. And if their share continues to increase at this rate, pressures will grow for an adjustment of market share between public sector and private sector in financial markets.

Conventional wisdom has it that as incomes rise, individuals will seek to diversify their investments increasingly in favour of risky assets such as bonds and stocks. In the case of Japan, however, securities holdings of individuals as a percentage of personal financial assets have decreased by 7.4 per cent, from 21.8 per cent at the end of fiscal 1969 to 14.4 per cent at the end of fiscal 1992, despite the fact that per capita GNP increased from ¥720,000 ($7,200) to ¥3,780,000 ($37,800) at the end of fiscal 1992.

Broken down, the share of individuals' holdings of public bonds increased from 2 per cent at the end of fiscal 1974 to 3.9 per cent at the end of fiscal 1984. In the past, interest income earned by an individual from a deposit of up to ¥3 million (known as 'the *maruyu* system') and investment of up to ¥3 million in government bonds were exempted from income tax (called 'the *tokuyu* system'). In 1976–85, the government issued deficit-covering bonds on a massive scale, and those bought by individual investors increased markedly in the process. However, as the government curtailed its debt offering and the trade frictions with the United States escalated in the second half of the 1980s, the high savings rate of Japan, which fuelled the growth in its exports, came under fire, forcing the

Japanese government to abolish the tax-exempt small amount savings (*maruyu* and *tokuyu*) system. As a result, purchases of government bonds by individuals have since decreased rapidly.

During these years, the Long Term Credit Bank, the Bank of Tokyo, the Central Bank for Agriculture and Forestry, and the government run Central Co-operative Bank for Commerce and Industry raised funds by offering bank debentures. The bulk of discount debentures (with a maturity of one year) which accounted for 28 per cent of the total bank debentures were sold to individuals over the counter by commercial banks and securities companies. As the years rolled on into the 1980s, these long term credit banks sold to individuals five year debentures called 'Wide' which carried an interest compounded twice a year, payable in a lump sum at maturity. However, the share of bank debentures in personal financial assets has changed little during the past 20 years, and nor has the share of industrial bonds. As a result, the share of bonds in personal financial assets decreased by 1.5 per cent from 5.4 per cent at the end of fiscal 1969 to 3.9 per cent at the end of fiscal 1992.

As purchases of bond investment trusts, the main investment vehicles of which are incorporated government notes and bonds (such as the medium term government bond fund), increased in the second half of the 1980s, the share of investment trusts in personal financial assets increased from 1.7 per cent at the end of fiscal 1979 to 3 per cent at the end of fiscal 1984. As the years advanced into the second half of the 1980s, the outstanding balance of stock investment funds increased sharply thanks to continued rises in stock prices, and the share of investment trusts as a whole in personal financial assets rose higher still, to 4.5 per cent at the end of fiscal 1989. Come the 1990s, however, a collapse in stock prices took a heavy toll in stock investment trusts, with the result that the share of investment trusts dropped back to 3.6 per cent at the end of fiscal 1992. More recently, the outstanding balance of money market fund (which is somewhat less liquid than the MMF of the United States) has been increasing markedly.

As the shares of investment trusts and bond holdings have not changed much, the decline in the share of securities as a whole in personal financial assets may be explained by a fall-off in the ratio of stock holdings. Among financial assets held by individuals, the share of stock, which stood at 14.8 per cent at the end of fiscal 1969, has since declined consistently, and after a brief recovery in the second half of the 1980s, it dropped to 6.9 per cent at the end of fiscal 1992 – a drop-off of 7.9 per cent during the past 20 years.

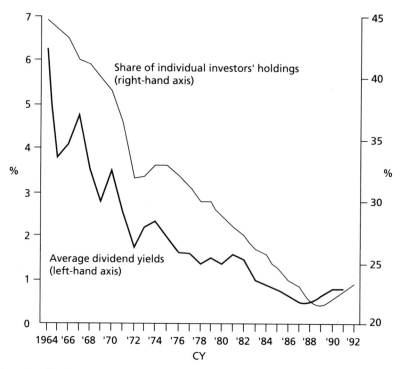

2.2 Ratio of individual investors and average dividend yield (source: Tokyo Stock Exchange).

As the data of the flow-of-funds account prepared by the Bank of Japan are based on the market price of stocks, changes in stock prices produce a large swing in the share of stock holdings in personal financial assets. Fig. 2.2 shows the relationship between the ratio of individuals' shareholdings to the total number of outstanding shares on the basis of 'Changes in the Distribution of Stock Ownership' compiled by the Tokyo Stock Exchange and dividend yields. As shown in Fig. 2.2, the ratio of individuals' shareholdings has decreased consistently since the war, and part of the blame for the decrease rests with the low dividend yields. As explained in Chapter 1, after the 'PER revolution' of the early 1970s, the PER (price–earnings ratio) of Japanese stocks continued to climb until the second half of the 1980s, and it is believed that the high PERs discouraged individuals from acquiring shares.

One characteristic distinguishing the Japanese stock market from others is the practice of cross-shareholding by corporations. As a growing number of companies have issued their shares at market price since the start of the 1970s, the cost of acquiring new shares has risen sharply compared with that of new shares issued at par

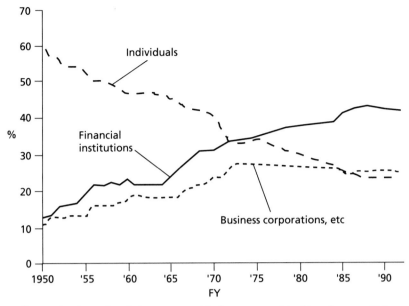

2.3 Change in the ratio of share ownership by groups of holders (source: Tokyo Stock Exchange).
Note: Financial institutions do not include investment trusts.

value. This has made it difficult for businesses to acquire new shares of other firms in cross-shareholding since 1970, and the ratio of shares held by business corporations has continued virtually flat. It is financial institutions which have offset the slack demand for equity, and the ratio of their stock holdings increased from 35 per cent in March 1974 to 43.3 per cent in March 1989 (Fig. 2.3). In the process, the ratio of financial institutions' shareholdings increased. Factors that contributed to the rise in the shareholdings of financial institutions include the following:

1 As business firms diversified their sources of financing away from bank borrowings, banks sought to strengthen their ties with their corporate clients by acquiring their shares.

2 Life insurance companies and trust banks managing pension funds beefed up their stock holdings to make up the slack in their business lending.

3 Stock investment by fund trusts (a fund entrusted to trust banks for its management at their discretion) and *tokkin* funds (a fund entrusted with specific instructions for investment) has increased sharply.

As the years wore on into the 1990s, however, a collapse in stock prices cut deeply into the unrealised capital gains in shares held by life insurance companies, and the problem of bad loans of leading banking institutions surfaced. All this has taken a heavy toll of stock investment by life insurance companies, commercial and long term credit banks, and trust banks. Indeed, Fig. 2.3 clearly points up the falling ratio of stockholdings by financial institutions – so much so that the Tokyo stock market will have to make strenuous efforts in the remaining years to 2000 to create a new structure of share ownership by seizing on a turnaround in corporate earnings. The real test facing the stock market of Japan will be: Can it lure individual investors back to the stock market? Or, how much will – and can – the long term debt driven financial institutions such as life insurance companies and pension funds devote their assets to stock investment exclusively based on the performance (dividend yields and capital gains) of stocks instead of business relationships (cross-holding of shares)?

The central bank and its monetary policy

Characteristics of Japan's monetary policy

The monetary policy the Bank of Japan has pursued since 1985, the year in which the yen started to climb steeply following the Plaza Accord, has a number of features distinguishing it from those of other industrial nations.

The ultimate objectives of Japan's monetary policy – stability of prices and sustainable economic growth – are no different from those of its Western counterparts. However, the operating target for Japan's monetary policy differs from those of Western countries in that while the latter countries place emphasis on high powered money (cash in circulation plus private bank reserve deposits with the central bank), the Bank of Japan attaches importance to short term rates (call rates and bill discount rates established in the interbank market, see Chapter 8 for details). For the intermediate target, Western central banks closely watch the movement of money supply, but the attitude of the Bank of Japan towards money supply is somewhat ambiguous. Until the 1960s the Bank of Japan attached importance to increases in loans made by private banks, and since around 1975, it has started following the movement of money supply. However, while Western central banks set and announce in advance their target ranges of money supply growth to be attained about a year down the road, the Bank of Japan only started publishing as late as July 1978 a forecast covering a three month period at the beginning of each quarter.

In operating its monetary policy, the Bank of Japan, as its Western counterparts do, employs three standard tools, namely, lending policy, open market operations (purchase or sale of bonds, notes, and commercial paper), and the change of reserve ratio. Of these, the Bank of Japan, unlike its Western counterparts, gives special weight to its lending policy. And this in effect is tantamount to giving banks a subsidy, because in Japan, the discount rate has invariably been lower than the overnight call rates formed in the interbank market, with the result that banks which borrow money from the central bank at the discount rate stand to earn the spread between the discount rate and the call rate. In the past, the overnight call rate has reliably been 0.5 per cent to 1 per cent higher than the discount rate, regardless of the conditions in the financial markets. Since 1994, however, the spread has narrowed to 0.25 per cent, prompting a spokesman from the Bank of Japan to observe that 'I wouldn't be surprised even if the two rates converged temporarily.' This marks a departure from the Bank's traditional monetary policy (Fig. 3.1).

As a complement to the three traditional policy tools, the Bank of Japan had been using window guidance, but in July 1991 it discontinued the practice. It was a practice which the Bank of Japan had employed since the mid-1960s to persuade major private banks through the discount window to hold down quarterly increases in their lending within a certain limit which the central bank saw appropriate in light of the economic conditions then prevailing. However, as the liberalisation of the financial markets took hold, and the pricing function of interest rates strengthened, giving the management of banking institutions a greater scope for their discretion, the practice was dropped in 1991.

A key point to watch in examining the operation of monetary policy by the Bank of Japan is its relations with call brokers and the Treasury investment and loans programme. As noted earlier, the Bank of Japan has closely followed the movement of call rates formed on the interbank market for clues for the development of its monetary policy. The bulk of fund transactions on the interbank market are brokered by call brokers. Their number is held down to

---

3.1 Difference between discount rates and other rates.
(A) Difference between the discount rate of Japan and the call rate (source: compiled by Nomura Research Institute on the basis of data drawn from *Economic Statistics Monthly* of the Bank of Japan).
Note: Monthly average of unsecured overnight call rates.
(B) Difference between the discount rate of the United States and the federal fund (FF) rate (source: compiled by Nomura Research Institute on the basis of data drawn from the statistics of the Federal Reserve Board).
Note: Monthly average of the FF rate.

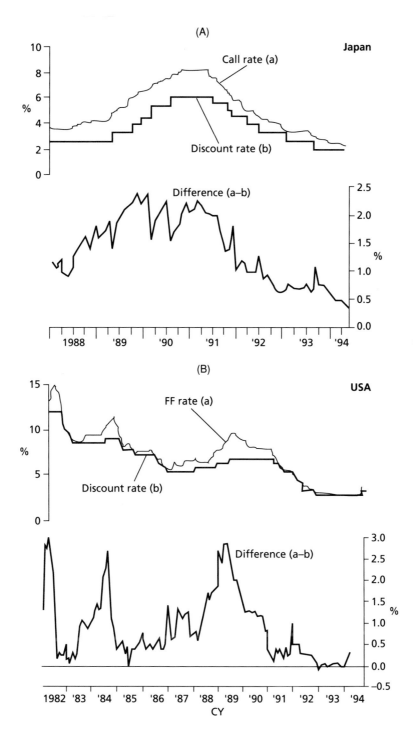

six and entry of additional participants is not allowed. As key managers of call brokers have hailed from the central bank or are closely related with it, communication between the central bank and call brokers works smoothly.

The Treasury investment and loans programme is financed with funds drawn from postal savings and governmental pensions, etc, which are invested in government and municipal bonds or lent to government run financial institutions. As postal savings are in competition with private bank deposits, the relationship between postal savings rates (which are set by the Ministry of Posts and Telecommunications) and private bank deposit rates (which are largely under the influence of the Bank of Japan) has long been a ticklish issue. As indicated in Chapter 2, if, for example, the Bank of Japan engineered a cut in the deposit rates of private banks to a level lower than the postal savings rate, it would trigger a shift of household deposits to postal savings (disintermediation). Therefore, the scope of the central bank for manipulating deposit rates is necessarily limited. When the funds pooled from postal savings and publicly run pension funds by the Trust Fund Bureau exceed the amounts of funds disbursed in Treasury investment and loans, it temporarily parks its surplus funds in bonds bought on the securities market or government bonds bought from the inventories of the Bank of Japan. If, in such cases, the Trust Fund Bureau purchases or sells large amounts of bonds at one time, such purchases or sales would affect bond yields, so the Bureau must exercise due care not to upset the monetary policy of the central bank. In fiscal 1992 and 1993, increases in lending by government run financial institutions to which the Bureau supplied funds outpaced those in lending by private banking institutions. This is another factor which the Bank of Japan cannot afford to ignore.

The governor of the central bank is appointed by the Prime Minister (for a term of five years), and its directors by the Minister of Finance (for a term of four years). Therefore, the independence of the central bank from politics or the Ministry of Finance is open to doubt. However, as politicians and bureaucrats are sufficiently cognisant of the statutory guarantee that 'the operation of monetary policy is an exclusive province of the Bank of Japan', there is a foundation for the central bank to maintain the independence of its policy thinking to a considerable degree. How much independence it can assert depends largely on personal relations between the governor and the Prime Minister or the Finance Minister then in office. Generally, an easy money policy meets with the warm support of the business community and no opposition from politicians, while a tight money policy often runs into resistance from the business community and politicians. If the central bank becomes too chary of ruffling politicians' feathers, it might miss a good opportunity to relax its credit reins because it fears the inevitable tightening in the future.

The monetary and credit control mechanism since 1985

Answers to the question as to what caused the steep growth in the money supply in 1986 through 1990 and then an equally steep decline in 1991 through 1994 will provide a clue to a correct evaluation of the performance of the monetary policy of the Bank of Japan in recent years. As we have seen, during these periods, Japan's economy went through an economic bubble and a serious recession that followed its bursting. The linkage between the recession and the wild swing that occurred in the money supply poses for economists an important question to which an easy answer does not lend itself (Fig. 3.2). However, the wild swing that occurred in money supply growth clearly shows that something is amiss with the nation's money and credit control mechanism, and it is necessary to examine why and how it went wrong. There are two schools of thought. One is led by Kunio Okina[1] and represents the views of the Bank of Japan, and the other, led by Professor Kikuo Iwata,[2] represents the views widely held by academics. Okina's view enjoys broad, if not monolithic, support of policymakers in the Bank of Japan. Policy decisions at the Bank of Japan are currently taken rather flexibly according to the dictate of changing situations. Nevertheless, Okina's view provides a suitable framework for evaluating the monetary policy of the Bank of Japan and may, therefore, be characterised as the dominant view within the circle of its policymakers.

---

1 Kunio Okina, *Kin'yu Seisaku: Chuoginko no Shiten to Sentaku* (*Monetary policy: Perspectives and policy choice of the central bank*), Tokyo (Toyo Keizai Shimposha), 1992.

2 Kikuo Iwata, *Kin'yu Seisaku no Keizaigaku: Nichigin Riron no Kensho* (*Economics of monetary policy: A critical examination of the monetary theory of the Bank of Japan*), Tokyo (the Nihon Keizai Shimbun), 1993.

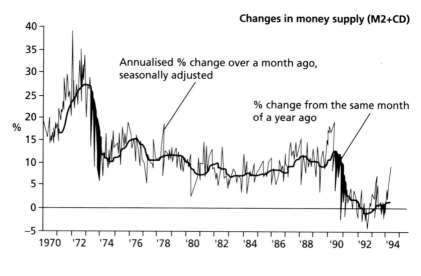

Changes in money supply (M2+CD)

Annualised % change over a month ago, seasonally adjusted

% change from the same month of a year ago

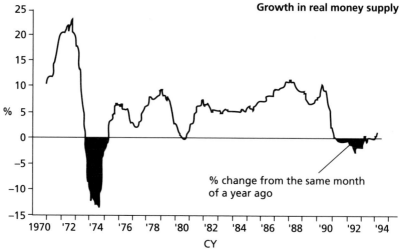

Growth in real money supply

% change from the same month of a year ago

CY

3.2 Money supply, stock prices and economic growth (source: compiled by Nomura Research Institute on the basis of data drawn from various sources).

The first point relates to the initial manoeuvres aimed at achieving policy objectives in the central bank. Iwata argues, as the textbook preaches, that a proper monetary policy should start with a mechanism of controlling the money supply based on high powered money. Okina contends that the standard monetary theory is not amenable to day-to-day manoeuvring of monetary policy at the central bank, and asserts that the money and credit control mechanism based on interbank rates is the right tool. According to Okina, high powered money is not something that can be thrust into the lap

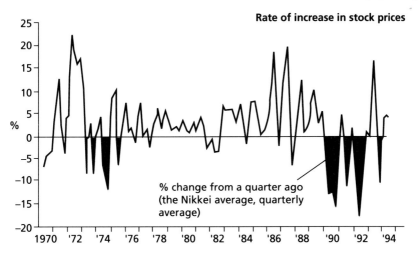

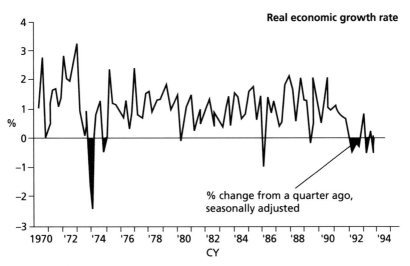

3.2 *Continued.*

of the central bank; it is an end-product of economic activities. Therefore, under the current system (reserves are deposited only after the underlying deposits have been established), it is difficult for the central bank to control in advance changes occurring in high powered money.

The second point concerns how the central bank can shepherd interbank rates to a desired level. Iwata maintains that the central bank cannot move interbank rates one way or the other without changing the level of supply of high powered money. In response,

Okina argues that high powered money has no close relationship with the interest rates formed through day-to-day or monthly interbank transactions, and that interbank rates can be moved by accelerating or decelerating the pace of deposit of reserves or by sending a signal indicating the policy stance of the central bank to the interbank market by other means, without actively moving high powered money.

The third point has to do with the characterisation of money supply as an intermediate target for evaluating the relevance of a given monetary policy. While Iwata maintains that the level of money supply is closely related to the vigour of the economy, and that therefore money supply should be closely watched as an intermediate target, Okina argues that the relationship between the two has become tenuous in recent years, and he doubts the wisdom of using money supply as an intermediate target on the grounds that the immediacy of effectiveness of money supply has increasingly weakened. In fact, opinions are divided on this point, but the views favouring money supply as an intermediate target cannot be lightly dismissed. It must also be remembered that mainstream opinion within the Bank of Japan has been changing rather radically according to shifting economic situations. More specifically, prior to 1975, the Bank of Japan did not define money supply as an intermediate target; instead, it stressed the importance of increases in lending by private banks as an intermediate target. After having experienced virulent inflation in the wake of the first oil crisis of 1973 and a radical change in the flow of funds triggered by massive offerings of government bonds after 1975, the central bank began to take money supply seriously as an intermediate target. And it did not change its stance until around 1988, despite the wrenching changes brought about by the speculative bubble in the second half of the 1980s. For example, in the May 1988 issue of *Chosa Geppo* (*Monthly Survey*), the Bank of Japan had this to say:

> *While it is true that the currency demand function has become somewhat unstable, a change of this magnitude is not particularly serious when compared with the current growth rate of money supply or its nominal aggregate demand. Therefore, one may judge that it is not so serious as to make the evaluation of money supply levels impossible (p 42). . . . When viewed from the standpoint of ensuring sustained growth in domestic demand on the basis of stable prices, money supply is an important indicator. . . . The*

Bank of Japan feels that it should endeavour to steer its
monetary policy in a proper direction, keeping an eye on
the growth rate of money supply and the velocity of money
circulation. (p 44)

The differences between Okina and Iwata should be weighed, first, in terms of the length of the period which a given monetary policy is intended to cover. The longer the period the policy is intended to cover, the more relevant the standard theory is likely to be, and the shorter the period, the better the current view of the Bank of Japan is likely to work.

Second, their differences should be weighed in terms of the behaviour of banking institutions and their corporate clients. If the banking institutions put a premium on long term business relationships with their clients, they will seek to adjust their supply of funds to the demand of their clients by manipulating the price and quantity of such funds in a way different from the way they would deal with their short term customers. It is against this background that the Bank of Japan attaches importance to the effects of signals rather than relying on the volume of supply of high powered money when it moves interbank rates.

Third, whether the relationship between interest rates and the economy or between money supply and the economy is stable or not varies from country to country and depends on the economic conditions then prevailing. Therefore, the current view of the Bank of Japan should be weighed in terms of whether or not it is appropriate to cases where the relationship between money supply and the economy is unstable.

Fourth, the differences between Okina and Iwata should be weighed in terms of whether the procedure for formulating a desirable money policy should be worked out on the basis of the existing systems, including the current reserve deposit system, or on the assumption that they should be overhauled.

For now, the Bank of Japan does not explicitly adopt money supply or real interest rates as an intermediate target. Instead, the central bank develops its monetary policy with the aim of leading nominal interbank rates to a desirable level on the basis of its overall view of the movement of the financial market.

In reality, however, unexpected things can happen in the market, and regulatory restraints make it impossible to effect business and financial transactions in an efficient manner. As the behaviour of the people is unpredictable under such circumstances, it is difficult to

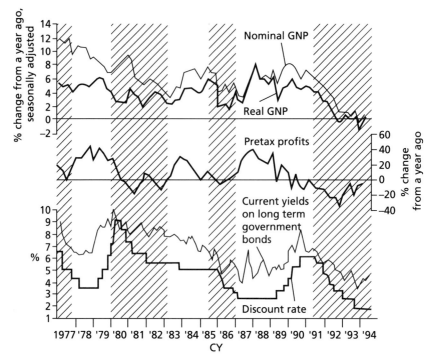

3.3 Long term government bond yields and the economy (source: Nomura Research Institute).

Note: Shaded areas indicate recessionary periods. Percentages relating to GNP represent three-quarter moving averages of annualised percentage change from a year ago, seasonally adjusted. Those relating to pretax profits represent changes from the same quarter of a year ago compiled on the basis of data drawn from the Statistics of Business Corporation, Ministry of Finance and those relating to yields on long-term government bonds represent month-end yields on government bonds with a remaining life of close to ten years. The latest readings are as of 30 June 1994.

determine an interbank rate that is most suitable for the attainment of policy objectives. Furthermore, when the central bank implements its monetary policy on the basis of its overall judgement of the health of the economy, the nation's monetary policy may become vulnerable to political intervention. The foregoing suggests that the current policy framework of the Bank of Japan is hardly the best one, and this calls for the creation of a new framework which is designed to stabilise as much as possible the movements of both money supply and real interest rates.

In this case, it is necessary to reform the regulatory system of contractual savings, such as insurance and pensions, which constitute the mainstream of the current flow of funds in such a way as to

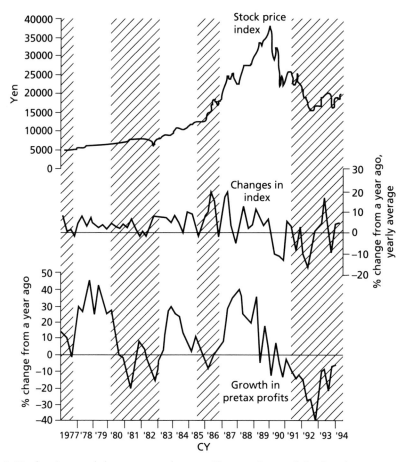

3.4 Stock prices and the economy (source: Nomura Research Institute).
Note: Shaded areas indicate recessionary periods. Monthly average of the Nikkei 225 stock index. The latest reading was taken on 30 June 1994. Percentages represent quarterly changes from a year ago and are based on the *Statistics on Business Corporations*, Ministry of Finance.

facilitate efficient financial transactions. For instance, insurance companies should be required to disclose information concerning the entire range of their management, and pension funds should be allowed to manage their funds freely. To ensure consistency between the interest rates charged by government run financial institutions and those charged by private banking institutions, the whole structure has to be overhauled. Liberalisation has to be pushed further and the government has to put an end to the long term prime rate system.

In sum, it is true that liberalisation of the financial markets has come a long way, and Western countries can be familiar with

the monetary policy operation in Japan. However, some regulatory reforms mentioned above must be implemented in order to
increase the efficiency of financial transactions further (Fig. 3.3 and
3.4).

The government and the public bond new issue market

4

A make-believe fiscal rehabilitation

AN ARDUOUS JOURNEY TO THE DISCONTINUATION OF DEFICIT-COVERING BONDS

In an effort to make up for the sharp drop-off in tax revenues that occurred during the recession in the wake of the first oil crisis of 1973, the Japanese government continued to issue deficit-covering bonds after fiscal 1975. In 1985, having set its sights on 'weaning the government from its habit of relying on deficit-covering bonds', the Ministry of Finance (MOF) was steadily slashing budget deficits, and finally succeeded in achieving its first stage goal of discontinuing deficit-covering bonds in fiscal 1990 for the first time in 15 years (Table 4.1).

Under the slogan 'fiscal rehabilitation without tax hikes' advocated by the Provisional Administrative Research Committee of 1981–3 (a task force charged with responsibility for recommending measures for administrative reforms), the government sought to implement administrative reforms as an integral part of its programme for rehabilitating public finances. By pronouncing cuts in deficit-covering bonds to be a political imperative, the MOF sought to curb general account spending by imposing a zero to minus ceiling on the budget proposals of all ministries and agencies.[1] Its strategy for rehabilitating government finance was to reduce the amount of deficit-covering bonds by ensuring reductions in fiscal

---

1 General account spending equals total spending less debt servicing costs, grants-in-aid to local public bodies, and transfers to the Industrial Investment Special Account.

Table 4.1 Changes in financial balance and the amount of government bonds issued (trillion yen)

Fiscal year	General account			Balance (B)	Bonds issued (C)	New cash (D)	Construction bonds (E)	Deficit-covering bonds (F)	Refinance (G)	Outstanding amount
	Expenditure	Income	Excl. debt (A)							
1965	3.7	3.8	3.6	−0.1	0.2	0.2	0.0	0.2	–	0.2
1966	4.5	4.6	3.9	−0.6	0.7	0.7	0.7	0.0	–	0.9
1967	5.1	5.3	4.6	−0.5	0.7	0.7	0.7	0.0	–	1.6
1968	5.9	6.1	5.6	−0.3	0.5	0.5	0.5	0.0	–	2.1
1969	6.9	7.1	6.7	−0.2	0.4	0.4	0.4	0.0	–	2.5
1970	8.2	8.5	8.1	−0.1	0.3	0.3	0.3	0.0	–	2.8
1971	9.6	10.0	8.8	−0.8	1.2	1.2	1.2	0.0	–	4.0
1972	11.9	12.8	10.8	−1.1	1.9	1.9	1.9	0.0	–	5.8
1973	14.8	16.8	15.0	0.2	2.4	1.8	1.8	0.0	0.6	7.6
1974	19.1	20.4	18.2	−0.9	2.8	2.2	2.2	0.0	0.6	9.7
1975	20.9	21.5	16.2	−4.7	5.7	5.3	3.2	2.1	0.4	15.0
1976	24.5	25.1	17.9	−6.6	7.6	7.2	3.7	3.5	0.4	22.1
1977	29.1	29.4	19.9	−9.2	9.9	9.6	5.0	4.5	0.3	31.9
1978	34.1	34.9	24.2	−9.9	11.3	10.7	6.3	4.3	0.6	42.6
1979	38.8	39.8	26.3	−12.5	13.5	13.5	7.1	6.3	0.0	56.3
1980	43.4	44.0	29.9	−13.5	14.5	14.2	7.0	7.2	0.3	70.5
1981	46.9	47.4	32.0	−14.9	13.8	12.9	7.0	5.9	0.9	82.3
1982	47.2	48.0	34.0	−13.3	17.3	14.0	7.0	7.0	3.3	96.5
1983	50.6	51.7	38.2	−12.5	18.0	13.5	6.8	6.7	4.5	109.7
1984	51.5	52.2	39.4	−12.1	18.1	12.8	6.4	6.4	5.4	121.7
1985	53.0	54.0	41.7	−11.3	21.3	12.3	6.3	6.0	9.0	134.4
1986	53.6	56.5	45.2	−8.4	22.7	11.3	6.2	5.0	11.5	145.1
1987	57.7	61.4	52.0	−5.8	24.9	9.4	6.9	2.5	15.4	151.8
1988	61.5	64.6	57.5	−4.0	21.1	7.2	6.2	1.0	13.9	156.8
1989	65.9	67.2	60.6	−5.2	21.7	6.6	6.4	0.2	15.1	160.9
1990	69.3	71.7	64.4	−4.9	26.0	7.3	6.4	1.0	18.7	166.3
1991	70.5	73.0	66.3	−4.3	25.6	6.7	6.3	0.0	18.9	171.6
1992	70.7	70.7	59.6	−11.1	31.0	9.5	9.5	0.0	21.5	176.0
1993(E)	76.9	76.9	58.5	−18.5	38.0	16.2	16.2	0.0	21.8	191.0
1994(F)	75.6	75.6	56.8	−18.8	41.8	18.8	13.5	3.1	23.0	210.0

Notes: 1 (A) = Total income − debt (includes government bonds); (B) = (A) − expenditure; (C) = (D) + (G); (D) = (E) + (F).
2 The figures for fiscal 1990 include provisional special government bonds issued to finance the contribution Japan made in fiscal 1990 to the war chest of the allied forces operating in the Gulf area.

Source: Ministry of Finance; estimate and forecast by Nomura Research Institute.

spending through an overhaul and rationalising the administrative structure and procedures.

Thanks to these reform measures, the growth rate of general account spending, at least that of the original budget, has been held down across the board. In addition, administrative reform measures, such as an overhaul of the social security system (the introduction of a basic pension and old-age medical insurance) and the privatisation of three public corporations (Japan National Railways, Nippon Telegraph & Telephone Corporation, and Japan Tobacco Monopoly) – projects which would have been difficult even to launch in the absence of a financial crisis – have been carried out successfully.

Successes achieved in reducing budget deficits in the second half of the 1980s may be attributed to three factors:

1 The new system of budget compilation backed by the prestige of the Provisional Administrative Research Committee (the Special Committee) mentioned earlier.

2 The political imperative of increasing revenues without raising taxes.

3 The determined drive mounted by the government for regulatory reforms and extraordinary measures, but with a few twists.

The strategy for cutting government spending

The most important recommendation submitted by the Special Committee was the unrelenting enforcement of ceilings on government spending.[2] It was in fiscal 1982 that the toughened ceilings began to bite. Following a zero increase ceiling across the board in fiscal 1982, it was further tightened to a minus growth ceiling in fiscal 1983 through fiscal 1987. As a result, the growth rate of general account spending has consistently been lower than the economic growth rate projected since fiscal 1980 (Fig. 4.1). This serves to show that the government has been strongly committed to cutting its budget deficits.

2 In its final report submitted to the Prime Minister on 14 March 1983, the Provisional Administrative Research Committee states, in part, that 'in an effort to achieve the goal of fiscal rehabilitation and encourage Ministries and agencies to carry out reforms on their own, a ceiling should be imposed on the increase in budget proposals before they are submitted and steps should be taken to ensure their observance of the ceiling'.

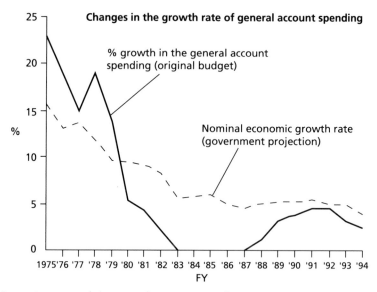

Changes in the growth rate of general account spending

% growth in the general account spending (original budget)

Nominal economic growth rate (government projection)

FY

4.1 Percentage growth in general account spending.

In truth, however, when viewed from the standpoint of the basic line laid down by the Special Committee, cuts in budget deficits have been made rather erratically both in budgeting and financing tax reductions. More specifically, if the minus growth ceiling was the chief strategic tool for cutting deficit-covering bonds, it should normally have been shown in the original budget (the budget adopted at the beginning of a fiscal year). However, a comparison of the original budget, the supplementary budget(s), and the year-end settlement of accounts with those of a year ago shows that it often was the year-end settlement of accounts that showed the largest cut in deficit-covering bonds (Fig. 4.2).

Figure 4.3, which sums up the sources of funds used for financing cuts in deficit-covering bonds, shows that the cuts in deficit-covering bonds were financed not by savings made through spending cuts but by increases in tax receipts. Furthermore, despite cuts in policy-dictated general account spending in the original budget, it actually increased by the time the general account was closed. This suggests that both reductions of deficit-covering bonds and increases in policy-dictated spending were made possible by increases in tax revenues.

Of course, credit should be given to the government for its determined effort to cut spending, but there is no denying that it has veered considerably from the line it originally laid down.

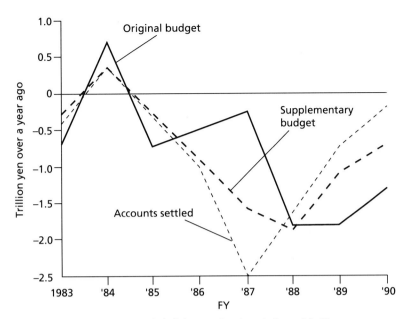

4.2 Changes in the amounts of deficit covering bonds issued (trillion yen over a year ago).
Note: The post-supplementary budget figures for fiscal 1990 do not include ¥968.9 billion worth of special bonds.

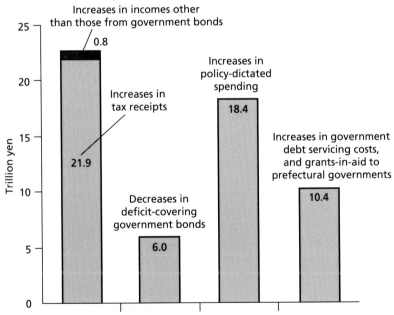

4.3 Changes in major categories of revenue and expenditure in fiscal 1985–90 (trillion yen) (source: Ministry of Finance).
Note: The figures for fiscal 1990 do not include ¥968.9 billion worth of government bonds issued to finance the contributions the Japanese government made in support of the allied forces' operations against the Iraqi invasion of Kuwait.

Increases in tax revenues without tax hikes

Thus, natural increases in tax revenues (increases developed over and above the government's original projection) have played a key role in reducing deficit-covering bonds.[3] The frustration that the government experienced in the course of its efforts to rehabilitate its finances in the first half of the 1980s was blamed on an overly optimistic estimate of tax revenues which made subsequent shortfalls even more pronounced. Conversely, the success the government achieved in rehabilitating its finances in the second half of the 1980s was brought about by a large natural increase in tax revenues.

Direct tax revenues (income taxes of both corporations and individuals) started to increase in the second half of fiscal 1986 and cumulative natural increases in tax revenues during the five years to fiscal 1990 came to ¥18.7 trillion ($187 billion at the rate of ¥100 to the dollar, Table 4.2). This was borne out by the tax elasticity, which jumped to 3.3 points in fiscal 1987, up from an annual average of 1.1 points in fiscal 1976 through 1985.

Largely responsible for the natural increases in tax revenues are such non-current factors as the sharp rises in stock and land prices fuelled by speculative bubbles. But there is no denying that the government's deliberate tactics aimed at rehabilitating its finances also had a hand in boosting natural increases in tax revenues. In other words, the MOF spurned requests for increased spending and tax cuts by conservatively estimating tax revenues – all with a view to securing funds for financing shortfalls in revenues caused by cuts in deficit-covering bonds.

As implied in the slogan 'fiscal rehabilitation without tax hikes', the government shunned tax hikes throughout the 1980s.[4] However, it was possible that income taxes did in effect increase through a bracket creep.[5] Also, the social security burden shouldered by work-

---

3 The term 'natural increase' means increases in taxes actually received over and above the estimates made at the time the budget was compiled. (The term is sometimes used to indicate automatic increases that occur owing to an unexpected growth of the economy.)

4 When the consumption tax was introduced in December 1988, an income tax cut was implemented before the consumption tax took effect, with the result that the year ended with a net income tax cut of ¥1.8 trillion ($18 billion at the rate of ¥100 to the dollar).

5 This refers to an increase in tax receipts generated by an automatic rise in tax rates (bracket creep) caused by economic growth or inflation.

Table 4.2 Changes in natural increases in tax receipts, by categories of taxes (100 million yen)

Fiscal year	1986	1987	1988	1989	1990	1991	1992	1993	1994 (estimated)
Total of direct taxes	6,574	52,080	47,348	39,505	31,691	−11,236	−79,213	−70,274	−31,589
Income tax	77	9,551	5,098	32,095	46,235	10,113	−40,476	−33,595	−9,531
Corporate tax	3,851	39,868	45,071	6,303	−13,274	−26,719	−44,084	−38,141	−21,364
Inheritance tax	2,646	2,661	−2,821	1,107	−1,270	5,370	5,202	2,387	−767
Others	—	—	—	—	—	—	145	−925	73
Total of indirect taxes	6,594	3,959	10,017	−387	−10,672	−8,280	−1,374	−1,494	478
Consumption tax	—	—	—	−3,481	−6,973	323	2,729	1,285	−753
Liquor tax	−15	1,455	1,361	−149	210	−258	−640	−986	−125
Securities trading tax	7,334	5,910	4,599	1,171	−4,861	−5,770	−3,025	651	−519
Others	−725	−3,406	4,057	2,072	952	−2,575	−438	−2,444	1,875
Total of tax receipts	13,168	56,039	57,365	39,118	21,019	−19,516	−80,587	−71,768	−31,111

Note: Indirect taxes include stamp duty.
Source: Compiled by Nomura Research Institute based on data from various budget reports submitted by the Ministry of Finance.

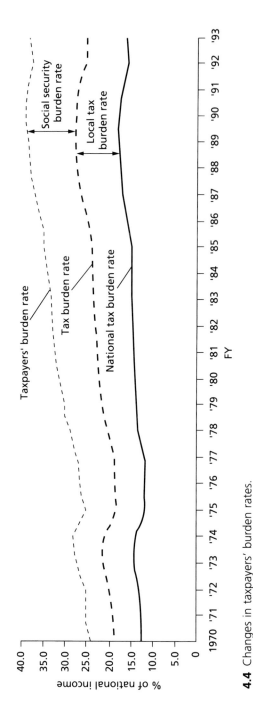

4.4 Changes in taxpayers' burden rates.

Notes: 1) The figures for years to fiscal 1992 are actual results and those for fiscal 1993 are estimates made by Nomura Research Institute.

2) Figures for the years to fiscal 1978 include increased revenues which resulted from a reclassification of categories of incomes belonging to different fiscal years.

3) The national tax includes funds transferred from the government-owned Japan Tobacco Monopoly, but these were not included in the general-account revenues.

4) Tax burden rates are based on tax revenues and they are different from rates computed on the basis of national economic accounting.

ers has increased. This is evident from the fact that the taxpayers' burden rate has increased consistently throughout the 1980s (Fig. 4.4). In view of this, the fiscal rehabilitation could not have been accomplished without tax hikes.

'Hidden borrowing' through special measures and non-tax revenues

What role did the institutional reform and special measures play in accelerating fiscal rehabilitation? What really matters in this connection are (1) the size of the so-called 'hidden borrowing' that has developed in the course of dealings between the special account and prefectural finance, (2) deferred spending, and (3) the size of non-tax revenues. A non-tax revenue of a special nature is the proceeds of gold coins (worth ¥370 billion or $3.7 billion) issued in commemoration of the 60th anniversary of the reign of the late Showa Emperor (Hirohito). In addition, the sale of government holdings of NTT shares generated about ¥10 trillion ($100 billion) in fiscal 1986 through 1988. (As this is closely linked to the Debt Consolidation Fund, it will be discussed further later.) It might be mentioned that part of the proceeds went to social capital construction projects, thereby helping the government to save the general account funds which otherwise would have been spent on public works projects.

The term 'hidden borrowing' refers to such portions of general account spending that were deferred in one form or another to the next fiscal year, and such action, as a rule, is taken in the form of a special measure. As shown in Table 4.3, spendings were deferred in various forms of the order of ¥2 trillion to ¥3 trillion each year in an effort to maintain the momentum of fiscal rehabilitation.

Most serious in implication is the suspension of the mandatory transfer of funds to the Debt Consolidation Fund ('the Fund') which is not usually counted as a hidden borrowing. During the eight years from fiscal 1982 through 1989, suspended transfer of funds to the Fund amounted to ¥15.57 trillion ($155.7 billion). (It was resumed in fiscal 1990 to 1992.) The transfer of general account funds at a fixed rate to the Fund is based on the government's debt redemption plan. As long as the Fund has sufficient funds to redeem maturing debts, temporary suspension of the transfer of funds does not cause a serious problem. As the Fund has been running short of funds to redeem maturing government bonds, the suspended transfer may be characterised as a broadly defined hidden borrowing.

Table 4.3 Measures taken to reduce deficit spending included in the budgets since fiscal 1982 (100 million yen)

Fiscal year	Special deferment of the transfer to welfare annuity special account	Temporary deferment of interest subsidies to the Housing Loan Corp	Deferment of the transfer to the national annuity special account	Transfer of funds from the special account of automobile liability insurance	Reduction of Treasury subsidy to the government run health insurance	Funds borrowed for the special account of roads	Deferred liability resulting from measures taken for prefectural finance (of which, those covered by past memoranda)	Amounts of suspended fixed rate transfer to government debt service costs
1982	The state liability of	517	–		–	–	–	11,984
1983	¥1,507.8 billion in fiscal	778	3,180	2,560	–	–	–	13,973
1984	1982–5 (principal and	1,045	3,221	–	–	–	△300 (960)	16,127
1985	interest) was disposed of by the supplementary of fiscal 1988	1,034 (△103)	2,556	–	939	1,200	1,855 (855/ supplementary budget △1,395)	18,627
1986	3,040	1,084 (△259)	1,917	– (△55)	1,300	3,460 (△1,200)	2,977 (857)	20,738
1987	3,600	857 (△468)	1,252	– (△2,505)	1,350	3,037	1,923 (653/ supplementary budget 500)	23,168
1988	3,600	1,147 (△468)	601	–	650	(△6,497)	2,534 (804)	25,036
1989	3,240	1,297 (△468)	0	–	400	–	2,584 (1,059)	26,081
1990	–	484	△528	–	–	–	2,969	–
1991	–	1,189	△995	–	–	–	4,671	–
1992	–	670	△1,409	–	–	–	2,938	–
1993	–	238	△1,772	–	1,300	–	4,317	(supplementary budget 30,487)
1994	–	–	–	8,100	1,200	–	5,735	30,849
Total	13,480	2,581	12,727 (△4,704)	10,660 (△2,560)	7,139	0	38,191 (△1,695)	(217,070)
Balance	10,440	2,581	8,023	8,100	7,139	0	36,496	(217,070)

Notes: **1** The triangle denotes the amounts repaid (in the case of measures for prefectural finance, it means a government loan to prefectural governments).
2 With the abolition of new borrowings in fiscal 1984, the responsibility of the government and the prefectural governments for redeeming past liabilities then outstanding was specifically defined.
3 The temporary additions to deferred liabilities defined by law were disposed of as they occurred in each fiscal year. As the amount of debt reduced in fiscal 1982 (¥113.5 billion) was added to that of fiscal 1983, it was omitted.
4 The total of deferred liabilities of prefectural governments does not include the government loans made to prefectural governments and the amount repaid in fiscal 1988 and 1989 (a total of ¥46 billion).
5 In addition, there are long term liabilities of Japan National Railways Liquidation Corporation (¥28.5 trillion).

In any event, the cumulative total of fixed rate transfer suspended so far is equal to about 70 per cent of the natural increases in tax revenues developed in fiscal 1986 through 1989. This suggests that the revenues saved from suspending the transfer to the Fund helped avert, at least on the surface, additional issuance of deficit-covering government bonds. The balance of hidden borrowing (excluding the liabilities of the now defunct Japanese National Railways but including the suspended transfers to the Fund) outstanding at the end of fiscal 1989 stood at ¥25.9 trillion ($259 billion). This is equal to 40 per cent plus of the balance of outstanding deficit-covering government bonds – meaning that the total debts had actually increased by more than 40 per cent without authorisation by these special enabling measures.

In sum, the fiscal rehabilitation achieved in the second half of the 1980s turned out to be a windfall generated by a bubble-induced increase in tax revenues and hidden borrowing, although the government effort to cut spending did have a hand in it. More will be said later about the problems which have resulted from this fluke and from government efforts.

MASSIVE OFFERING OF GOVERNMENT BONDS AND THE DEBT CONSOLIDATION FUND

As noted in the preceding section, the Debt Consolidation Fund (and the Debt Consolidation Fund Special Account which runs the Fund) is closely linked with the sinking fund system of Japan. Both construction bonds and deficit-covering bonds are issued under the general account and redeemed with the funds drawn from the Debt Consolidation Fund. The Fund receives, manages, and disburses all funds earmarked for the redemption of government bonds.

The Debt Consolidation Fund draws funds from (1) the general account of the annual budget – in three forms, namely (1a) fixed rate transfer of a sum equivalent to 1.6 per cent of the government bonds outstanding at the beginning of the preceding fiscal year, (1b) transfer of one-half of the surplus registered in the general account, and (1c) transfer of an amount decided by the government in its budget – (2) the proceeds of rollover bonds, and (3) the proceeds from the privatisation of NTT and other government owned enterprises. Of these, the most reliable source of funds for the Debt Consolidation Fund is the fixed rate transfer of funds from the general account.

As noted above, in fiscal 1982 through 1989, the fixed rate transfer of funds was suspended. However, as the Fund had an ample balance in those years (in 1982 the Fund had a balance of ¥4.3 trillion as against ¥96 trillion worth of outstanding government bonds), it was thought that a suspension of the fixed rate transfer would not cause any serious problem.[6]

In those years, the suspension of the fixed rate transfer enabled the government to cut ¥1 trillion to ¥2 trillion in its spending and cover the budget deficit to a certain degree. However, if the fixed rate transfer is suspended when tax revenues do not increase or government spending cannot be cut, a resumption of the fixed rate transfer would directly necessitate the issuance of additional deficit-covering bonds. Such having been the situation, it was difficult to discontinue the suspension of the fixed rate transfer.

To make the situation even worse, large amounts of government bonds issued in the second half of the 1970s fell due in the mid-1980s. As cash had to be drawn down from the Debt Consolidation Fund to meet cash redemptions of these government bonds, the Fund rapidly ran out of cash in 1985, raising the possibility of having to change the government bond redemption programme. According to a provisional estimate released in 1985 by the MOF, the balance of funds held by the Debt Consolidation Fund would be depleted, unless the fixed rate transfer was resumed once again in fiscal 1986.

Coming as it did at such a critical juncture, the sale of government holdings of NTT shares helped bail the Fund out of the situation (Fig. 4.5). Acting on a report submitted by the Special Committee, urging the government to privatise government owned enterprises, the government transformed Nippon Telegraph & Telephone Corporation (NTT) and Japan Tobacco Monopoly (JT) into stock companies in fiscal 1985 and Japan National Railways (JNR) in fiscal 1987. Although the government had to assume the large debts which JNR had accumulated over the years, the privatisation of these public corporations has been instrumental in revitalising business firms and industries related with them.

NTT, in particular, had been running large surpluses over the years thanks in part to the monopolistic control of the market it had enjoyed and it had huge net assets. The sale of the first tranche of NTT shares held by the government was carried out in 1986 just when speculation in stocks and land began to bubble over and it

---

6 It actually started with the supplementary budget of fiscal 1982. The suspension of the fixed rate transfer must be authorised by a special exemption law each year.

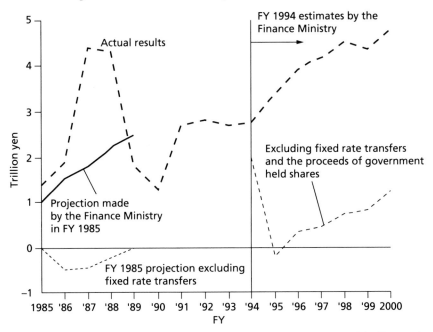

4.5 Changes in the balance of funds of the Debt Consolidation Fund (trillion yen) (source: compiled by Nomura Research Institute on the basis of data drawn from the Ministry of Finance).

helped the government net about ¥10 trillion in capital gains ($100 billion).

The government decided to transfer the proceeds of its NTT shares to the Debt Consolidation Fund. Subsequently, however, the government used part of the proceeds to finance the construction and improvement of social capital to the extent that it did not impede the management of the Debt Consolidation Fund.[7] At any rate, the transfer of the proceeds of NTT shares to the Fund helped stave off the depletion of its funds and allowed the government to take a breather in the management of its finances.

PRESSURE FOR A STIMULATION OF DOMESTIC DEMAND AND TREASURY INVESTMENT AND LOANS

From around 1985, most of the industrial nations had to contend with growing trade deficits, and pressure grew on Japan to cut its

7 Since fiscal 1987, the Debt Consolidation Fund has made loans with no interest. Such loans made in fiscal 1987 through 1994 amounted to about ¥9.6 trillion ($96 billion).

trade surpluses by stimulating its domestic demand and boosting its imports. Although Japan's trading partners pressed Japan to stimulate its domestic demand by boosting its fiscal stimulus, Japan found it difficult to increase its fiscal spending on account of the political imperatives of reducing its budget deficits throughout the 1980s.

Under such circumstances, Treasury investment and loans (financed by postal savings and publicly run pension funds) were playing a complementary role in support of general account fiscal spending (1) by subscribing to up to 30 per cent of the government bonds issued each year and (2) by financing part of the public works projects and making business and housing loans through government run financial institutions.

As the interest rates payable on deposits of the Fund Trust Bureau were set by law, its deposit rates could not be changed nimbly in step with changes occurring in market rates, and it took time for the government run financial institutions such as Housing Loan Corporation to adjust their mortgage rates. Meanwhile, pressure grew on the government to allow the postal life insurance system and publicly run pension funds greater freedom in managing their assets. In response, the government in 1987 amended the Trust Fund Law to allow the Bureau to change its deposit rates by a Cabinet order, and authorised the postal savings system, publicly run pension funds, and the postal insurance system to manage a certain percentage of their assets at their discretion (Table 4.4) rather than deposit at the Trust Fund Bureau.

As a result, the flexibility of the Treasury investment and loan system was enhanced in terms of both the size of amounts it could manage as it saw fit and the operation of its management policy. During the recession that followed the bursting of the economic bubble, particularly in fiscal 1991 when the funds available for the Trust Fund Bureau increased sharply on account of a shift of bank deposits to postal savings in search of higher yields, Treasury investment and loans played a pivotal role in stimulating the economy. In the process, the amount of funds that flowed into the market from the Trust Fund Bureau in investment and loans relative to the size of the general account appropriations rose from about 50 per cent in the first half of the 1980s to 65 per cent early in fiscal 1994.

While increases in loans made by private banking institutions slowed down after the bursting of the economic bubble, the government boosted its Treasury investment loans with the funds of the Trust Fund Bureau, with the result that the weight of loans made by government run financial institutions has increased (Fig. 4.6). As the

Table 4.4 Securities investment by Treasury investment and loans programme (100 million yen)

	1987	1988	1989	1990	1991	1992	1993
Funds raised from:	326,361	322,239	352,050	378,139	495,274	480,937	467,706
Trust Fund Bureau	263,808	256,744	277,345	298,175	412,778	401,978	376,595
Postal life insurance	38,994	42,211	55,815	60,333	62,872	60,248	70,534
Industrial investment special account	1,438	824	843	638	626	721	577
Government-guaranteed bonds and government-guaranteed loans	22,121	22,460	18,047	18,993	18,998	17,990	20,000
Funds invested in securities market:							
Share of government bonds held by the Trust Fund Bureau	23.0%	12.4%	11.1%	8.3%	4.5%	7.3%	3.9%
Projects for the operation of postal life insurance	3,500	5,000	14,000	16,500	16,500	14,000	20,000
Projects for strengthening the financial base of pension funds	10,000	23,700	15,300	18,000	20,500	23,900	24,250
Postal savings special account	20,000	25,000	30,000	35,000	40,000	47,500	47,500

Notes:
1 The breakdowns are based on the amounts actually raised, and those for fiscal 1993 are based on plans.
2 The share of government bonds held by the Trust Fund Bureau is based on actual amounts, the flow of government bonds in fiscal 1993 is based on plans, and their stock is as of the end of January 1994.
3 The breakdowns of investments are based on plans.

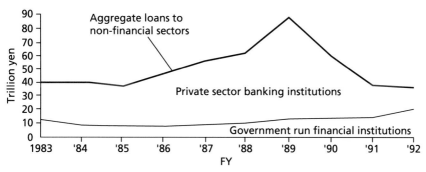

4.6 Fund transactions (source: compiled by Nomura Research Institute on the basis of data drawn from the fund flow account, Bank of Japan).

government run financial institutions made deep inroads into the market for mortgage loans to individuals, some of the private banking institutions complained about the public sector's growing dominance of the market.

These government run financial institutions raise funds through four channels:

1 The Trust Fund Bureau (postal savings, publicly run welfare pensions and the national annuity fund);

2 The postal insurance system;

3 Government-guaranteed bonds and borrowings; and

4 The Industrial Investment Special Account.

Funds that can be drawn in loans from the Trust Fund Bureau (because the amounts obtainable from the postal insurance system are not predictable) and those that can be drawn from the Industrial Investment Special Account (because they are determined by the government according to its policy needs) may be characterised as 'passive' financing, and those that can be raised through the offering of government-guaranteed bonds as 'active' financing.

In consequence, the Treasury investment and loan system had no difficulty in financing its programme when postal savings increased sharply as they did in fiscal 1991–2, and the need to offer government-guaranteed bonds was less strong. Conversely, when the balance of postal savings decreases or when the publicly run pension funds have to pay out more in benefits than they take in contributions, government run financial institutions will have to resort more heavily to active financing.[8]

In addition to investment in or loans to government run financial institutions, the Treasury investment and loan system also plays the role of financing the budget deficits of local public bodies. On average, the Treasury and loan system buys each year 60 per cent to 70 per cent of the bonds issued by municipalities. However, as the growth in the amounts of investment and loans made by the system

---

8 At present, few government run financial institutions raise funds by offering government-guaranteed bonds. The one that issues the largest amount of government-guaranteed bonds is the publicly run Enterprise Financial Corporation, which accounts for about one-half of the government-guaranteed bonds outstanding. The proceeds are used to buy municipal bonds, which in effect amounts to guaranteeing municipal bonds by the government.

is likely to slow down owing to a slower increase in postal savings, there will be a limit to the amount of budget deficit of local public bodies the system can finance, and the necessity to finance their deficits directly on the capital markets will grow in coming years.

Moreover, the role the system plays – pooling funds through postal savings and lending them at cheaper interest rates to finance housing projects – has come under growing criticism for the distortion it causes to financial transactions. Therefore, it is necessary for the government to take a second look at the system to see if it will function as effectively as it has done in the past or whether government finance can shoulder the burden in coming years.

What comes after fiscal rehabilitation?

THE BURSTING OF THE ECONOMIC BUBBLE AND INCREASES IN BUDGET DEFICITS

The government appeared to have succeeded in reining in budget deficits, but the scenario of fiscal rehabilitation it had stitched together has come seriously undone under the recessionary pressure that emerged in the wake of the economic bubble. Factors responsible for this development are (1) an unexpectedly large shortfall of tax revenues, and (2) the fiscal drains caused by repeated implementation of fiscal stimulus packages. This suggests that the double-edged sword which had cut budget deficits in the second half of the 1980s is now cutting the other way, boosting budget deficits.

The natural increase in tax revenues that occurred in the second half of the 1980s was brought about by a sharp increase in direct tax receipts from bubble-induced active asset transactions and swollen corporate earnings. With the bursting of the speculative bubble in 1990, direct tax receipts collapsed and fell below year-ago level for three consecutive years. They are likely to decrease further owing to an income tax cut implemented in fiscal 1994 (Fig. 4.7).

Since fiscal 1991, the government has implemented fiscal stimulus packages four times for a total of ¥45 trillion ($450 billion), and they have added a heavy burden to government finances. To finance the social capital construction programmes carried over from the 1980s and new public works projects envisioned in these fiscal stimulus packages, a large amount of construction bonds were issued. However, except for the government bonds to be issued to finance the income tax cuts, the government managed to make do

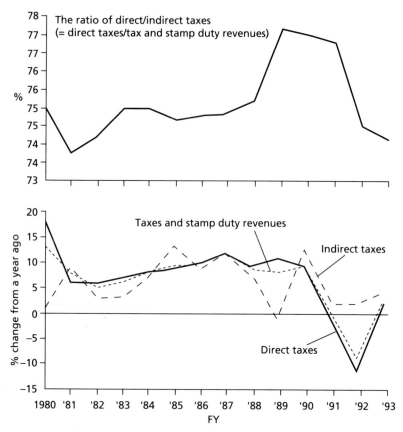

4.7 The ratios of direct and indirect taxes (source: Ministry of Finance).
Note: The figures for fiscal years to 1992 are actual results and those for fiscal
1993 are based on post-supplementary data.

without issuing deficit-covering government bonds, prompting some
to remark that the situation is not as tight as it was in the 1980s.
However, in fiscal 1993 alone, the government ran as much as ¥16
trillion ($160 billion) in budget deficits, boosting the degree of
reliance on government bonds to more than 20 per cent. When
measured in terms of reliance on debts, the situation has worsened
to a degree comparable to that which existed in 1985 when fiscal
rehabilitation had not begun in earnest (Fig. 4.8).[9] Since fiscal 1993,

9 In an effort to obviate the necessity for issuing deficit-covering government
bonds, the government suspended the fixed rate transfers to the Debt
Consolidation Fund and employed a measure bordering on window-dressing –
replacing the interest-free loans made with the proceeds of NTT shares through
the general account.

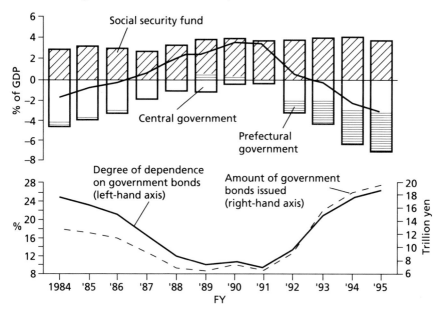

4.8 Investment–savings balance of the government sector.
Note: Percentages for fiscal 1994 and 1995 are projections made by Nomura Research Institute.

the fixed-rate transfer of funds from the general account to the Debt Consolidation Fund has been suspended. Even the government has admitted that if the fixed rate transfer is not resumed and/or the remaining government holdings of NTT shares are not sold, the Debt Consolidation Fund will face another crisis.[10]

THE GREYING POPULATION AND TAX, ADMINISTRATIVE AND FINANCIAL REFORMS

In order to engineer fiscal rehabilitation in the post-bubble years, the government must strive to (1) stabilise the structure of its tax revenues, (2) cut government spending through sweeping reforms of its administration and finance, and (3) steadily reduce 'hidden borrowings'.

10 See the Ministry of Finance report entitled 'Provisional Statement of the Debt Consolidation Fund Accounts', released in April 1994. The proceeds of shares of JR East Japan realised in the autumn of 1993 have been appropriated to the repayment of the debt of the now defunct Japan National Railways and no funds have been transferred to the Debt Consolidation Fund.

The percentage of the aged population will grow higher still in coming decades, and a slowdown in the increase of the size of the workforce is highly likely to lower the potential growth rate of the economy, creating a vulnerable structure of tax revenues which is highly dependent on direct taxes. Under such a structure, tax revenues will become increasingly unstable. Moreover, unless the aged population shoulders the tax burden, an increasing tax burden will dampen the urge of the working population to work, thereby sapping the vitality of the economy. It is for this reason that pressures for increasing the weight of indirect taxes and raising the consumption tax have been mounting in recent years.

Meanwhile, if the government seeks to cut its budget deficit only through tax hikes, such moves would give an added spin to the spiral of budget deficit necessitating further tax hikes. Therefore, unless government spending is cut further, the government cannot make a dent in budget deficits. Measures the government could take to achieve spending cuts include phasing out the practice of allocating public works projects according to the vested interests of different ministries and agencies and overhauling the social programme spending.

The problem of hidden borrowing should be addressed from long and medium term standpoints. As hidden borrowing means deferment of government spending or payment, it simply cannot be eliminated. Under the one year budgeting system, the government tends to focus its attention on the flow of deficits, but now that the outstanding balance of government debts exceeds 40 per cent of gross domestic product (GDP), it may have to pay more attention to the stock of deficits.

The same is true of local (meaning prefectural) finance. Local public bodies (meaning prefectural governments) have played an important role in taking up the slack developed in the economy during the post-bubble recession by sharply boosting their public works spending in lieu of government spending.[11] Meanwhile, prefectural finance has increasingly been squeezed on account of fall-offs in their tax revenues. Luckily, prefectural governments had built a fat fall-back in the form of financial adjustment funds when they had unexpectedly large increases in tax receipts in the 1980s. In

---

11 A total of about ¥16 trillion (public works project costs undertaken by prefectural governments on their own, the costs of land they acquired for public works projects, and inhabitant tax cuts) was borne by prefectural governments.

recent years, however, their financial adjustment funds have been drained steadily (see Fig. 4.8).

CHALLENGES FACING THE PUBLIC BOND NEW ISSUE MARKET AND ITS OUTLOOK

A flexible approach to the liberalisation of the financial markets and changing situations in the government bond trading market has caught on among the government debt managers.

Except for those issued to finance income tax cuts, the government has not issued deficit-covering bonds since 1990, but the balance of outstanding government bonds has been increasing steadily in recent years. The government issued about ¥39.4 trillion ($394 billion) worth of bonds including refundings in fiscal 1994 and plans to issue about ¥40.8 trillion ($408 billion) worth of bonds in fiscal 1995 (Table 4.5). That includes the resumption of the issuance of deficit-covering bonds.

In fiscal 1985 to 1990, the amount of government bonds issued each year was held down. As it was necessary to maintain the depth of the bond trading market and expand the scale of the money market in keeping with the liberalisation of the financial markets, the government sought to maintain a balanced supply of government securities by increasing the volume of Treasury discount bills (TB) to the extent consistent with its necessity for issuing 10 year bonds.

However, as budget deficits began to swell once again, and the Debt Consolidation Fund had only limited funds to buy government bonds, the market became flooded with government bonds – to such an extent, in fact, that the government had to change the structure of maturities of its securities. To cushion the impact of the increased supply of government bonds, the government sought to diversify the maturity mix of its securities by increasing the issuance of 20 year bonds, by resuming the issuance of four year notes, and by issuing notes with a new maturity of six years.[12]

At least for several years yet, the issuance of government bonds in large amounts is likely to continue, and it will pose a formidable

12 The MOF calls the six year note a long term bond, but the market considers it as a medium term note. The Ministry also explains that it does not issue five year coupon notes to avoid competition with bank debentures having a maturity of five years.

Table 4.5 Changes in planned issuance of government bonds (100 million yen)

Fiscal year	1982 Original	1983 Original	1984 Original	1985 Original	1986 Original	1987 Original	1988 Original	1989 Original	1990 Original
Private sector									
Underwriting syndicates	52,800	67,000	69,000	76,000	83,000	93,000	88,000	82,000	79,000
10 year bonds	49,800	64,000	64,000	NA	NA	88,000	83,000	79,000	77,000
5 year notes	3,000	3,000	5,000	NA	NA	5,000	5,000	3,000	2,000
Auctioned	28,752	53,219	54,102	62,318	60,849	79,368	69,933	74,886	92,518
20 year bonds	—	—	—	—	NA	20,000	20,000	18,000	12,000
Medium term notes	28,752	53,219	54,102	NA	NA	39,432	27,357	16,000	14,000
Treasury bills	—	—	—	—	NA	19,936	22,576	40,886	66,518
Private sector total	81,552	120,219	123,102	138,318	143,849	172,368	157,933	156,886	171,518
Share	59.5%	67.3%	68.2%	67.0%	64.1%	65.7%	67.6%	70.3%	72.9%
Public sector									
Trust Fund Bureau	35,000	37,000	36,000	50,000	50,000	40,000	35,000	23,000	20,000
Self managed account of postal savings	—	—	—	—	—	10,000	12,500	15,000	17,500
Over the counter sales by the postal savings system	—	—	—	—	—	10,000	10,000	9,000	7,500
Switchover to the Bank of Japan	(*)	(*)	(*)	(*)	(*)	14,000	(*)	—	—
Switchover to the Trust Fund Bureau	20,576	21,377	21,302	18,055	30,535	15,849	18,079	19,263	18,659
Public sector total	55,576	58,377	57,302	68,055	80,535	89,849	75,579	66,263	63,659
Share	40.5%	32.7%	31.8%	33.0%	35.9%	34.3%	32.4%	29.7%	27.1%
Total	137,128	178,596	180,404	206,373	224,384	262,217	233,512	223,149	235,177
Bonds for new financing	104,400	133,450	126,800	116,800	109,460	105,010	88,410	71,110	56,300
Refundings	32,728	45,146	53,604	89,573	114,924	157,207	145,102	152,039	178,877

Notes: **1** (*) indicates that breakdowns of switchover to the Trust Fund Bureau and to the Bank of Japan are not available.
    2 Medium term notes include two, three, four, and six year notes.
    3 The five year notes underwritten by syndicates are discount notes.
Source: The Ministry of Finance.

challenge to the market to handle such a bloated supply of government debts. Although the government will offer some 'sweeteners' for its debts, the question is whether the market can absorb all those government debts without upsetting its normal function.

Investors do have the need to secure the liquidity of their holdings with a remaining life of four to seven years. And this has given rise to the necessity for creating a medium term benchmark

1991 Original	1992 Original	1993 Original	Post-supplementary budgets	1994 Original	Post-supplementary budgets	1995 Original	Post-supplementary budgets
84,000	90,000	90,000	114,000	122,000		122,000	122,000
82,000	88,000	88,000	112,000	120,000		120,000	120,000
2,000	2,000	2,000	2,000	2,000		2,000	2,000
106,489	119,202	122,160	156,438	365,604		184,648	207,908
10,000	10,000	10,000	13,000	10,000		12,000	12,000
12,316	15,063	12,000	43,438	46,000		52,000	75,260
84,173	94,139	100,160	100,000	109,604		120,648	120,648
190,489	209,202	212,160	270,438	287,604		306,648	329,908
80.5%	72.9%	70.9%	71.2%	78.7%		80.7%	80.9%
6,000	6,000	10,000	10,000	17,000		20,000	25,000
20,000	23,750	23,750	23,750	25,000		25,000	25,000
7,500	7,500	7,500	7,500	7,500		7,500	7,500
4,227	4,227	2,000	9,560	28,206		20,609	20,609
8,500	36,350	43,913	58,460	—		—	—
46,227	77,827	87,163	109,270	77,706		73,109	78,109
19.5%	27.1%	29.1%	28.8%	21.3%		19.3%	19.1%
236,716	287,029	299,323	379,708	365,310	393,718	379,758	408,018
53,430	72,800	81,300	161,740	136,430	164,900	125,980	154,240
183,286	214,229	218,023	217,968	228,880	228,818	253,778	253,778

issue or futures contract that facilitates hedging medium term holdings against risks.[13]

On the other hand, the amounts of outstanding municipal bonds and government-guaranteed bonds are much smaller than govern-

13 Regrettably, no serious debate about the possibility of trading such futures has taken place as yet.

ment securities and they are less liquid than the latter. In order, therefore, to offer incentives to investors to hold them for the longer haul, it is necessary to equip them with a liquidity premium or issue them in larger quantities. As municipal bonds are often placed privately with institutional investors at a par value of ¥100, many of them carry a coupon rate reaching down to three decimal places, making ordinary investors wary of buying them. Furthermore, prefectural governments issue municipal bonds as necessity arises, instead of in large lots, with the result that each of their issues tends to be small in amount with the approval of the central government. And as they decide to issue debts as the necessity arises, the timing of issue tends to converge towards the end of the fiscal year. With a view, therefore, to evening out the issuing calendar, studies are being made to explore the feasibility of issuing municipal bonds as a group, instead of individually by prefectures or project by project.

In any event, municipal issuers should rearrange their issuing schedules and methods to facilitate the trading of their debts and reduce their issuing costs, and the chances are that their issuing schedules will be redesigned in this direction.

5 Corporate finance

The revaluation of assets

When World War II ended, Japanese firms found their net worth shrivelled to a dismal level. Some data put the equity to total asset ratio at 11.8 per cent – down from 60 per cent before the war. The worsening of their balance sheet is blamed – on top of sloppy management of their financial resources during the war and rampant inflation after the war – on the fact that since around 1935 the government, pursuant to its wartime policy that favoured indirect financing, had pressured businesses into financing their capital investment with bank borrowings.

Following the enforcement of the Asset Revaluation Law in 1949, enacted on the recommendations of the Shoup Mission invited by the occupation authorities, businesses' equity ratio rose sharply to 40.1 per cent in 1955. The Shoup Report pointed out that despite the inflation-induced sharp rises in the value of their production facilities after the war, Japanese firms had continued to depreciate their plants and equipment on the basis of their pre-war book value and showed inflated earnings in their books, and that the government, in turn, generated revenues by levying corporate taxes on fictitious profits businesses had thus made on paper. And it urged the government to introduce a fair and adequate depreciation system designed to enable business firms to replace worn-out or obsolete machinery and facilities. In response, the Asset Revaluation Law allowed businesses to increase the book value of their assets on the basis of their market price. And the net worth ratios of Japanese firms recovered after a fashion to a level close to that which had existed before the war.

Rapid economic growth and deterioration of balance sheets

The indirect financing system which had been introduced during the war continued into the post-war period. As explained in Chapter 1, with a view to rehabilitating the war-torn economy and catching up with Western economies, the government, by design or otherwise, sought to create an indirect financing system aimed at pooling cheap money into the hands of banks by tightening its control of the financial markets and by regulating interest rates and financial products.

Meanwhile, the domestic market was shielded from foreign competition to ensure the protection of Japanese firms, and the government sought to nurture them by pursuing an industrial policy. Japanese firms drew heavily on the experience of Western countries in defining problems which were likely to arise with economic development and in mapping out the future courses of their industries. By closely analysing American data, Japanese firms were able to predict what would happen in the Japanese markets for television, automobiles and so on. In other words, there were low risk growth opportunities for many industries while competition among domestic participants in each of these industries was fierce.

Rapid expansion of a company tends to put a great strain on the company's resources, particularly when its equity capital fails to keep pace with the expansion. When a company grows at a fast pace, boosting its balance sheet more rapidly than its internal equity growth can cope with, it has to issue new shares to raise the necessary capital. However, if its shareholders or the investors at large do not come up with the needed cash, the company has no choice but to go to a bank for a loan. If it repeats the same practice often enough, it is bound to become overleveraged. Indeed, this was the case with Japanese firms during the years of rapid economic growth.

Table 5.1 shows the growth rates of shareholders' equity and gross assets in each of the five year periods from the latter half of the 1950s. Until the first oil crisis hit them in 1973, sales and gross assets of Japanese firms were growing by more than 15 per cent each year, while their internal growth (increases in capital through retained earnings) inched ahead only about 5 per cent. This suggests that pressure bearing down on their internal growth had been at work all these years.

Table 5.1 Growth rates of Japanese manufacturers

	Sales	Total assets	Internal equity
1955–9	20%	21%	6%
1960–4	13	19	4
1965–9	18	16	8
1970–4	14	13	6
1975–9	11	6	6
1980–4	4	4	6
1985–9	5	8	5

Note: Calculated from Bank of Japan, *Shuyo Kigyo Keiei Bunseki* (*Financial Analysis of Major Firms*).
Source: Shigeru Watanabe, *ROE Kakumei* (*The ROE Revolution*), Toyokeizai Simposha, 1994.

The relatively rapid rate of internal growth witnessed in the second half of the 1960s was brought about by an exceptionally high (3 per cent) increase in the ratio of after-tax profits to sales. After the first oil crisis, however, the growth rate of after-tax profits slumped sharply notwithstanding a rapid growth in sales. As the firms could not cut dividends in keeping with their falling after-tax profits, their internal growth had to slow down. Meanwhile, their gross assets, though they grew somewhat slower than in the second half of the 1960s, continued to increase by two-digit percentage points. As a result, the equity to total asset ratio of Japanese firms had hit the lowest point during this period.

The most critical task facing corporate treasurers during the rapid growth period was how to secure loans from their banks on a steady basis to finance the growth of their business. On the other hand, the most important task facing bankers was how to increase deposits and lending volume as interest rates and financial products were tightly regulated. Under such circumstances, the top priority of corporate money managers was to build good and stable relations with banks which provided a steady flow of credits, while that of the bankers was to build long term business relations as 'main bank' with blue chip and growth companies whose demand for business funds was likely to increase steadily in the years to come.

Against this background, six major business groups (Mitsui, Mitsubishi, Sumitomo, Sanwa, Fuyo (Fuji) and Dai-ichi Kangyo) including those which had been affiliated with former *zaibatsu* (big pre-war industrial or financial combinations) were formed, each centring around a city (large commercial) bank. Short term loans made by these city banks were in effect converted into long term loans by rolling them over and over again and by a tacit agreement made by their clients not to repay their loans against the bank's interest. As businesses were perennially hard pressed for funds, they had to rely heavily on their main banks and were not averse to disclosing their business information and future plans to their main banks.

Such having been their relations, the banks have been closely involved in the management of their client businesses, not just to protect their own exposures but also to bolster the growth of their clients' business, because the banks felt that growth of their clients would directly translate into an increase in their own loans and profits. These banks were not interested in companies which were stable but not growing. Therefore, the banks were willing to extend financial and managerial assistance even to a company which ran into a temporary financial difficulty, if it had a long term growth potential.

According to textbook theory, those who take the risk and commit their funds to a company with growth potential and reap the fruits of its growth are shareholders, and the wherewithal which serves as a buffer in bad times is shareholders' equity. However, under the closed indirect financing system that developed after the war, a large part of the role usually played by shareholders was taken over by the banks. In other words, under the traditional corporate governance system that ruled post-war Japan, the banks played the role of shareholders keeping an eye on the management of the company, and their loans served as a stable source of funds just as equity capital would normally have done.

In consequence, the weight which the shareholders' equity carried in corporate finance has declined gradually, and the equity to total asset ratios of manufacturing firms, which had exceeded 30 per cent in early post-war years, dropped to the pre-asset revaluation level of 16.6 per cent in 1975, after the first oil crisis hit them hard. By US standards, this is as bad as the financial position of American firms which issue high risk junk bonds (Fig. 5.1).

An economic slowdown and surplus funds

After the oil crisis-induced recession, the equity to total asset ratios of businesses began to rise consistently. When interest rates shot up during the oil crisis, businesses awoke to the ruinous effect of the large debt, and reduction of their debt became their top priority.

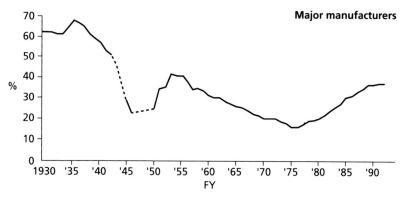

Major manufacturers

5.1 Equity to total asset ratio (source: *ROE Kakumei*).
Note: Calculated from Mitsubishi Economic Institute, *Honpo Jigyo Seiseiki Bunseki* (*Performance analysis of Japanese corporation*) and *Shuyo Kigyo Keiei Bunseki*.

They sought to whittle down their debt load by a ruthless squeeze of assets.

Business firms owe the improvement in their capital structure in the second half of the 1970s to a sharp increase in the turnover rate of their gross assets. While sales continued to increase at an annual rate of 10 per cent plus, the growth rate of their gross assets was held down to the 5 per cent area, reflecting their determined efforts to downsize assets. When viewed in terms of five year periods, it was only during this period that the growth rate of gross assets fell sharply behind that of sales. Through such improvement of asset usage, the growth rate of gross assets was held down below that of internal equity growth, that is, the growth rate of shareholders' equity boosted by profits. And this triggered the improvement in the equity to total asset ratios.

Come the first half of the 1980s, the rapid economic growth wound down to a slower but sustainable growth track, the ratio of after-tax profits to sales improved somewhat, the high turnover rate of gross assets was sustained, and a lower payout ratio helped improve the capital structure.

The largest factor which has contributed consistently over the past 20 years since the first oil crisis to the improvement in the financial structure of Japanese firms is the slower but sustained growth of the economy that followed the rapid growth.

Figure 5.2 shows the percentage of capital investment financed by cash flow (depreciation charges and retained earnings) during the past 40 years. The graph clearly shows the transition from the cash-short period to the cash-rich period. Before 1970, the ratio fell below

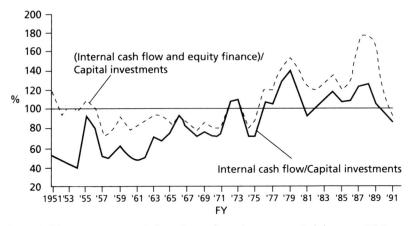

5.2 Capital investment vs cash flow (manufacturing companies) (source: *ROE Kakumei*).
Note: Calculated from *Shuyo Kigyo Keiei Bunseki*.

100 per cent, necessitating borrowing from outside sources, mainly from banks. As the years rolled on into the second half of the 1970s, businesses had enough cash flow to finance their capital investment. Even when their capital investment increased sharply in the second half of the 1980s, they were able to finance it with their internal funds. As they did not need bank loans for their capital investment, they were spared the constraint of going through banks' examination on investment projects.

Liberalisation of the capital markets

In addition to increases in their cash flow, the rapidly progressing liberalisation of the capital markets has drastically changed the environment surrounding corporate financing. As financing vehicles diversified markedly in the process, quantitative constraints of financing and debt servicing costs have decreased dramatically. Sharp increases in the amount of equity-linked financing (convertible and warrant bonds) in the second half of the 1980s were sparked not only by the strong equity market, but also by measures taken by the regulatory agencies: the relaxation of the eligibility standards for issuing corporate bonds, and the abolition of the rule mandating corporate issuers to return to shareholders' premiums earned through issuing new shares at market price.

As noted in Chapter 1, the post-war financial and capital markets built around the pre-war indirect financing system had been shielded from foreign markets, and the government strictly regulated domestic financial transactions. Furthermore, as the government had enforced ceilings on deposit interest rates, low cost funds flowed into the banks, enabling them to play a dominant role in supplying funds to businesses. Thanks to the regulation of deposit rates, the earnings position of the banks improved markedly, helping them to build a solid financial base which has made them virtually insolvency-proof. But some argued that businesses' financing costs had not decreased, because there was no competition among the banks. For example, Osamu Shimomura, a leading brain behind the government's rapid growth policy, repeatedly pointed out that corporate financing costs in Japan were higher than in other countries or before the war. And the Ministry of International Trade and Industry (MITI) and the business community also joined the chorus calling for a cut in the spread between the banks' deposit and lending rates and the relaxation of regulation of bond offerings on overseas markets.

What directly prompted the Japanese government to liberalise the financial and capital markets was foreign pressure. Since the Japan–US Yen/Dollar Committee released its report in May 1984, liberalisation has made headway at a rapid pace (see also Table 1.3).

With the deregulation of the Euro-yen market, such as the lifting of the ban on issuing Euro-yen bonds and the abolition of the principle requiring demand based on trade for foreign exchange transactions, the way for Japanese firms and financial institutions freely to raise funds on overseas markets was opened. These liberalisation measures were followed by the lifting of the ban on issuing unsecured straight bonds and commercial paper, the relaxation of the regulation of issuing corporate bonds, the liberalisation of issuing terms of corporate bonds and the introduction of market-dictated deposit rates (the liberalisation of interest rates on large denomination time deposits, and the lifting of the ban on developing new financial products such as money market funds, etc).

Of these, the measure which had far-reaching impacts on corporate financing was the liberalisation of equity-linked equity financing. High levels of cash flow, and the ample and low cost funds which Japanese business firms have been able to raise through equity and equity-linked financing have spurred them to acquire foreign firms, develop new business and information systems, and invest in research and development and corporate housing projects for employee fringe benefits.

Following the collapse of the stock market in 1990, the volume of equity-linked financing decreased sharply, but it is still on a high plateau when compared with the years before the late 1980s. Equity-linked financing has caught on among business corporations as the major option for financing.

Equity-linked financing

Soon after the war, convertible bonds were issued at the par value of their underlying stocks, and it was in 1962 that the first convertible bond with a conversion price based on the market price of its underlying stock was issued. And the first warrant bond was issued in 1981 following an enabling amendment of the Commercial Code. Characteristic of the Japanese practice of issuing convertible bonds is the setting of their conversion price at a level quite close to (5 per cent higher than) the market price of their underlying stock prevailing at the time of their issue – to encourage their conversion into shares.

The amount of capital raised each year by companies listed on the Tokyo Stock Exchange through equity-linked financing increased sharply from ¥2 trillion ($20 billion at the rate of ¥100 to a dollar) to ¥4 trillion ($40 billion) in the first half of the 1980s to ¥11 trillion ($110 billion) in fiscal 1987 to ¥24 trillion ($240 billion) in fiscal 1989, which matched the amount of capital raised during the seven years from 1980 to 1986 (Fig. 5.3).

In 1989, Japanese firms raised ¥6 trillion ($60 billion) through offering new shares, ¥8 trillion ($80 billion) through offering convertible bonds, and ¥10 trillion ($100 billion) through offering warrant bonds. The bulk of these warrant bonds were issued in dollars on the Euro market where regulation was much looser than on the domestic market. From 1992, no warrant bonds were issued on the domestic market for two consecutive years. As a rule, Japanese firms which issue foreign currency-denominated warrant bonds make an arrangement through a contract of forward rate of exchange or currency swaps to ensure the payment of interest and principal in yen. Thus, they are, in effect, using foreign currency-denominated convertible and warrant bonds as a vehicle for raising yen funds.

As issuers of foreign currency-denominated convertible bonds do not have to redeem their principal if their holders convert them into

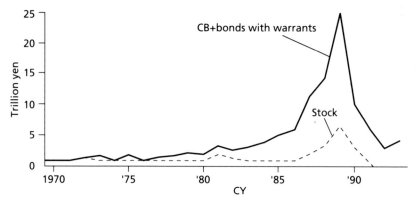

5.3 Equity finance by Tokyo Stock Exchange listed companies (source: *ROE Kakumei*).
Note: Calculated from Tokyo Stock Exchange *Shoken Token Nempo (Annual Statistics)*.

shares, there are difficulties for their issuers to contract a forward rate of exchange or currency swaps for the payment of principals or interest, and therefore, exchange risks commonly remain uncovered. The value of foreign currency-denominated convertible bonds issued by Japanese firms in the 1980s averaged at about ¥1 trillion ($10 billion) a year, and their value has not increased as much as those of other vehicles. Most of the issuers are small companies registered with the over the counter (OTC) market or listed on a national stock exchange, and the bulk of them are Swiss franc-denominated convertible bonds offered on the Swiss market. This is because the requirements for issuing such bonds on the domestic market are prohibitively stringent for small companies to meet, and in the case of OTC companies, they are barred from publicly offering warrant bonds.

With a view to meeting the equity ratio imposed by the Bank for International Settlements (BIS), Japanese banks actively made offerings of equity-linked securities in the second half of the 1980s. Most of their offerings were rights issues which were a sure way to pile up equity, and banks' rights issues accounted for one-half of the total volume of rights issues in the market.

With the increase in the amount of convertible and warrant bonds issued, the amount of new capital resulting from the conversion of convertible bonds or the exercise of warrants increased sharply in the second half of the 1980s. The amount of capital raised through such roundabout routes by companies listed on the Tokyo

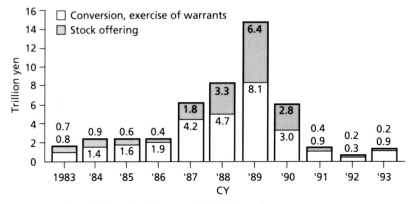

5.4 Increase in paid-in capital (source: *ROE Kakumei*).
Note: Shaded areas indicate amount raised through public offering etc. White areas indicate amount of roundabout financing. Calculated from Tokyo Stock Exchange *Shoken Token Nempo* (*Annual Statistics*).

Stock Exchange increased from ¥1 trillion ($10 billion) in each of the three years from 1984 to 1986 to ¥4 trillion ($40 billion) in 1987 to ¥8 trillion ($80 billion) in 1989. However, as the prices of a large majority of stocks fell sharply below the conversion and exercise prices of their convertible bond and warrants thereafter with the bursting of the speculative bubble, the amount of capital raised through such roundabout routes also decreased sharply, to a 10 year low of ¥0.3 trillion ($3 billion) in 1992. The amount of capital raised through direct rights issues also peaked out at ¥6.4 trillion ($64 billion) in 1989 and dropped steeply thereafter on account of the suspension of new issues imposed by the regulatory agency to support stock prices. The total amount of shareholders' equity raised through the offering of new shares, the conversion of convertible bonds, and the exercise of warrants has increased sharply from ¥2 trillion ($20 billion) in each of the three years from 1984 to 1986 to ¥14 trillion ($140 billion) in 1989 (Fig. 5.4) and then dropped to less than ¥1 trillion ($10 billion) thereafter.

The total value of new shares to be issued against outstanding convertible and warrant bonds amounted to ¥30 trillion ($300 billion) at the end of 1989. It grew larger gradually to ¥37 trillion ($370 billion) at the end of 1992 as their holders balked at exercising their right on account of steep falls in the prices of their underlying stocks, and then decreased to ¥30 trillion ($300 billion) at the end of 1993 because the rights of four year warrants issued in 1989 expired unexercised.

Capitalisation

By combining with surplus cash flow and the accumulation of retained earnings, the improved access to the capital markets has generated a force that has profoundly changed the structure of capitalisation in Japanese companies.

The share of bank borrowings in the capitalisation of large manufacturing firms shrank from 67 per cent in fiscal 1975 to 25 per cent in fiscal 1992. In the process, the share of shareholders' equity increased from 25 per cent to 54 per cent during the same period. And the sum of outstanding corporate bonds which carried fixed interest rates and shareholders' equity also increased from 33 per cent to 76 per cent. In other words, the share of long term funds in the capitalisation increased markedly, suggesting a shift of corporate financial structure to one which is less vulnerable to changes in interest rates. While this is largely due to a slowdown in economic growth, it is also true that equity and equity-linked financing in the second half of the 1980s had a hand in a big way in turning around the financial structure of Japanese firms.

Thanks largely to slower growth in gross assets and accumulation of retained earnings, the equity to total asset ratio increased until around 1985. By contrast, gross assets increased at a rapid rate of close to 10 per cent in each of the three years starting from fiscal 1987, and the increase in externally raised capital outpaced that of retained earnings.

Meanwhile, businesses have whittled down their debts. In the second half of the 1980s, the funds which business firms raised internally (retained earnings and depreciation charges) and those raised on the capital markets consistently outstripped their capital spending and investments to their affiliated companies, and they used the difference to repay debts and beef up their cash holdings and deposits. As a result, the total amount of their bank borrowings decreased for seven years running (Fig. 5.5).

As their cash holdings and deposits increased, their share in gross assets which had long steadied at about 10 per cent began to increase and rose to 15 per cent in fiscal 1988. As business firms reduced bank loans, cash and deposits finally exceeded the amount of their borrowings from banks in fiscal 1989. As a result, the relationships of large firms with their banks reversed from net borrowers to net lenders. And the net financial income of large manufacturing firms turned positive in fiscal 1989 for the first time since the war.

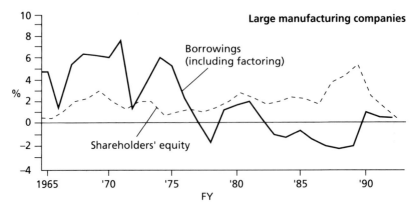

5.5 Relative growth rates of borrowings and shareholders' equity (source: *ROE Kakumei*).
Note: Increase in each category is divided by total assets. Calculated from *Shuyo Kigyo Keiei Bunseki*.

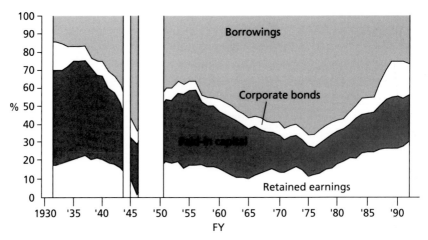

5.6 Composition of capitalisation (source: *ROE Kakumei*).
Note: Calculated from *Honpo Jigyo Seiseiki Bunseki* and *Shuyo Kigyo Keiei Bunseki*.

Thus, the overleveraged financial structure of Japanese firms which had been formed under the controlled economy during the war and reinforced during the rapid growth years after the war has been effectively demolished, and their capital structure has returned to the one based on shareholders' equity and direct (debt and equity) financing which had existed in pre-war years (Fig. 5.6).

Changes in the banks' role and the loss of financial discipline

As large sums of funds flowed back to the banks from their blue chip borrowers, the banks were pressed by the necessity of finding new borrowers and had to change their stance from one of waiting for customers to come to them with hat in hand to one of reaching out to their prospective customers with specific project proposals to cultivate and stimulate their loan demand. They had aggressively to seek out business opportunities for lending, for example to such real estate projects as the construction of office buildings, speculative investment in land lots, and the development of resort facilities, in Japan and abroad; to financial engineering schemes aimed at making capital gains by stock market speculation; and to help with the acquisition of foreign business firms by Japanese companies. But as the bubble burst, the banks found themselves holding the bag loaded with bad loans (see Chapter 7).

In the process, the banks lost their clout as a key element of corporate governance of Japanese companies. Even if they had not lost their prestige with the bursting of the speculative bubble, the banks would have been eased out of their dominant position in the corporate governance of Japanese firms, given the changes in the flow of funds caused by the end of fund shortages and freer access to the financial and capital markets, because the leverage they had enjoyed in corporate governance came from the lender's power; when the borrower's position has strengthened, that power has gone forever.

But nothing has replaced banks. Now that equity-linked financing has come to take on the largest weight among the corporate financing vehicles, shareholders should impose discipline on corporations. However, they, including institutional investors, are not up to the task. For the conventional wisdom – both business firms and the stock market used the size of pretax profits as sole benchmark for evaluating business corporations, and companies which pursued an increase in their pretax profits were considered good companies – which was established during the period when indirect financing had played a dominant role has outlived its relevance to the changed market reality where equity-linked financing has taken hold. Even per-share profits and dividend burden are not high hurdles under a high price–earnings ratio (PER).

In the United States, conventional wisdom sees the issuance of new shares by a company as its management's negative message about its business outlook. Therefore, the issuance of new shares could more often than not work as a signal with a negative implication on the stock price of the issuer. By contrast, the stock markets in Japan tend to take the issuance of new shares at market price as a positive message from the issuer, because the issuance of new shares has long been contingent upon having a good prospect for increasing its pretax profits in coming years. Although having a good prospect for increasing pretax profits is merely a condition to be met in regulatory screening of applicants, not a guarantee of their increase, in Japan, unlike in the United States, the mere fact a company issues new shares at market price helps create an image of such a company as a blue chip corporation.

One lesson which the experience with the speculative bubble holds out is that if business firms make excessive capital investment simply because investors are willing to provide their funds, both the business firms and their investors end up with a loss. This serves to point up the necessity for Japanese business firms to establish basic financial goals on their own. In fact, a growing number of business firms have since set goals for their return on equity (ROE).

Straight bonds and credit rating

It was in 1974 that a Japanese firm obtained a credit rating of its bond, the first ever among Japanese firms to do so. It was Mitsui & Co which obtained from an American agency a credit rating of BBB for the purpose of offering its bonds on overseas markets. In those days, credit rating was not known in the capital markets of Japan, nor was there any credit rating agency.

In the days when Mitsui & Co obtained a credit rating for the first time, the corporate bond market of Japan was tightly regulated. The size of the shareholders' equity above a certain level was the most critical element required by the eligibility standards for issuing corporate bonds, and on account of this requirement, the bond market was virtually closed to those with a small amount of capital. In addition, corporate bonds had to be secured by collateral, and interest rates and other issuing terms were decided uniformly according to the standards established by the *Kisaikai* (New Issue Committee) composed of members drawn from banks and securities companies. So tight was the regulation of the market that only a trickle of bonds were available for trading on the market, and there was little incentive for creating credit rating agencies which provide investors with impartial and professional information concerning the credit standing of bond issuers. Credit information provided by credit rating agencies becomes meaningful only in developed capital markets. This was why credit rating agencies failed to make their debut in a tightly regulated market.

During the Depression in the 1930s, many companies in Japan defaulted on their bonds as American firms did. In contrast with the United States, where credit rating agencies continually updated the credit standing of each and every corporate bond, Japan simply adopted in 1933 a principle (called 'corporate bond cleansing campaign') which required securing all bonds by collateral. The different approaches taken by the two countries in reaction to the massive default on debts reflected the difference in maturity of the two markets, and the practice of requiring collateral against all bonds survived many years. It took 52 long years before the practice of issuing bonds without requiring collateral was revived on the capital markets of Japan in 1985.

In 1979, the first credit rating agency, called Japan Bond Research Institute, was established, and credit ratings assigned by the agency have been used as eligibility standards since the turn of the 1980s. Prior to that, the *Kisaikai* composed of members drawn from 36 banks and 7 securities companies worked out eligibility standards on the basis of net asset value and other data on applicants. At monthly meetings, the *Kisaikai* picked candidates from among the applications introduced by its members and decided on issues, their amount of issue and issuing terms (interest rates) in consultation with the Ministry of Finance and the Bank of Japan.

During the early years that followed the establishment of the credit rating agency, underwriters used the numerical standards established by the *Kisaikai* in conjunction with the credit ratings assigned by the agency. Since 1990, however, the eligibility standards have been unified into the credit ratings given by rating agencies. In determining the eligibility of commercial paper (which was liberalised in 1987 as a vehicle for short term financing), credit rating was used as a sole criterion. While the practice of assigning credit ratings was started in the United States as a source of information for investors, the credit rating system was introduced in Japan as a replacement for outdated eligibility standards.

Although the regulatory requirements have been eased year after year, some of the requirements established by the *Kisaikai* – the size of net asset value and per-share dividends – still remained on the rule book in 1994. Nevertheless, there is no mistaking the fact that liberalisation of eligibility standards has made progress since the introduction of the credit rating system. Under the old eligibility standards that remained in effect until November 1990, 30 per cent of the firms rated AAA, 50 per cent of those rated AA, and 80 per cent of those rated A as of 1992 would have been barred from issuing unsecured straight bonds. By contrast, any company with a credit rating of BBB or higher is currently authorised to issue unsecured straight bonds.

In the second half of the 1980s, the weight of financing on the capital markets of Japan shifted sharply from indirect to direct financing, and the balance of funds raised by leading manufacturing firms through bond offerings increased to a level neck and neck with their bank borrowings. As the bond thus gained increasing weight as a vehicle for financing from a marginal tool to a major source of financing, corporate issuers came to pay closer attention to the credit ratings of their debt securities. Reflecting this tendency, the number of business corporations which have obtained credit ratings for their bonds and commercial paper increased to 850 and 300, respectively, by 1994. In the process, the credit rating agencies have become widely known in the capital markets, particularly in the new issue market, during the 10 or so years of their existence. It is fair to say that the introduction of the credit rating system has played a vital role in modernising capital markets and in freeing the bond market from the strangulation of arbitrarily imposed regulation. The role of the credit rating system as a lever for accelerating the regulatory reforms has almost come to an end, and now it will take on the role of a provider of information on the credit standing of debt and equity issuers to help investors make informed decisions.

The balance of straight bonds issued by business corporations outstanding at the end of April 1993 outstripped utility bonds and rose to ¥12.6 trillion ($126 billion); efforts are being made to streamline their trading market. And the experience of the United States clearly shows that credit information will play a critical role in developing an efficient secondary market that enjoys the confidence of investors. Already there has emerged a difference in yields among the bank debentures on the secondary market since 1990.

Sooner or later, a bond secondary market where yields on corporate bonds are determined according to their credit rating will emerge.

Split ratings

When two credit rating agencies assign different ratings to a bond issued by one and the same corporation, it is called a 'split rating', meaning that their evaluations are divided. While credit ratings of a Japanese bond issue given by the three Japanese agencies (the Japan Bond Research Institute, the Japan Credit Rating Agency Ltd and the Nippon Investors Service Inc) vary from one another mostly by a notch (either plus or minus), those assigned by the two American rating agencies sometimes differ from those given by Japanese agencies, on average, by one full grade. The split rating issue has been noticed since Moody's Investors Service started to assign credit ratings to a large number of Japanese firms and publish them on its own without specific requests from the Japanese firms.

As of July 1993, the number of Japanese firms to which Standard & Poor's and Moody's Investors Service had assigned credit ratings on their own stood at 154. A total of 35 of them were assigned by these two American agencies credit ratings more than two grades lower than those given by Japanese agencies, and 20 of them were assigned credit ratings below BB (Ba), which is considered below investment grade. The credit ratings assigned to these 154 firms by Japanese agencies averaged at AA-, while those assigned by the US agencies averaged at A3, a difference of one full grade.

The lower the credit standing, the larger the difference in credit ratings. One of the Japanese firms which is rated A by a Japanese rating agency got a rating below Ba. And all the Japanese firms rated by the Japanese agency as BBB got ratings below Ba from American rating agencies in 1993. This suggests that while Japanese rating agencies have strong confidence in the safety of bonds issued by Japanese firms, Moody's considers a broad range of Japanese bonds unfit for investment.

Credit rating agencies in Japan and their US counterparts are also divided on the evaluation of industries. Their evaluations diverge most widely on the steel and textile industries. The American rating agencies assigned to all six Japanese steel makers and four out of seven textile companies ratings two grades below those assigned by the Japanese agencies, while the ratings assigned by them to transportation equipment (autos) and precision machinery makers are not much different from those given by Japanese agencies. Only 2 out of the 13 electrical machinery makers got ratings two grades below those given by Japanese agencies. For example, Japan Bond Research Institute assigned ratings in the range of AA to transportation equipment and steel makers, whereas Moody's assigned an average of A1 to transportation equipment makers and Baa2 to steel makers, one grade lower than those given by the Japanese agency. The average credit ratings given by American agencies to Japanese industries which enjoy a competitive edge in the world markets are not much different from those given by Japanese agencies, while those assigned to former leading industries (steel and textiles) are distinctly lower than those given by Japanese agencies. Meanwhile, credit ratings given by American agencies to non-manufacturing sectors (housing and property developers, and construction) are much lower than those given by Japanese agencies. Ratings given by the US agencies to three out of five housing and property developers, and five out of nine construction companies are two grades lower than those given by Japanese agencies, owing in part to the fact that these types of businesses are operated under different schemes in other countries, and in part to the fact that US agencies take seriously the shaky balance sheets of these companies caused by steep falls in land prices. Ratings given to utilities and banking institutions which carry little risk thanks to government protection are not much different from those given by Japanese agencies. Those to which the American agencies assigned ratings two grades below those given by Japanese agencies are three trust banks and two regional banks out of a total of 32 banking institutions they covered in 1993. In the area of transportation, American agencies gave much lower ratings to shipping companies which faced fierce international competition, but those given to railway companies are not much different from those given by Japanese agencies (Fig. 5.7).

The three Japanese credit rating agencies tend to assign greater weight to the scale of operations than the American agencies. In short, Japanese agencies are soft on big firms. A comparison of the credit ratings assigned by the American agencies to S&P 500 and those given by the Japanese agencies to NRI400 firms selected by Nomura Research Institute shows that there is no striking difference in ratings in terms of their minimum net asset values, and the American agencies assigned BBB or A even to small companies. One striking difference in their attitude is that while the American agencies assigned relatively lower ratings even to large companies, the larger the scale of operation, the higher the ratings given by the Japanese agencies tend to be. In the case of the Japanese agencies, the larger the net asset value on average, the higher the ratings. By contrast, the ratings assigned by the American agencies have less direct relationship with net asset values (Fig. 5.8).

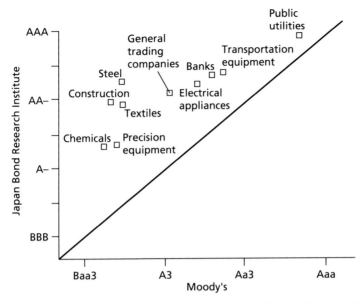

5.7 Split ratings (source: Watanabe et al, *NRI Corporate Finance Research Report*, vol. 3).

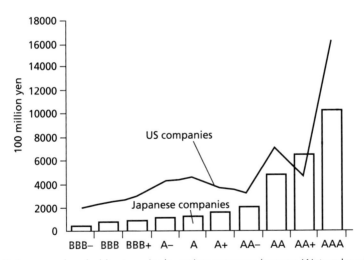

5.8 Average shareholders' equity by rating category (source: Watanabe et al, 'Credit Ratings of Japanese Companies', *Zaikai Kansoku* (*Business Outlook*), Nomura Research Institute, Jan. 1993).

As the credit rating system was introduced as a yardstick for measuring the eligibility of issuers, initially it was the concern mostly of issuers of debt securities. However, as the volume of straight bonds traded on the market grew in recent years, and since the problem of bad loans plaguing the banking institutions came to light, the interest in credit ratings which show the safety of bonds has risen among investors and self-regulatory organisations. However, as the rating assigned to a Japanese firm by American agencies (say, Ba) often diverges from that given by a Japanese agency (A), the difference in ratings often confuses investors, and this stands in the way of active utilisation of credit ratings as a reliable source of information for their investment decisions.

Some hold the view that as the two American rating agencies rate Japanese firms from a global perspective, their evaluation of even a Japanese blue chip corporation tends to be conservative. Others argue that the meaning of the grades used by American agencies differs from that used by their Japanese counterparts. Still others contend that American agencies evaluate Japanese firms on the basis of management parameters of American firms and do not take into account factors contributing to financial stability which are unique to Japan, such as the special relationships Japanese firms have with the government, banking institutions, and member companies belonging to one and the same business group. The penchant of Japanese rating agencies for giving larger weight to the scale of operation is justifiable at least from this point of view. Historically, the incidence of default on corporate bonds in Japan is not large.

What is more, unlike other American rating agencies, Moody's rates the credit standing of business firms in many cases on an unsolicited basis, and because it assigns ratings to companies without the benefit of their proprietary information, its ratings might tend to be conservative because of the dearth of information.

An official of a large American bank who is responsible for rating the credit standing of its customers had this to say about the background to split ratings:

> *In the United States where we have a large collection of data on the relationships between financial information and default, even unsolicited ratings made exclusively on the basis of publicly available data are highly reliable. Banks' internal rating of the credit standing of their customers is made on the basis of a model that incorporates the relationship between the financial data of a target company and its credit rating given by leading rating agencies. In Japan where the rating agencies are often divided on their evaluation of the credit standing of one and the same company and data on defaults are scarce, it*

is difficult to formulate a rating model compared even with other Asian and European countries.

There are strong grounds for such a view, and establishing a standard for evaluating the credit risks of Japanese firms is an important task which the capital markets of Japan must come to grips with in coming years.

6 Cross-border money flow

Factors determining the pattern of money flow to and from Japan

The relationship between Japan's current account balance and the pattern of money flow to and from Japan has changed markedly since the first half of the 1980s. Until the 1970s, Japan's foreign currency reserves changed almost in lockstep with changes that occurred in its current account balance. This suggests that cross-border movements of private capital had a minor role. In fact, except for 1972–4 – a period during which the financial markets of the world were seriously in confusion on account of the collapse of the Bretton Woods agreement and the eruption of the first oil crisis – the gross amounts of long and short term capital to and from Japan were smaller than the level of current account balance.

Since 1980, however, private capital moving to and from Japan has increased sharply, far outpacing its current account balance, and has had big impacts on interest and exchange rates, in Japan and abroad. One of the factors behind this development was a sharp increase in the current account imbalances among industrial nations, particularly between the United States and Japan. The expansionary fiscal policy pursued by the first term Reagan Administration and the tightening of credit reins by the Federal Reserve Board (FRB) combined to push up the dollar rate and boost America's current account deficits. At the same time, the disinflation caused by these fiscal and monetary policies of the United States pushed down international commodity prices, weakened the clout of oil exporting countries on the world's capital markets and exacerbated the debt crunch of developing countries. Meanwhile, Japan, whose economy had emerged much leaner from the oil crisis-bred recession ahead of other industrial nations, piled up current account surpluses year after year. And thanks to the weakening of the financial clout of oil producing countries and much reduced lending power of US banks on account of their swollen bad loans to developing countries, Japan (and its banks and institutional investors) took on sharply increasing importance as a capital provider. As a result, the money flow to and from Japan has come under the sway of changes occurring in the current account balances of industrial nations, particularly, the United States, and the way they finance their current account deficits, on the one hand, and the policies which the Japanese fiscal and monetary authorities pursue in response to such external developments, on the other.

The second factor was the measures the Japanese government took (see Chapter 1) pursuant to the amended Foreign Exchange Control Law (enforced in December 1980) and the recommendations made by the politically powerful Yen/Dollar Committee in 1984 which deregulated foreign currency transactions and foreign investment by institutional investors. The pace and substance of deregulation measures have since come under the influence of the movements of the market.

From the foregoing, it may be said that the pattern of money flow to and from Japan has been largely determined by the movement of Japan's current account balance and changes that have occurred in the macroeconomic environment – fiscal, monetary, and currency policies – of other countries in response to the movement of Japan's current account balance. Moreover, as the Yen/Dollar Committee demonstrated (see below), macroeconomic conditions and movements of deregulation have been influencing one another.

In the following pages, we will divide the 15 years that followed 1980 into three periods – 1980–4 (when the dollar was strong), 1985–9 (when the dollar weakened), and after 1990 – reviewing the characteristics of money flow to and from Japan during these periods, and the relationship between the macroeconomic environment and deregulation of the financial markets, and then briefly examine the outlook.

The strong dollar period (1980–4)

Except for a short spell of market confusion that developed in the wake of the second oil crisis of 1979, the first half of the 1980s was marked by the recycling of huge amounts of Japan's current account surpluses to the United States in the form of long term portfolio investment by Japanese institutional investors. The amount of long term capital that flowed out of Japan increased from $8.7 billion in 1981 to $49.7 billion in 1984. In addition, issuance of yen-denominated foreign (*samurai*) bonds, limited though their amounts were compared with Japanese institutional investors' investment in US bonds, also played a role in boosting the outflow of capital from Japan (see also Chapter 2).

One of the factors which triggered the outflow of long term capital from Japan was the difference in interest rates between Japan and the United States. Owing to the tightening of credit reins by the FRB in 1980, and the huge budget deficit under the Reagan Administration in 1981, both long and short term interest rates rose sharply in the United States. On the other hand, business demand for funds in Japan remained weakened as Japan's business sector tried to reduce borrowings in order to improve profitability, with the result that the spread of interest rates between the two countries widened to 3–6 per cent.

The outflow of capital from Japan pushed down the yen rate against the dollar. But the monetary authorities of both countries did not take any strong action to arrest the fall in the yen rate, creating the impression that they acquiesced in the weakening of the yen.

The second factor which encouraged the outflow of capital from Japan was the easing of regulation of foreign capital transactions by the Japanese regulators at a time when the spread of interest rates between the two countries tended to widen. As noted earlier, the Japanese government amended the Foreign Exchange Control Law to liberalise foreign exchange transactions. The amendment to the Foreign Exchange Control Law did not specifically change the regulation of foreign bond investment by institutional investors, but changed its stance from one prohibiting in principle to one liberalising in principle. This allowed the monetary authorities to ease their administrative guidance on foreign investment by institutional investors. More specifically, in January 1981 pension trusts were allowed to invest up to 10 per cent of their gross assets in foreign currency-denominated assets, and in May 1983 the postal insurance system also was allowed to invest up to 10 per cent of its gross assets in foreign bonds. However, as the yen continued to weaken, the regulators imposed a cap on increases in foreign investment by life insurance companies during the period from April 1982 to August 1986 with a view to reducing the speed of capital outflow from Japan.

Obviously, Japanese institutional investors stepped up their investment in foreign assets not merely to take advantage of the difference in interest rates but also for the purpose of spreading the risks of their exposures. In addition to their need to diversify their portfolios, insurance companies sought to prepare themselves for a massive increase in claims in consequence of a widely predicted earthquake in the Tokai area by stepping up their investment in foreign assets. And this was also a factor contributing to sharp increases in foreign investment by Japanese institutional investors.

On the new issue market, Japan's current account surplus and deregulations worked to increase the issue of *samurai* bonds, which amounted to ¥1.2 trillion to ¥1.3 trillion (about $4 billion in 1984 dollars) in 1984–5. The increase in *samurai* bonds is attributed to low interest rates under a burgeoning current account surplus in Japan, and the relaxation of the eligibility standards effected on the recommendation of the Yen/Dollar Committee submitted in July 1984.

The change in capital flows in and out of Japan in this period had very important implications not only for Japan but also from global perspectives. First, the capital that flowed from Japan to the United States was used to finance the current account deficit of the United States, strengthened the dollar, and thus played a pivotal role in creating what is known as 'an imperial cycle' – a cycle in which a strong dollar boosts the structural current account deficit of the US. In the second half of the 1980s, with a view to correcting the strong dollar, pressure was brought to bear on Japan to ease its monetary control sharply on a long term basis, and this led to the development of an economic bubble. Second, the United States blamed the undervaluation of the yen caused by the closed nature of the Japanese financial markets for its widening current account deficit, and called for the appointment of a Yen/Dollar Committee to address the problems; the Committee had a series of meetings from February to May 1984. In retrospect, the United States' blaming of the closed nature of the Japanese financial markets for its growing current account deficit was not met with support, and the aim of the United States was not simply to correct the undervaluation of the yen but also to help US financial institutions make inroads into the Japanese market. However, the liberalisation of capital transactions in Japan was accelerated by the activities of the Committee. And its effects began to show up after 1985, except in the *samurai* bond market, and markedly changed the pattern of money flow to and from Japan during the strong yen period in the second half of the 1980s.

The strong dollar correction period after the Plaza Accord (1985–9)

Japan's current account surplus continued to increase until it hit a peak in 1987 and has since remained on a high plateau. But the money flow to and from Japan during the weak dollar period which started in 1985 showed a much more complex structure compared with the first half of the 1980s. The outflow of long term capital outpaced current account surpluses, while short term funds flowed into Japan through banks, creating a structure of short term borrowing and long term lending. In 1987, for example, Japan's current account surplus was widened to $87 billion, while outflow of long term capital soared to $136.5 billion. On the other hand, inflow of short term capital (broadly defined, short term capital includes funds flowing into Japan through foreign exchange banks – Japanese banks authorised to deal in foreign exchange – and the margin of error in the statistics) rose to $88.8 billion.

Under this structure, international money flows concerning Japan during this period had the following five characteristics. First, despite the weakness of the dollar, long term investment in the United States made by Japanese institutional investors stayed at a high level. Second, in the new issue market, issuance of Euro-yen bonds by non-residents increased sharply, and investment in these bonds by Japanese investors played a role in boosting the outflow of Japanese long term funds. On the other hand, the issuance of *samurai* bonds tended to decrease and their importance as the vehicle to facilitate capital export from Japan decreased. Third, direct investment by Japanese firms in foreign countries also increased sharply from 1987.

Fourth, the flow of short term funds into Japan mainly took the form of borrowing of dollar funds by Japanese banks from the Euro market. This was because Japanese institutional investors began to hedge their exchange risks and Japanese banks invested actively in long term dollar bonds with the short term dollar funds they borrowed in the Euro market.

The fifth characteristic is the fact that capital transactions between Japanese institutions through foreign markets – roundabout transactions – increased during the period. The roundabout transactions are listed statistically as an outflow and an inflow of funds with a certain time lag, and they are largely divided into two kinds. One, as explained in Chapter 5, is a two part transaction consisting of the issuance of equity-linked securities on a foreign market by Japanese firms (inflow of long term capital) and purchases of such bonds by domestic investors (outflow of long term capital). The value of foreign bonds issued by Japanese firms net of redemptions reached a peak of $75.7 billion (on a balance of payments basis) in 1989. The other is Euro-yen 'impact loans'. An impact loan is a yen-denominated loan given by a foreign banking institution to a Japanese firm without specifying its use. In reality, however, a Japanese bank transfers its short term funds to its branch in a South-East Asian country, which, in turn, lends the funds back to a Japanese firm as short term loans.

One of the factors which prompted Japanese banks to borrow short term funds to make long term loans was the fall in long and short term rates in Japan caused by the relaxation of credit reins by the Bank of Japan to counteract the weak dollar and excess liquidity developed by the easy money. Since 1987, the money supply in Japan has increased by double digit percentage points, fuelling the rise in stock and property prices. The cost of raising funds in Japan dropped steeply, and investment in foreign securities and real estate by Japanese firms (statistically, the latter is included in direct investment) and direct investment in foreign markets by Japanese manufacturing firms to cope with the rising yen have increased sharply.

As the prices of domestic assets Japanese institutional investors had acquired increased their hidden (unrealised) profits, they played an important role in luring Japanese investors to foreign property markets. As the unrealised profits were large enough to absorb exchange losses, they continued to pour billions of dollars into foreign assets while the difference in interest rates persisted. In the case of life insurance companies, they are authorised to use only interest and dividend incomes for distribution among their policy holders under Article 87 of the Insurance Business Law, while they are required to set aside capital gains in reserves under Article 86 and these gains can be used only when they run an evaluation or liquidation loss. While they sought to increase their interest income by investing in the high yielding bonds of the United States and other countries, life insurance companies converted capital gains earned from stock and land holdings into income gains to offer high dividend products (such as single premium endowment insurance). And this has been a factor sustaining their investment in foreign securities at a high level despite the strong yen (see also Chapter 7).

Another factor was the effect of the deregulation of the market which began to take hold after the recommendations of the Yen/Dollar Committee. The regulation of investment in foreign assets by institutional investors was eased step by step, and even the Fund Trust Bureau (a government agency responsible for managing funds pooled from postal savings, national and employees' welfare pension funds, and surplus funds of the government) was authorised to invest up to 10 per cent of its assets in foreign securities in April 1987. And the relaxation of the official guidelines for issuing Euro-yen bonds in 1986 also helped accelerate the issuance of Euro-yen bonds.

Where short term money flow is concerned, the principle of 'genuine' demand (a principle authorising forward exchange contracts only for the purpose of meeting genuine, as opposed to speculative, demand such as the payment of import bills, etc) and the restriction of *enten* (to convert the dollar funds raised on the Euro-dollar market or on the Tokyo call dollar market into yen funds) were abolished in April and June 1984, respectively. This enabled institutional investors to hedge their foreign securities positions with futures, and the banks to raise short term foreign currency funds and invest them in foreign securities. In addition to the relaxation of monetary conditions, the liberalisation of movement of short term funds was responsible for having produced a unique pattern of money flow – borrowing short term funds to finance long term loans – in the second half of the 1980s.

As more and more Japanese firms sought to circumvent the regulation still remaining in Japan, money flow of the roundabout type, sparked by advancing relaxation of the financial markets and deregulation of money flow to and from Japan, gathered pace. With the cost of raising funds by offering equity-linked securities falling sharply thanks to a rise in the price of their underlying stocks, the volume of debt securities offered on much less regulated foreign markets and the purchases of such securities by domestic investors increased. While there was a strong demand for short term funds, domestic banks were not able to meet such demand because of the window guidance (regulation of loans made by the central bank to commercial banks through a discount window, which was practised until June 1991) and shortage of funds. The relaxation of regulation of capital transactions – the liberalisation of impact loans of Euro-yen (short term loans in June 1984 and long and medium term loans in June 1989), and the opening of the Tokyo offshore market (December 1986) – coming as it did at such a juncture has given a boost to roundabout transactions through their overseas branches which are not subject to the window guidance of the central bank. The relaxation of regulation of the issuance of Euro-yen bonds, although technically not roundabout transactions, has diminished the relative utility of *samurai* bonds and has reduced the volume of their offerings.

The relaxation of credit reins by the Bank of Japan in the second half of the 1980s came about in consequence of a series of concerted interest rate cuts and currency market interventions aimed at controlling the fall in the dollar and counteracting the deflationary pressure brought about by the rising yen. In the months that followed a rise in the discount rate by the Bundesbank and the occurrence of Black Monday in 1987, pressure mounted on Japan to take measures designed to stave off a worldwide deflation and arrest the fall in the dollar, in response to which the Bank of Japan cut its discount rate several times, finally to as low as 2.5 per cent by May 1989. There is no denying that the deregulation of foreign investment by Japanese investors had in effect served to support the US bond market and the dollar. As a result of the policy pursued by Japanese banks of borrowing short term funds to finance their long term loans under such circumstances, Japan has built a huge surplus in its long term external asset position, while Japanese banks have run large external short term liabilities. This suggests that Japan has played a role in international finance as a net capital exporter in the aftermath of an 'imperial cycle' and as an engine of maturity transformation. And such one-sided flow of money, together with a fallen dollar and worldwide deregulation of the financial markets, has led to a period of large adjustments of the money flow to and from Japan in the 1990s, described in the next section.

The adjustment period since 1990

Japan's current account surplus decreased to $35.8 billion in 1990 owing in part to a contribution of $11 billion made to the United Nations to cover part of the cost of the Gulf War. In response to the decrease in Japan's current account surplus, the yen depreciated in 1989 through the first half of 1990, and it appeared that the adjustment of the overvaluation of the dollar and the excessive current account surplus which had started since the Plaza Accord of 1985 had run its course. However, in the second half of 1990, Japan's current account surplus began to expand once again and rose past the $100 billion mark for the first time in 1992, to $111.1 billion. This triggered upward pressure on the yen in the second half of 1990.

The pattern of money flow to and from Japan developed since 1990 has the following characteristics.

1 The roundabout capital transactions have decreased.

2 The outflow of short term funds from Japan through the banks has outstripped their inflow, and the pattern of short term borrowing of foreign funds has disappeared.

3 The outflow of long term capital through Japanese investment in foreign securities has decreased below that of the 1980s and its pattern has changed violently.

4 The preference of Japanese investors for yen-denominated assets, both short and long term, has grown stronger than before. Particularly, the issuance of yen-denominated bonds by non-residents has increased in response to the preference of Japanese institutional investors.

The volume of foreign bonds issued by Japanese firms (a form of roundabout financing) peaked at $85.5 billion in 1989, and after decreasing sharply to $33.5 billion in 1990, has hovered within the range of $40 billion to $60 billion. And while the balance of outstanding debt securities net of redemptions of those issued in the second half of the 1980s rose to $75.7 billion in 1989, it decreased to $30.8 billion in 1993 and continued to fall below a year ago in 1994. The outstanding balance of impact loans also has been on the decline since 1992 after rising until 1991.

The inflow of short term funds through the foreign exchange banks also decreased to zero in 1990 from the peak at $68.8 billion recorded in 1987, and they have since been flowing out of Japan – of the order of $84.4 billion in 1991 and $71.9 billion in 1992 and continuing to outflow thereafter. This is mainly due to cutbacks in their foreign short term borrowing by the foreign exchange banks. And their short term debts, both yen- and dollar-denominated, have decreased from $620.6 billion at the end of 1990 to $467.5 billion at the end of 1993.

The pattern of flow of long term capital has been fluctuating wildly, from a net outflow of $43.6 billion in 1990 to a net inflow of $37.1 billion in 1991 and it outflowed again in 1992 and 1993. This was due to the fact that while investment in foreign securities by Japanese institutional investors in the second half of the 1980s decreased sharply from $80–$100 billion to $30–$60 billion, investment in Japanese securities by foreign institutional investors, mainly

US pension funds, has increased sharply. Outflow of long term capital through direct investment in foreign markets by Japanese firms has also been decreasing each year, from $46.3 billion in 1990 to the $10 billion area since 1992.

Meanwhile, the value of Euro-yen-denominated bonds issued by non-residents has stayed above the ¥4 trillion mark ($40 billion at the rate of ¥100 to the dollar) since 1991 after rising to ¥4.45 trillion ($44.5 billion) in fiscal 1989 and hit an all-time high of ¥4.78 trillion ($47.8 billion) in fiscal 1993. In addition, the value of *samurai* bonds issued by foreign borrowers has stood above the ¥1 trillion mark ($10 billion) except for 1991. While foreign currency-denominated short term loans made by Japanese banks have been decreasing in parallel with their short term liabilities, yen-denominated loans have been on the rise – sharply boosting the share of yen-denominated loans in their total short term assets.

The factor which contributed to such changes in the pattern of money flow was the evaporation of excessive liquidity from the Japanese capital markets. Owing to (1) repeated hikes of the discount rate during the period from 1989 to 1990 (from 2.5 per cent to 6 per cent) and a sharp decrease in Japan's foreign exchange reserves, and (2) worldwide rises in real interest rates triggered by the reunification of the two Germanys, the growth in Japan's money supply (measured in terms of M2+CD) has sharply slowed down from a two digit increase in the years to 1990 to almost zero percentage points, and this was accompanied by a collapse in stock and land prices.

In the course of such developments, the hidden (unrealised) profits of Japanese institutional investors have shrunk sharply on top of huge exchange losses they had suffered, making it difficult for them to absorb further exchange risks arising from acquiring additional foreign assets. Therefore, their chances of making fresh investment in US bonds are limited to a phase of market development where the yen depreciates and overseas interest rates come down. Increases in demand for non-residents' Euro-yen bonds and *samurai* bonds which offer higher yields than exchange risk-free domestic bonds reflect the strong aversion of Japanese institutional investors to exchange risks.

Sharply fallen stock prices have made it difficult for Japanese firms to raise funds by offering equity-linked securities on foreign markets, and have reduced roundabout capital transactions and acquisition of real estate in foreign markets which they used to finance with low cost funds. With their earnings shrunken on account of the recession, direct investment of Japanese firms has been limited to South-East Asian countries aimed at offsetting the effect of the strong yen by taking advantage of cheap labour available in these countries.

The decrease in liabilities of foreign exchange banks is blamed on cutbacks in the credit line available to them on the Euro market reflecting the increase in their bad domestic loans.

The second factor that should not be overlooked is the monetary situation of the United States. In that country, the real short term rate was cut close to zero with a view to turning around the economy and salvaging the near-bankrupt savings and loan associations. Funds flowed into the equity and debt markets through mutual funds, stock prices rose continually, and yields on bonds dropped sharply in the autumn of 1993. This narrowed the difference in interest rates between Japan and the United States, boosted the outflow of US long term capital, part of which to the equity market of Japan, and helped change the long term capital balance of Japan.

The third factor is a change in the regulatory stance that began in the 1990s. While cross-border capital transactions have been liberalised, the regulation for risk control was toughened, reinforcing the moves outlined in the foregoing.

The universal primary capital ratio rule for banking institutions agreed at the Bank for International Settlements (BIS) in 1992 heightened the effect of decreased hidden profits from their stock and land holdings, and squeezed the balance of foreign liabilities and assets of Japanese banks (see Chapter 7 for a more detailed explanation). What is more, a solvency margin rule, the equivalent of banks' primary capital ratio rule, is expected to be enforced on life insurance companies, an investor group having the largest exposure to foreign securities in Japan, and Article 87 of the Insurance Business Law which prohibits the distribution of capital gains in dividends to policy holders is expected to be revised, both by 1996. Given such prospects, an investment strategy aimed at raising the coupon rate on the assumption of exchange losses widely followed in the 1980s no longer makes investment sense.

Meanwhile, where deregulation of capital transactions is concerned, a number of measures have been taken – the relaxation of the eligibility standards for issuing Euro-yen and *samurai* bonds, a phasing out of what is known as 'Three Bureau Guidance' (an administrative guidance jointly issued by three bureaux – the International Finance Bureau, the Securities Bureau, and the Banking Bureau – of the Ministry of Finance in August 1975 which bars locally incorporated foreign securities subsidiaries of Japanese banks from assuming the lead managership of underwriting bonds issued by Japanese firms on overseas markets), the lifting of the ban on distributing Euro-yen-denominated sovereign bonds among Japan's resident investors, and the institution of the shelf registration system – giving a boost to the issuance of Euro-yen and *samurai* bonds.

Such a pattern of cross-border money flow took shape in reaction to the speculative bubble that developed in the second half of the 1980s – the collapse of asset prices and the toughening of risk control such as the enforcement of the BIS primary capital ratio – which, by combining with the weakened capacity of investors to absorb exchange risks, has led to swollen current account surpluses and upward pressure on the yen. As a result, Japan found itself no longer able to export capital exclusively denominated in dollars, while maintaining its position as a net capital exporter. And the necessity for nimbly diversifying its assets in response to changes occurring in the movements of the dollar and other major currencies and for increasing its investment in yen-denominated assets has mounted. This meant that Japan had to seek further liberalisation of the Tokyo market to equip it with stronger market intelligence gathering capabilities and the internationalisation of the yen for capital transactions and cross-border investment, proposed by the Yen/Dollar Committee as tasks confronting the regulators of Japan in the 1990s.

The key to meeting these challenges effectively lies in engineering a consistency between deregulation of cross-border money to and from Japan and that of the domestic market. The lack of such consistency became apparent when Japanese banking institutions employed a roundabout method of capital transactions, and the realisation has grown even keener as a growing number of debt offerings have been lured away to overseas markets in the form of Euro-yen bonds. In the case of Euro-yen bonds and *samurai* bonds, for example, for reasons of (1) the lack of transparency of placing due to the underdevelopment of Tokyo's bond market, and (2) the high cost including fees for fiscal agents (according to a survey by the Ministry of Finance, fees for fiscal agents on the first time issue of five year sovereign bonds worth ¥30 billion with a credit rating of single A issued by an OECD member country are 90 basis points in the case of a *samurai* bond issue and 28 basis points in the case of a Euro-yen bond issue), blue chip issuers prefer the Euro market over the Tokyo market. As a result, the volume of *samurai* bond issues came to only one-third of that of Euro-yen bond issues, and those offered by issuers with a credit rating of BBB accounted for 36.5 per cent of the total volume issued in fiscal 1993. These problems also exist in foreign exchange and stock transactions. Therefore, the liberalisation of cross-border money flow, while leaving the slowness of deregulation unremedied, could lead to a hollowing out of the Tokyo market. Compared with the 1980s when capital transactions became active thanks to super-easy monetary conditions and the ratio of dollar transactions was high, the overall capital transactions have decreased and the weight of yen-denominated transactions has increased – further magnifying the gravity of these problems.

Outlook

A weakened dollar and ballooning current account surpluses in Japan in the first half of the 1980s gave rise to an internationally concerted effort to prop up the dollar, which set the stage, if unwittingly, for an economic bubble in Japan in the second half. And as the economic bubble burst in 1990, the Japanese economy had to undergo painful adjustments, in the course of which the nation's political and business leadership has come to realise the growing relevance of the prescription recommended by the Yen/Dollar Committee – internationalisation of the yen. The key points to be borne in mind in divining the future movements of the Japanese economy are (1) the macroeconomic environment (how long Japan will continue to run current account surpluses and whether it can maintain its position as a net exporter of capital), and (2) regulatory reforms (how much Japan can – or will – do to accelerate the internationalisation of the Tokyo market and the yen).

In 1994, Japan ran a current account surplus of more than $130 billion. As Japan's imports have been increasing at an annual rate of double digit percentage points owing to a sharp rise in the yen rate and as the government is expected to run a large budget deficit this year and thereafter, its trade surplus will decrease in coming years. The Kobe earthquake of January 1995 will also reduce Japan's current surpluses by $10–20 billion for the next two to three years. However, with the domestic financial markets still beset by uncertainties, and as exports of capital goods and industrial raw materials to overseas transplants of Japanese firms are expected to increase, its trade surplus will shrink only marginally. It all depends on the movements of the yen rate and the size of government spending for health care and the welfare of the aged, which is expected to increase sharply in the second half of the 1990s, but Japan is likely to hold on to its position as a net exporter of capital in the remaining years to 2000.

The critical question is whether Japan can – or will – accelerate the deregulation of its market to a degree consistent with the liberalisation of cross-border money flow and to what extent it will internationalise the Tokyo market and the yen while it maintains its position as a net exporter of capital. In this sense, moves Japan takes in the next five years to overhaul its market will decide whether it will maintain a prominent position or be consigned to a marginal position in the international market in the twenty-first century.

7 Financial institutions of Japan

Domestic private financial institutions

The financial institutions in Japan are divided into two groups: those providing long term credits and ordinary (commercial) banks (Table 7.1). The former consist of long term credit banks, trust banks, and life insurance companies. There are three long term credit banks and they raise funds mainly by offering coupon debentures (maturing in two or five years) and discount debentures (maturing in one year) to make long and medium term loans primarily to large corporations. Loans made by long term credit banks accounted for 6.6 per cent of the total loans made by private financial institutions at the end of FY 1993.

There were seven trust banks (Nihon Trust was acquired by Mitsubishi Bank and now the number is six) and the services they provide are largely divided into five areas:

1 Ordinary banking service;

2 Long term loans to business corporations financed by funds collected from individuals by selling 'loan trust accounts' (with a maturity of two or five years);

3 Asset management of corporate pension funds;

4 Investment advisory service; and

5 Custodian business of securities investment trusts, and *tokkin* trust funds.

Trust banks' managing funds increased rapidly, mainly in the form of 'Fund Trusts' in the 1980s. The balance rose to ¥30 trillion

Table 7.1 Highlights of the financial institutions of Japan (31 March 1993) (trillion yen, %)

	No. of institutions	Loans (A)	Securities (B)	Assets (C) = (A) + (B)	Ratio of securities (B)/(C) × 100
Long term credit banks	3	47.6	14.2	61.8	23.0
Trust banks	7	59.8	76.5	136.3	56.1
Life insurance companies	27	61.1	67.4	128.5	52.5
Property and casualty insurance companies	25	7.2	12.3	19.5	63.1
City (commercial) banks	11	223.2	46.5	269.7	17.2
Regional banks	64	126.5	32.5	159.0	20.4
Second-tier regional banks	66	50.9	9.5	60.4	15.7
Credit associations	435	64.7	12.4	77.1	16.1
National Federation of Credit Associations	1	4.3	4.9	9.2	53.3
Subtotal	436	69.0	17.3	86.3	20.0
Credit unions	428	18.3	1.7	20.0	8.5
National Federation of Credit Unions	1	1.6	0.6	2.2	27.3
Subtotal	429	19.9	2.3	22.2	10.4
Agricultural co-operatives	3,118	17.4	3.7	21.1	17.5
Federation of Agricultural Credit Unions	47	10.3	11.0	21.3	51.6
The Central Bank for Agriculture and Forestry	1	13.3	14.3	27.6	51.8
Agricultural financial institutions	3,166	41.0	29.0	70.0	41.4
Federation of Agricultural Mutual Aid Co-operatives	48	8.4	9.6	18.0	53.3
Workers' credit unions	47	4.4	1.3	5.7	22.8
Federation of Workers' Credit Unions	1	0.2	1.7	1.9	89.5
Subtotal	48	4.6	3.0	7.6	39.5
Total of private financial institutions	4,329	717.6	319.5	1,037.1	30.8
Postal insurance		25.9	29.8	55.7	53.5
Trust Fund Bureau		210.4	92.2	302.6	30.5
Total of publicly run financial institutions		236.3	122.0	358.3	34.0
Total of private and public financial institutions		953.9	441.5	1,395.4	31.6
(Reference)					
Investment trusts				43.6	
Balance of postal savings				170	

Note: Includes numbers for the National Federation of Agricultural Mutual Aid Co-operatives.
Source: Bank of Japan.

($300 billion) during the latter half of the decade. However, as stock prices collapsed in the 1990s, it decreased sharply. Meanwhile, Public Investment Funds deposited part of their funds with trust banks in the form of *shiteitan* trusts, and their balance outstanding at the end of March 1993 increased to ¥20 trillion ($200 billion). Stock investment of 'Public Investment Funds', which is an issue drawing considerable public attention today, is carried through trust banks.

During the years of rapid economic growth, long term commercial lending was the main business of trust banks. However, upon the contraction of fund demand among large corporations since the 1980s, the weight of their business has shifted dramatically to the management of corporate pension funds and Public Investment Funds. The balance of loans made by trust banks outstanding at the end of March 1993 accounted for 8.3 per cent of the total loans made by domestic private financial institutions, while their share in securities holdings rose to 23.9 per cent. This suggests that the trust banks have become major institutional investors in the securities market of Japan.

Insurance companies collect insurance premiums from individuals pursuant to insurance agreements and at the same time manage corporate pension funds. In Japanese life insurance companies, the proceeds of life insurance and corporate pension funds are not managed separately. Long term commercial loans were the bulk of their operating assets until the mid-1970s, but since the 1980s, their security holdings have been increasing sharply. The share of business loans made by life insurance companies in the total balance of loans among domestic private financial institutions outstanding at the end of March 1993 stood at 8.5 per cent, while their share in securities holdings stood at 21.1 per cent, almost neck and neck with trust banks (see the next section for details).

Interest rates charged on long term loans in Japan are based on the long term prime rate and are set at a level 0.9 per cent above the coupon rate of five year bank debentures. While long term credit banks apply a fixed long term prime rate, trust banks revise their long term prime rate every six months and apply the prime rate of the long term credit banks at each revising month as a floater. The rates charged by life insurance companies vary from one company to another, but long term floaters seem to be popular.

In Western countries called commercial banks, the main players in the Japanese financial markets are named 'ordinary' banks. These include city banks, regional banks, and second-tier regional banks.

Such classifications are not based on statutory divisions but are due to their historical background, their locations, and customer bases. At present, there are 11 city banks which locate most of their branches in the nation's three economic centres (Tokyo, Nagoya, and Osaka), providing short term credits to large corporations. (The Bank of Tokyo which specialises in foreign exchange services is also included in the city banks but will be merged with Mitsubishi Bank, one of the largest city banks.) Recently, however, small business and consumer lending has been on a consistent rise.

As a group, city banks account for 31 per cent of the total loans made by private financial institutions as of 31 March 1993, the largest share of the domestic lending market. Interest rates charged by city banks are determined on the basis of the short term prime rate then in effect. Until the 1970s, when deposit rates were regulated, short term prime rates were set at a level 0.25 per cent higher than the discount rate. However, as interest rates have been liberalised since 1980, funds borrowed at deregulated interest rates increased, which widened the spread between the discount rate and short term prime rate to 0.5 per cent in 1981 and to 0.75 per cent in 1986, so they changed the practice of setting the short term prime rate to one which adds a certain spread to interbank rates. As the short term prime rate is changed on the initiative of city banks, it can vary from one region to another.

The government of Japan is subdivided into 47 prefectures. There are large banks called regional banks based in their respective prefecture capital, which provide loans to individuals and business corporations in their prefecture, underwrite municipal bonds issued by their local government, and handle the receipt and payment of local government funds. In most cases, there is only one regional bank in a prefecture, but in some prefectures where economic activity is diversified, there are two or more regional banks. All told, there are 64 regional banks in the country. As a group, regional banks account for 18 per cent of the total loans made by domestic private financial institutions, the second largest after the city banks.

Pursuant to the 1988 amendment of the Mutual Banking Law, mutual banks, which had been catering exclusively to small to medium-size businesses were converted into ordinary banks called 'second-tier regional banks'. Ordinarily, regional banks and second-tier regional banks serve different niche markets, the former catering to the financing needs of larger business corporations in a prefecture and the latter serving small to medium-size business firms. Second-tier regional banks as a group account for 7 per cent of the total loans made by domestic private financial institutions. Both regional banks and second-tier regional banks are stock companies, and a majority of their shares are listed on major exchanges.

In addition, there are credit associations and credit unions which are banking institutions owned by their members and cater to the banking needs of small business firms. Founded under the Small Business Co-operatives Law of 1949, credit unions are co-operative banking institutions devoted to mutual assistance among small businesses and workers. Following the enactment of the Credit Association Law in 1951, those credit unions which had taken on the characteristics of general banking institutions were allowed to embark themselves on banking business as a credit association.

Services provided by credit associations are not much different from those of ordinary banks, and the only difference is that credit associations are not allowed, in principle, to give loans to non-members or operate outside their designated areas. As of 31 March 1993, there were 435 credit associations, and they formed a national federation, the National Federation of Credit Associations, as their umbrella organisation. As demand for funds varies from one credit association to another or from one region to another, the Federation acts as co-ordinator of fund flow by accepting deposits of surplus funds from cash-surplus associations in different regions and lending them to cash-short credit associations in other regions. In addition, it seeks to invest funds effectively to offer a relatively higher yield deposit to members' financial position. Likewise, credit unions have formed a national federation of their own to perform roles similar to those of the National Federation of Credit Associations. Loans made by credit associations, credit unions, and their national federations account for 12.4 per cent of the total loans of private financial institutions.

Catering to the financial needs of farmers is a three-tier system of agricultural financial institutions. A total of 3,100 agricultural co-operatives across the country provide financial services to their members. In the case of agricultural co-operatives, the balance of deposits net of loans is defined as a surplus, and they are required to deposit more than two-thirds of their surplus with their regional superior organisation called the Federation of Agricultural Credit Co-operatives. Agricultural production has been slowing down in recent decades, and the loan–deposit ratio of agricultural credit co-operatives declined to 27 per cent as of December 1993, with the result that their idle cash is supposed to have been deposited with the Federation (this is called 'the system deposit'). There are 47 federations of agricultural credit co-operatives (one in every prefecture), and their primary function is to co-ordinate the flow of funds among their member co-operatives and invest surplus funds in securities instruments. These federations are obligated to deposit with the Central Bank for Agriculture and Forestry (Norinchukin Bank) more than 50 per cent of their surplus (deposits less loans). As demand for loans from these federations remains weak, they are investing in securities the funds left over after the obligatory deposits with the Norinchukin Bank. The Norinchukin Bank, in turn, lends the funds collected from these federations and those raised by issuing debentures, to businesses engaged in agriculture, forestry, and fisheries, and invests surplus funds in securities markets. At the end of March 1993, these three-tier agricultural thrift institutions held a total of ¥29 trillion ($290 billion) worth of securities, which accounted for 9 per cent of the total value of securities held then by domestic private financial institutions.

In addition to deposits and loans, agricultural co-operatives sell policies of life insurance and property and casualty insurance over the counter. Premiums collected by agricultural co-operatives are pooled at their prefectural federation of agricultural mutual aid co-operatives and invested in various securities, and part of the funds is deposited with their superior organisation called the National Federation of Agricultural Mutual Aid Co-operatives. Thus, the insurance business of agricultural co-operatives is also structured in three tiers. The total balance of operating assets of these federations and the National Federation stood at ¥18 trillion ($180 billion) at the end of March 1993, accounting for 14 per cent of the total balance of assets of private life insurance companies. The agricultural insurance system is allowed to provide policies of life insurance and property and casualty insurance, while no other private life insurance company is allowed to provide property and casualty insurance, and vice versa.[1] However, an amendment to the Insurance Business Law planned for 1997 would allow insurance companies of one sector to provide insurance coverage of the other sector through a subsidiary of their own.

Operating assets of private property and casualty insurance companies outstanding at the end of March 1993 accounted for 2 per cent of the total operating assets of private financial institutions.

---

1 Non-agricultural and non-public sector is called 'private' sector in Japan.

In addition, there is a special banking institution called the workers' credit union. These unions provide the services of financing the welfare and mutual aid projects undertaken by labour unions and consumers' livelihood co-operative associations. There are 47 workers' credit unions across the country, and they provide mortgage loans and consumer loans to their members with funds collected through deposits of their members. They, too, have their superior organisation called the National Federation of Workers' Credit Unions. Operating assets of workers' credit unions and their national federation outstanding at the end of March 1993 stood at ¥7.6 trillion ($76 billion), accounting for 0.7 per cent of the total operating assets of private financial institutions.

Thus, the characteristics of Japan's small financial institutions are that all of them – credit associations, credit unions, agricultural thrift institutions, federations of agricultural credit co-operatives, and workers' credit unions – have their own superior organisations, which play the role of co-ordinating the flow of funds between cash-surplus and cash-short member organisations and managing their surplus funds effectively. As their subordinate organisations perennially run surplus in most cases, these superior organisations have become key players in the bond market of Japan.

Net assets of the investment trusts outstanding at the end of fiscal 1992 (ended 31 March 1993) stood at ¥43.6 trillion ($436 billion), 47 per cent of which are in stock investment trusts and 39 per cent in bond investment trusts. More recently, net assets of money market funds (MMF) have been increasing markedly, while those of stock investment trusts have been on the decline continuously due to the weak stock market (Table 7.2).

Table 7.2 Changes in the net assets of Japan's investment trusts (¥100 million, %)

Fiscal year	Stock investment trusts		Bond investment trusts		Subtotal		MMF		Total
75	19,643	57.4	14,548	42.5	34,191	100.0			34,192
80	41,516	67.4	20,037	32.6	61,553	100.0			61,553
85	116,782	52.8	104,533	47.2	221,315	100.0			221,315
90	356,890	76.3	110,861	23.7	467,751	100.0			467,751
91	251,989	65.0	135,935	35.0	387,924	100.0			387,924
92	204,096	46.8	168,874	38.7	372,970	85.6	62,929	14.4	435,899
93	189,419	41.4	178,383	39.0	367,802	80.5	89,321	19.5	457,123

Source: The Investment Trusts Association.

Government run financial institutions

In addition to these private financial institutions, there are 24,000 postal offices across the country which take deposits and sell insurance policies. The balance of postal savings outstanding at the end of March 1993 stood at ¥170 trillion ($1.7 trillion), and this accounts for 16.7 per cent of personal financial assets. That of postal insurance stood at ¥55.7 trillion ($557 billion) as of the same date, accounting for 6.4 per cent of personal financial assets. All told, postal savings and insurance account for a total of 23 per cent of personal financial assets.

Postal savings and contributions to public pension funds are transferred to the Trust Fund Bureau of the Ministry of Finance. At the end of March 1993, the Bureau had a balance of ¥302 trillion ($3.02 trillion). This and the balance of postal insurance totalled ¥358 trillion ($3.58 trillion) – 26 per cent of the total assets of the domestic financial institutions – which is managed by the Trust Fund Bureau of the Ministry of Finance and the Postal Insurance System of the Ministry of Posts and Telecommunications.

The funds of the Trust Fund Bureau and the postal insurance system, and the proceeds of government-guaranteed bonds, are used to finance Japan's Treasury investment and loans programme (see Chapter 4 for further details of this system). This section looks at the market operation which the Treasury investment and loan programme undertook in the second half of the 1980s.

Under the Treasury investment and loan programme, the funds collected by offering various financial products (postal time savings accounts – see Chapter 2, postal insurance coverage, public pension funds) and the proceeds of government-guaranteed bonds are used to finance the construction of social capital, loans to small businesses and agricultural and forestry operations, and various public works projects (public housing, highways, and hospitals). As interest rates have been liberalised in steps since the 1980s, and for the financial needs of these agencies, pressure has grown for generating higher rates of return on their investment. With the private financial institutions poised to take advantage of liberalised interest rates, the postal savings system has come under increasing pressure to raise the returns on its investment to meet their competition, and so has the postal insurance system. The public pension funds also had to improve the rate of returns on their investment in order to provide against increases in the ageing population. With a view to meeting these challenges, the postal savings system and the public pension funds sought to develop vehicles, other than internal deposits to the Trust Fund Bureau, to improve the rate of return on their investment. Under similar circumstances, the postal insurance system also tried to diversify its investments. In the course of such efforts, public pension funds were authorised in fiscal 1986 to invest part of their assets autonomously, and a similar measure was taken for the postal savings and the postal insurance systems in fiscal 1987. And these systems have come to participate directly in the securities market either on their own or through trust banks and insurance companies for the first time in their history.

The balance of public pension funds outstanding at the end of March 1993 rose to ¥97 trillion ($970 billion), that of the postal savings system to ¥173 trillion ($1.73 trillion), and that of the postal insurance system to ¥66 trillion ($660 billion) – the main source of funds for Treasury investment and loans – for a total of more than ¥300 trillion ($3 trillion). As of the same date, the balance of autonomous investment in securities stood at ¥16.1 trillion ($161 billion) for the public pension funds, ¥20.4 trillion ($204 billion) for the postal savings system, and ¥7.2 trillion ($72 billion) for the postal insurance system – for a total of ¥43.7 trillion ($437 billion). This was equal to 13.1 per cent of the total assets held by the three public institutions mentioned above and amounted to 20 per cent of the Treasury investment and loan programme (flow basis) in fiscal 1993 (Table 7.3).

First, the public pension funds were allowed to invest in the securities market as Public Investment Funds. In the past, public pension funds had had to deposit all pension premiums with the Trust Fund Bureau in the form of 'internal deposits'. As the yield of internal deposits fell in the 1980s following the liberalisation of interest rates, particularly in the wake of the Plaza Accord of September 1985, lowering returns on investment of internal deposits aroused growing complaints, and pressure mounted for the authorisation of autonomous investment. In response, the Ministry of Health and Welfare authorised in fiscal 1986 the Annuity Welfare Corporation, an auxiliary organisation of the Ministry (which is engaged primarily in building and running welfare facilities for the beneficiaries of the public pension system and in providing housing loans to them at below-market rates), to borrow funds from the Trust Fund Bureau at the same interest rate as that on the internal deposits and manage these funds in the markets. The Annuity Welfare Corporation invests part of the funds borrowed from the Trust Fund Bureau

Table 7.3 Funds managed by three publicly run systems (trillion yen)

Fiscal year	Public pension funds				Postal savings funds for coping with liberalised interest rates			Postal insurance	Total	(Reference) Balance of trust (*shiteitan*)
	Trust (*shiteitan*)	Life insurance	Autonomous investment	Subtotal	Trust (*shiteitan*)	Autonomous investment	Subtotal	Trust (*shiteitan*)		
85	0.5			0.5					0.5	0.5
86	1.6	0.3	0.1	2.0		2.0	2.0	0.4	4.4	2.0
87	3.0	0.9	0.3	4.1		4.5	4.5	0.9	9.5	3.9
88	4.5	1.7	0.5	6.7	0.3	7.2	7.5	2.3	16.5	7.1
89	5.9	2.9	0.8	9.6	0.8	10.2	11.0	3.9	24.5	10.6
90	7.4	4.2	1.0	12.7	1.5	13.5	15.0	5.6	33.3	14.5
91	9.4	5.5	1.2	16.1	3.1	17.3	20.4	7.2	43.7	19.7
92										

Note: Public pension funds = national pension funds + welfare pension insurance.
Sources: Bank of Japan, Ministry of Finance, and Ministry of Posts and Telecommunications.

in securities (it is not allowed to invest them in equities) on the advice of investment advisory service companies, and the rest are entrusted to trust banks (*shiteitan*) and life insurance companies (variable insurance for Annuity Welfare Corporation). When the term of a contract expires, the Corporation repays the principal of the loan together with interest accrued thereon to the Trust Fund Bureau, and the remaining profits, if any, are retained for the purpose of strengthening its financial base. Autonomous investment started with ¥500 billion ($5 billion) invested in *shiteitan* in fiscal 1986, and the fund grew to ¥16 trillion ($160 billion) by the end of March 1993: ¥12.4 trillion ($124 billion) managed by the Corporation on the advice of investment advisory service firms, ¥5.5 trillion ($55 billion) entrusted with life insurance companies, and ¥9.4 trillion ($94 billion) entrusted with trust banks (*shiteitan*).

Shiteitan is an abbreviation of *shitei tandoku kinsen shintaku* which means a money trust separately managed where the basic investment strategy is decided by a trustor. Money trusts offered by trust banks in Japan are divided into *shiteitan* and *tokutei kinsen shintaku* or simply *tokkin*. In the case of *shiteitan*, the trustor designates the basic strategy such as cash flow needs, asset allocation, etc. Selection of specific securities is left at fund managers' discretion. In the case of *tokkin* funds, the trust bank simply performs the administrative work in accordance with specific instructions given by the trustor. Depending on the method employed for managing a fund, money trusts are divided into those composed of funds provided by a single trustor and those composed of funds pooled from two or more trustors. In other words, *shiteitan* is a money trust aimed at large investors which is managed separately by fund managers of trust banks under the basic strategy designated by the trustor.

The authorisation of autonomous investment by the postal savings system was designed to help the system (1) establish its management base on the model of business corporations and (2) cope with liberalised interest rates. Although the postal savings system is run by the government, it came under pressure to establish a self-sustaining operation. However, as it is required to transfer the entire amount of money it collects in post offices to the Trust Fund Bureau, it was allowed little scope for improving its performance. To help the postal savings system cope with the competition unleashed by the liberalisation of interest rates, encourage the development of products and services tailored to meet the needs of depositors, and maintain self-sustaining power, a special account for coping with liberalised interest rates was created.

Under this special account, the system can borrow funds from the Trust Fund Bureau at the same interest rate to operate them on the open market. When the system earns any profits from securities investment, the profits are retained at the special account as reserves for coping with further liberalisation of the market. The ¥2 trillion ($20 billion) seed money with which the special account started in fiscal 1987 increased to ¥20.4 trillion ($204 billion) by the end of March 1993. Initially, the system managed the funds by itself (investment in equities was not authorised), but since fiscal 1989, it has been authorised to invest its funds in *shiteitan* money trusts through the Postal Insurance Welfare Corporation. As of the end of March 1993, ¥3.1 trillion ($31 billion) of its funds were invested in *shiteitan* and ¥17.3 trillion ($173 billion) were operated by this special account.

Although the postal insurance system serves as an important source of funds for the Treasury investment and loan programme, it was authorised to invest part of its funds in bonds to compete with private insurance companies for a higher rate of returns. However, it was not authorised to invest its funds in equities, while its private sector competitors were allowed to do so. To remedy this situation, the government authorised it in fiscal 1987 to invest its funds in equities through *shiteitan* offered by trust banks. As a result, the balance of its funds invested in *shiteitan* increased sharply from ¥350 billion ($3.5 billion) in fiscal 1987 to ¥7.2 trillion ($72 billion) at the end of fiscal 1992.

Since August 1992, public funds have come to attract the growing attention of the stock market, because the government authorised new *shiteitan* with no limit on the ratio of stock investment as part of its fiscal stimulus package announced in that month. In the past, the ratio of shares that could be allocated into *shiteitan* portfolios of public pension funds and the liberalisation special account of the Ministry of Posts and Telecommunications was limited to 30 per cent and that of the postal insurance system to 80 per cent. What is more, the method of interest payment to the Trust Fund Bureau discouraged stock investment. To get around this problem, the regulatory agency instituted a new facility called 'new *shiteitan*' worth ¥2,800 billion in addition to the existing *shiteitan* facility. Characteristics of the new *shiteitan* are (1) that there is no limit on the ratio of stock investment, and (2) that interest accruing to the Trust Fund Bureau can be paid in a lump sum once every five years. In a statement released together with the announcement of a fiscal stimulus package in May 1993, the government also said that it encourages efficient management of new *shiteitan*. In fiscal 1993, ¥2.8 trillion ($28 billion) worth of new *shiteitan* was launched. The balance of Public Investment Funds invested in *shiteitan* also increased to ¥23 trillion ($230 billion) at the end of fiscal 1993.

With the bursting of the bubble economy in 1990, private banking institutions found themselves saddled with huge amounts of bad loans, and their capacity for stock investment was reduced sharply. Meanwhile, funds converging on postal savings and postal insurance have increased steadily, sharply boosting the balance of *shiteitan*, with the result that purchases of shares by Public Investment Funds increased to a level matching those of foreign investors. Given the prospects for a slowdown in stock investment by domestic institutional investors in the next couple of years, market attention will be focused on the movement of publicly managed funds. Seen from a different angle, this spells a decline in the ratio of shareholdings of private financial institutions, and a rise in that of public pension funds, the postal insurance, and the postal savings system – suggesting a sharp change in the distribution of share ownership on the Tokyo stock market from private financial institutions to 'public' financial institutions.

Banks

THE BURSTING OF THE ECONOMIC BUBBLE AND BAD LOANS

During the period from the second half of the 1980s to early in the 1990s, leading Japanese banks have undergone a jolting change on account of the introduction of the capital adequacy ratio imposed by the Bank for International Settlements (BIS) and the emergence of huge amounts of bad loans in the autumn of 1991.

The regulation of the capital adequacy ratio enforced on the Japanese banks in compliance with the BIS rule is structured as follows.

Risk weight was assigned to major assets of the banks, ranging from 0 per cent (government bonds) to 100 per cent (business loans). The total of assets multiplied by their respective risk weight is called 'risk assets'. The BIS rule requires all participating banks to maintain the ratio of their equity capital to risk assets at a level equivalent to 8 per cent or more. The value of foreign currency-denominated assets must be translated into yen amounts. Therefore, the capital adequacy ratios of city and long term credit banks which have large amounts of foreign currency-denominated assets are vulnerable to swings occurring in the yen rate. Other conditions being equal, a rise in the yen rate pushes up their capital adequacy ratio, while a drop in the yen rate has the opposite effect.

Under the BIS definition of capital adequacy, almost all of the equity capital in financial statements is treated as Tier I (core) capital, and it increases with the issue of new shares and the accumulation of retained earnings. And 45 per cent of the unrealised profits in securities holdings and subordinated debt are called Tier II (supplemental) capital. As the rule requires that Tier II capital should not be larger than Tier I capital, the ratio of Tier I capital should be larger than 4 per cent in order to meet the BIS requirement. The bulk of the Tier II capital of Japanese banks is held in the form of unrealised profits of their securities holdings. Therefore, their Tier II capital is vulnerable to changes occurring in the prices of securities they hold. As their securities holdings are largely made up with listed government bonds and shares, a drop in interest rates boosts their unrealised profits in government bonds – and by extension, their capital adequacy ratio. On the other hand, an increase in interest rates has the opposite effect. A rise in the prices of shares they hold pushes up their capital adequacy ratio, while a drop in them has the opposite effect. In short, a rise in the yen rate and stock prices and a drop in interest rates boost their capital adequacy ratio, while a drop in the yen rate and stock prices, and a rise in interest rates push down their capital adequacy ratio. If market fluctuation decreases their capital adequacy ratio, they must curb the growth in their risk assets. As business loans carry a 100 per cent risk weight, the banks are tempted to curb their lending to hold down their risk assets. Another alternative is to issue subordinated debt which constitutes Tier II capital.

Figure 7.1 shows the growth rates of assets of the city and long term credit banks in the 1980s. The introduction of the capital adequacy ratio at a certain level usually tends to discourage the growth in banks' assets. However, the growth rate of assets of Japanese banks did not change despite the introduction of the capital adequacy ratio in the autumn of 1987. In fiscal 1989, their growth rate actually rose to 20 per cent. This is explained by the fact that a wide-ranging increase in stock prices occurred in that year which

7.1 The change in big banks' asset growth (source: Annual Reports).
Note: Big banks means city banks and long-term credit banks. Figure shows year on year basis.

automatically boosted the unrealised profits of their share holdings and therefore their capital adequacy ratio, and also the bullish stock market enabled Japanese banks to raise large sums of capital through stock offerings – ¥2 trillion ($20 billion) in fiscal 1988 and ¥2.6 trillion ($26 billion) in fiscal 1989. In other words, the sharp expansion of capital gave them extra scope for making additional loans. As the months rolled on into 1990, however, the unrealised profits in their share holdings shrank sharply following a collapse in stock prices in 1990, and it became difficult for them to raise fresh capital through stock offerings. To maintain their capital adequacy ratio in the face of shrunken unrealised profits, they took in large sums of money in subordinated debt – but to no avail. As a result, the growth rate of assets of the city and long term credit banks took a dive and finally turned negative in FY 1990.

In the second half of the 1980s, bank loans increased sharply. Where did they go? Table 7.4 sums up the net increase in loans made by the city, regional, long term credit, and trust banks during the five year period to March 1990. As noted in Chapter 5, while these banks were able to increase their equity capital easily during the period, large business corporations also actively raised their capital through equity and equity-related financing on an unprecedentedly large scale to trim their borrowings from banks and beef up their liquidity on hand. As a result, profitability of loans made to large corporations

Table 7.4 The net increase of loans in the late 1980s

	Change (trillion yen)			Share (%)		
	City, regional banks	**Long term credit banks, trust banks**	**All banks**	**City, regional banks**	**Long term credit banks, trust banks**	**All banks**
All corporations	65.4	31.2	96.6	69.5	93.4	75.8
Manufacturers	−1.5	−3.3	−4.7	1.5	−9.9	−3.7
Real estate/ construction	22.3	7.7	30.0	23.8	23.0	23.6
Non-banks	15.4	21.0	36.4	16.4	62.9	28.6
Others	29.1	5.8	34.9	31.0	17.3	27.4
Individuals	27.3	1.3	28.5	29.0	3.8	22.4
Others	1.4	0.9	2.3	1.5	2.8	1.8
Total	94.1	33.4	127.4	100.0	100.0	100.0

Note: During the period from March 1985 to March 1990.
Source: Bank of Japan.

by the city, long term credit, and trust banks deteriorated, compelling them to develop new groups of borrowers. And the new groups they found were property developers, non-banks, and individuals. As shown in Table 7.4, loans to non-banks accounted for 28.6 per cent, and those to construction companies and property developers 23.6 per cent, of the increases in loans of all banks. Adding those to individuals, loans made to new groups of borrowers accounted for 75 per cent of net increases in their loans. As prices of real estate rose due to lower interest rates, investment in commercial property increased sharply and triggered a wave of speculation in real estate. And banks themselves also jumped on the bandwagon and made property-related loans bypassing non-banks, sharply boosting their property-related loans. Mortgage loans to individuals, more particularly loans to individuals for the purpose of their acquisition of condominium units, golf course membership, and stocks, have increased dramatically. Such convergence of bank loans to the real estate market in this period has subsequently come to plague them as bad loans in the 1990s.

With a view to meeting the capital adequacy ratio imposed by the BIS, the city and long term credit banks sharply increased their equity capital (for a cumulative total of ¥10 trillion ($100 billion) in FY 1985 through FY 1989), but this has given rise to a serious hangover. As the prices of bank stocks had been controlled in the past, bank stocks' liquidity was very poor on the Tokyo Stock Exchange. Their prices remained little changed. However, as Sumitomo Bank abandoned its control over its share prices in the first half of the 1980s, other banks followed suit, and the number of their shares traded on the market has since increased gradually. Such relaxation of control notwithstanding, a much larger percentage of their shares remained locked up in the vault of their royal shareholders, with the result that the liquidity of their shares was much lower than those of business corporations. Although these banks offered large amounts of their shares on the market in the second half of the 1980s, a considerable portion of them remained unsold, so they had to ask their clients to purchase them. As it happened, business corporations themselves made equity financing on an unprecedentedly large scale, and they too had to solicit their loyal shareholders to acquire their shares. Banks held business corporations' stocks in compensation for selling bank stocks to business corporations. Thus, the shares issued by these banks to clear the BIS capital adequacy ratio requirements have given rise to, and strengthened, the relationship of cross-shareholding between banks and business corporations. In a majority of cases, big banks ended up holding twice as much as the shares they issued in equity financing. Thanks to the massive offerings of their shares in the second half of the 1980s, these banks have easily cleared the BIS standard. In reality, however, they have come to hold shares of their corporate clients worth far larger than their own equity capital, and have been forced to finance some part of their stock investments by deposits. As long as stock prices continued to rise as they had done in the second half of the 1980s, these banks could justify their investments by increases in unrealised gains from their stock holdings. However, when stock prices collapsed early in the 1990s, they could no longer justify such stock investment. Worse yet, they had to realise the hidden profits of their stock holdings to offset their charge-off on bad loans, with the result that the financial capacity of these banks to hold shares for the purpose of cross-shareholding has badly weakened. In other words, the relationship between issuers and their loyal shareholders which had long been a characteristic of the Japanese stock market since the war is now disintegrating with the weakening of the banking system.

In the autumn of 1991, the domestic stock market realised the seriousness of the bad loan problem besetting the banking system. During the four months to April 1992, bank stocks tumbled, and in an effort to calm the market, the Ministry of Finance disclosed in March 1992 the total amount of bad loans of the city, long term credit, and trust banks, which had a jolting impact on the financial market of Japan. The first reaction was shown in the form of downgrading the credit ratings of Japanese banks by foreign credit rating agencies. Japanese banks had not received below A ratings in the 1980s. Following the surfacing of the bad loan problem, the credit rating of some Japanese banks plunged to as low as BBB.

As the recession continued to cast gloom over the economy, the Bank of Japan cut the discount rate a number of times from the second half of 1991 and finally slashed it to an all-time low of 1.75 per cent (see Chapter 2). However, banks' bad loans continued to increase with the months, and their credit ratings were downgraded lower still. Faced with such pressures, the banks have become increasingly wary of making fresh loans, and the year-to-year growth rate of their loans continued to slow down despite the sharp cut in the discount rate during the period from 1993 to 1994. This was an experience unknown before.

Information disclosed by Japanese banks is still inadequate to pass a credible judgement. However, according to indicators related to the bad loans of the city banks (including estimates for some of them), the balance of loans of these banks as a group outstanding at the end of September 1993 stood at ¥272 trillion ($2.72 trillion), of which ¥16 trillion ($160 billion) – 5.9 per cent of their total outstanding loans – was estimated to be non-performing assets. This is equal to 6.9 years' worth of their annual net profits. And their ratio of non-performing assets to the unrealised gains from their land and stock holdings stood at 72 per cent. In FY 1992, some of the city banks began writing off their bad loans, and during the 12 month period ended March 1994 (FY 1993), city, long term credit, and trust banks have written off a total of ¥3.5 trillion ($35 billion) worth of bad loans. Leading Japanese banks are highly likely to write off their bad loans on a large scale during the next two to three years in order to recover the sound performance of their assets. Therefore, their capacity for holding shares of their corporate clients will contract sharply, and the recovery of their credit extension capacity will be delayed. While the banking sector has become weakened, the corporate bond market has increased 6.5-fold in five years, from ¥800 billion ($8 billion) in FY 1987 to ¥5.2 trillion ($52 billion) in fiscal 1992. However, government run financial institutions sharply boosted their shares in the lending market.

Figure 7.2 shows trends (fiscal 1979 = 100) among the fund positions of private banks, government run financial institutions (the postal savings system, the postal insurance system, and employees'

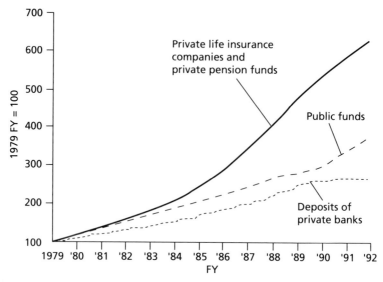

7.2 The change of funding in major financial institutions (source: Bank of Japan).
Notes: Public funds = postal insurance, postal savings accounts and employees' pension funds.
Private life insurance and pension funds = pension funds managed by trust banks, life insurance and federation of mutal associations.
Deposits of private banks = cash, demand and time deposits and certificates of deposit.

pension fund), private life insurance companies, and private pension funds managed by trust banks during the 14 years to fiscal 1992. As was the case in the United States, the entities which sharply increased their shares in the financial markets of Japan in the 1980s were insurance companies and private pension funds. Since 1990, however, private banks' fund attracting power has weakened sharply on account of the collapse of the stock market and the problem of swollen bad loans. In their place, government run financial institutions emerged and have attracted large amounts of funds from the market. While in the United States a weakened banking system led to a sharp expansion of the capital markets and a sharp increase in the assets of mutual funds, in Japan it boosted the market shares of government run financial institutions.

With their financial positions thus strengthened, government run financial institutions accounted for more than 50 per cent of the domestic financial transactions effected in fiscal 1993. In other words, the amounts of funds supplied to the market by Public Investment Funds and government run financial institutions' shares in the lending market have increased sharply. With the advent of a coalition government, calls for a sweeping overhaul of government regulation of the market have become increasingly vocal. However, the market shares of government run financial institutions are still rising, and pressure for an adjustment of market shares between government run financial institutions and private ones will grow stronger in coming years.

INTERNATIONALISATION STRATEGY IN FOR A CHANGE

Since 1975, Japanese banks have been very active in international markets. The foreign currency-denominated assets of Japanese banks have increased at an annual rate of 20–30 per cent, and as a percentage of total assets, they grew from about 10 per cent at the end of March 1975 to more than 30 per cent at the end of March 1990. The sharp increase in their foreign currency-denominated assets is attributed to the following three factors:

1 While the credit ratings of US banks were downgraded repeatedly in the 1980s on account of the recurring problems of bad loans, Japanese banks enjoyed the relative advantage of high credit ratings in the 1980s.

2 While the banks of major industrial nations had to curb the growth in their assets in the 1980s on account of the capital adequacy ratio requirement, Japanese banks, helped by a bull run of the stock market, were able to increase their capital through equity offerings, so they did not have to hold down the increase in their assets.

3 The appreciation of the yen against major currencies also helped boost Japanese banks' lending to overseas customers. When the yen appreciates from ¥240 to ¥120 to the dollar, the yen value of the foreign currency-denominated loans carried on their books is halved. Even when they increased foreign currency-denominated loans in the second half of the 1970s and the 1980s when the yen had risen consistently, this had little impact on their yen based assets.

Come the 1990s, however, the situation reversed. The depreciation of the yen that occurred in 1990 and 1991 sharply boosted the banks' yen based assets and cut into their capital adequacy ratios. On top of that, the collapse of the Tokyo stock market in those two

Table 7.5 The overseas assets of Japanese banks (trillion yen)

	Mar. 1991 (A)	Mar. 1992	Mar. 1993 (B)	(B)/(A)
The Industrial Bank of Japan	13.9	13.2	10.9	0.8
The Long Term Credit Bank of Japan	8.9	8.2	8.6	1.0
The Nippon Credit Bank	4.5	4.3	3.4	0.8
Long Term Credit banks total	27.3	25.6	22.9	0.8
Dai-ichi Kangyo	23.8	20.2	18.3	0.8
Mitsubishi	22.4	21.8	18.1	0.8
Fuji	19.5	18.1	15.5	0.8
Sanwa	21.8	21.4	17.8	0.8
Sumitomo	24.3	21.6	18.8	0.8
Sakura	16.4	14.8	12.6	0.8
Asahi	7.9	6.8	6.0	0.8
Tokai	12.3	11.0	8.0	0.7
Daiwa	5.7	5.2	5.0	0.9
Hokkaido Takushoku	2.9	2.6	2.0	0.7
Tokyo	17.0	16.1	12.0	0.7
City banks total	174.1	159.6	134.1	0.8
Mitsubishi Trust	9.4	8.4	6.9	0.7
Sumitomo Trust	8.2	7.4	7.3	0.9
Mistui Trust	7.1	6.5	5.5	0.8
Tokyo Trust	4.2	4.7	3.8	0.9
Yasuda Trust	6.7	5.7	4.4	0.7
Chuo Trust	2.3	2.0	1.8	0.8
Nihon Trust	0.6	0.5	0.4	0.7
Trust banks total	38.6	35.2	30.1	0.8
Banks total	240.0	220.5	187.1	0.8

Source: Based on annual reports.

years lopped off much of their unrealised gains from stock holdings and made it extremely difficult to increase their capital through offerings of new shares. This compelled Japanese banks to cut down on their assets. As the spreads earned by their international division narrowed below those earned by their domestic division, and as their foreign currency transactions carried volatility risk of capital adequacy ratio, it was very difficult to keep low spread overseas business.

From the second half of 1991, Japanese banks had to come to grips in earnest with the problem of bad loans, and their funding costs increased consistently in the overseas market. Faced with the requirement to meet the capital adequacy ratio, downgraded credit ratings, and increasing bad loans, in Japan and abroad, the assets of their international divisions have been shrinking continuously in recent years (Table 7.5). The immediate tasks they have to contend with are to dispose of their bad loans and win back their former credit ratings by improving their profitability. This spells a slowdown in the activities of the international divisions of Japanese banks in the next two to three years. However, their lending to Asian countries is likely to pick up. As shown in Table 7.6, Japanese banks have definitely shifted the weight of their expansion to these Asian countries. And the share of their Asian operations in their international business is expected to increase sharply in the remaining years to the twenty-first century.

In the 1980s, Japanese banks sought to strengthen their operations in all major regions. However, faced with the bad loan problem, they began to tone down their drive to establish their presence across the world early in the 1990s, and their commitment to different regions will become mixed in coming years depending on their financial strength. They are highly likely to seek to penetrate more aggressively some regions, particularly the Asian region, where the economies are expected to grow more rapidly than the rest of the world, where direct investment by Japanese firms will continue to grow in the years to come, and where the Japanese government maintains a high diplomatic profile. Already, Japanese investment in Asian stocks has been increasing dramatically, and fund demand of South-East Asian countries is growing stronger. Given these prospects, the ties between Asian countries and the international financial centre of Tokyo are bound to grow stronger in the remaining years to the twenty-first century.

Life insurance companies

Among the leading institutional investors participating in the financial market of Japan are life insurance companies. As a group, they account for about 10 per cent of the total assets of financial institutions and institutional investors. Measured in terms of the book value of securities held by them, their securities holdings account for as much as 20 per cent of those held by financial institutions and institutional investors (see Table 7.1). In the following sections, we would like to review the characteristics of life insurance companies.

Table 7.6 The overseas expansion of Japanese banks

	1990 (year end)				June 1993				Overseas expansion (b)/(a) − 1 (%)
	Branches	Local subsidiaries*	Offices	Total(a)	Branches	Local subsidiaries*	Offices	Total(b)	
ASEAN	5	11	48	64	10	14	44	68	6.3
NIES	67	59	45	171	78	74	44	196	14.6
Hong Kong	31	35	32	98	39	46	29	115	17.3
China	4	0	63	67	14	0	55	69	3.0
US	126	55	62	243	137	83	38	258	6.2
Europe	71	99	98	268	82	113	76	271	1.1
Total including others	309	280	446	1,035	355	362	365	1,082	4.5

Note: *Locally incorporated subsidiaries with a stake of 50% or more.
Source: Bank of Japan.

THE NUMBER OF LIFE INSURANCE COMPANIES

The number of life insurance companies catering to the residents of Japan stood at 30 at the end of FY 1993. Of these, 27 are based in Japan, and the remaining three (American Family, Alico, and National Life) are foreign companies based in other countries with branches in Japan. Some of the 27 life insurance companies based in Japan are partially owned by foreign life insurance companies (Table 7.7). Two of them (INA and Prudential) are subsidiaries of foreign life insurance companies, one (Saison) is a joint venture between a Japanese business firm and a foreign life insurance company, and another (Nicos) is partially owned by a foreign company. Of the remaining 23, 16 are mutual companies and 7 are stock companies owned by domestic shareholders. The 10 largest life insurance companies are mutual companies.

Table 7.7 Life insurance companies in Japan (as at the end of March 1994)

Name of company	Balance of total assets (¥ billion)	Legal status	Major shareholders
1 Nippon	34,719.0	M	–
2 Dai-ichi	24,494.6	M	–
3 Sumitomo	21,397.9	M	–
4 Meiji	14,824.7	M	–
5 Asahi	11,169.2	M	–
6 Mitsui	9,255.3	M	–
7 Yasuda	8,181.5	M	–
8 Chiyoda	6,316.6	M	–
9 Taiyo	5,828.4	M	–
10 Toho	5.353.4	M	–
11 Kyoei	5,064.1	J	NA
12 Daido	4,273.0	M	–
13 Nippon Dantai	3,735.6	J	Board members, Mitsui Mining (4%), Canon, Sumitomo Bank, Sumitomo Trust, Nippon Trust (2% each), (a total of 250 shareholders)
14 Fukoku	3,463.6	M	–
15 Dai-hyaku	3,363.1	M	–
16 Nissan	2,102.9	M	–
17 Tokyo	1,462.9	M	–
18 Heiwa	557.3	J	Board members, Chukyo Warehouse Co (10.5%), Tatsumi Syoji Co 7.5% (a total of 297 shareholders)

Table 7.7 *Continued*

Name of company	Balance of total assets (¥ billion)	Legal status	Major shareholders
19 Saison	404.0	J	All State International 5%, Saison Group 50%
20 Yamato	279.4	M	–
21 Taisho	222.3	J	NA
22 Sony	207.5	J	Sony Co 90%, Mitsui Trust 5%, Sakura Bank 5%
23 INA	173.0	J	GIGNA 90%, Yasuda Fire & Marine Insurance 10%
24 Nicos	111.9	J	Nippon Shinpan Co 70%, Equitable 30%
25 ORIX	50.2	J	ORIX 100%
26 Prudential	47.4	J	Prudential 100%
27 Orico	27.6	J	Orico 100%
Subtotal of cos established in Japan	167,086.8	–	
1 American Family	1,295.0	Branch	
2 Alico	655.8	Branch	
3 National Life	84.6	Branch	
Subtotal of branches of cos established in foreign countries	2,035.5	–	

Note: 'M' means a mutual company. 'J' means a joint stock company.
Source: Each company's annual report.

In addition to these 30 insurers, there are 10 foreign life insurance companies which cater to the insurance needs of foreigners resident in Japan (such as the US military forces in Japan).

THE VOLUME OF INSURANCE CONTRACTS HELD BY LIFE INSURANCE COMPANIES

At the end of FY 1993, the total value of life insurance contracts held by 27 insurers stood at ¥1,930 trillion ($19.3 trillion), the largest in the world. Table 7.8 shows the number of life insurance policies held by insurance companies in different countries, and its ratio to their respective national income in fiscal 1992. The amount of life insurance policies held by Japanese insurers is 1.4 times, and its ratio

Table 7.8 International comparison of balances of insurance policies (fiscal year 1992)

	Insurance policies in force (¥ trillion)	Ratio of insurance policies in force to national income (%)
Japan	1,840	528
US	1,298	220
France	228	207
Germany	168	99
Canada	129	257
UK	127	128
South Korea	93	313
The Netherlands	68	220
Spain	54	95

Source: Life Insurance Association 'Fact Book 1993'.

to national income 2.4 times, that of the United States. This is attributable to two factors:

1 Japan has a high savings rate by international standards, and Japanese savers have traditionally used life insurance as a substitute for saving.

2 While the investment preference of the American people has shifted from one for life insurance to one for pensions, the shift of Japanese investor preference for pensions has not occurred as much as in the United States.

THE SIZE OF ASSETS OF LIFE INSURANCE COMPANIES

As of 31 March 1994, life insurance companies had a total of ¥167 trillion ($1.67 trillion) worth of assets, of which they held ¥75 trillion in securities and money trusts (locally known as *tokkin* trust funds which invest their assets in securities for short term trading). These assets are valued either at the lower of cost or market or on the cost basis.

Figure 7.3 shows the rate of increase in the assets of life insurance companies and the amounts of their net increase since the war. As shown in the graph, the history of growth in their assets after the war may be largely divided into three periods.

The first period covers the years from FY 1945 to FY 1983. Although annual net increase in their assets continued steadily during this period, their rate of increase declined gradually, high

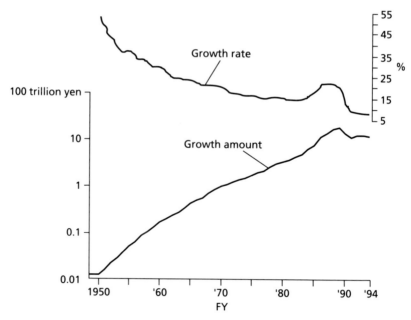

7.3 Growth and growth rate of total assets of life insurance companies (source: Life Insurance Association).

though it still was. On the whole, however, the life insurance industry grew steadily in step with the recovery and expansion of the economy.

The second period covers the years from FY 1984 to FY 1989. This was a period during which life insurance companies' assets increased at a rate far above the trend line in terms of both absolute amounts and the rate of increase. Net increases in their assets amounted to ¥19–20 trillion a year or at a rate of more than 20 per cent. Armed with such a rapid increase in their assets, life insurance companies actively invested their assets not only in domestic stock but also in foreign securities and real estate, so aggressively, in fact, that they spread their name, *Seiho* across the financial communities of the world.

The third period covers the years from FY 1990 to the present. During this period, the annual rate of increase in their assets dropped by as much as 30 per cent from the previous period to a single digit, to ¥13–14 trillion.

The changes that have occurred between the second and the third periods reflect the boom and bust the Japanese economy underwent during the period, and suggest a precipitous fall-off in the capacity of life insurance companies to attract funds and a sharp change in their investment attitude.

EXCESSES COMMITTED DURING THE BUBBLE YEARS

The low interest rate policy which the Bank of Japan pursued in the second half of the 1980s sharply pushed down the rate of return on financial products (notably, bank deposits and bank debentures). However, the rate of return on life insurance products stood at a relatively high level compared with deposits.

Generally speaking, when market rates drop, the down of returns on the assets of life insurance companies lags behind market interest rates, because much of their assets are locked into higher yielding long term loans and bonds. This is why the rate of return on their assets declined later than market rates did. As a result, life insurance products turned out to be more attractive than bank deposits, enabling the insurers to attract huge sums of money from the investing public.

In addition, life insurance companies in Japan had two advantages in attracting funds. One of them was the introduction of single premium endowment insurance policies with five year maturity which were managed jointly with the proceeds of other long term insurance products. The bulk of the assets of life insurance companies (97 per cent of their gross assets as of March 1994) are managed under one account (general account). In other words, insurance products of the same category or those with the same duration of contracts are not separately managed. As a result, policy holders, in principle, receive the same rate of return regardless of the kind or duration of their insurance contracts. A person who bought a short term policy during a period of declining market interest rates receives a high rate of return on his investment which is the same as the one received by the holder of a different kind of policy with a longer maturity. In the first half of the 1980s, life insurance companies offered an endowment insurance policy maturing in five years, and this has touched off a wave of disintermediation of funds from bank deposits, enabling the insurers to increase their funds dramatically.

Another advantage was a sharp appreciation of their stock holdings due to the consistent rise in stock prices in the second half of the 1980s. Although the rate of return on their loans and bond holdings was higher than market rates then prevailing, it had declined gradually. However, they used the capital gains they had

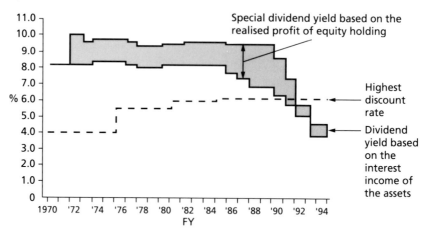

7.4 Discount rate and dividend yield of life insurance companies (source: Life Insurance Association).

made on stocks to make up for the fall-offs in the rate of return on other assets. (The listed shares which life insurance companies held were valued at the lower of cost or market and carried large sums of hidden profits.)

As shown in Fig. 7.4, holders of policies with a maturity of six years or longer received a rate of return close to 10 per cent a year throughout the 1980s. Meanwhile, life insurance companies had to contend with a serious problem – the high cost of their funds.

Since the end of the war, insurance premiums have been lowered consistently, and this is due to the fact that the discount rate – assumed yield on assets or the minimum expected rate of return on the funds which policy holders paid to the life insurance company – has been raised consistently since the war. The discount rate which started at 3 per cent immediately after the war was raised in stages until April 1985 – to 5.5 per cent in the case of policies with a maturity of 20 years or longer, 6 per cent in the case of those with a maturity of 10 to 20 years, and 6.25 per cent for those with a maturity of 10 years or shorter. This level of discount rate stood unchanged until March 1990. The reasons why the life insurance companies hiked the discount rate in the days of low interest rates are as follows:

> **1** The rate of return on the assets of life insurance companies had consistently been higher than the discount rate until the mid-1980s and they made a wrong decision that their rate of return of their asset management would continue to be higher than the discount rate in the future.

2 Life insurance companies had to compete with policies issued by the all-powerful post offices.

Eventually, the high funding costs imposed a heavy burden on life insurance companies in the management of their assets. Before going into that problem, we would like to review the characteristics of asset management of the life insurance companies.

CHARACTERISTICS OF ASSET MANAGEMENT IN THE YEARS TO 1989

Table 7.9 shows changes that have occurred in the composition of assets of life insurance companies. The Japanese economy grew at a rapid pace until around 1975. In those years, the capital markets of Japan were underdeveloped, and life insurance companies were major lenders of funds to business firms which needed long term funds to finance their investment in new plant and equipment. Therefore, lending was the principal vehicle of investment for life insurance companies, and their loans to business firms as a percent-

Table 7.9 Composition of assets held by life insurance companies (%)

As end of fiscal year	1955	1960	1970	1975	1980	1983	1985	1989	1990	1993
Cash and deposits	4	1	1	1	2	4	10	6	6	8
Call loans	2	1	1	1	1	0.2	0.3	0.3	1	2
Tokkin trust funds	–	–	–	–	–	–	2	3	4	4
Loans	49	62	67	68	60	54	54	35	38	38
Securities	33	25	22	22	30	35	35	47	44	41
(Domestic bonds)	(3)	(2)	(2)	(4)	(11)	(11)	(11)	(9)	(8)	(13)
(Domestic equities)	(30)	(23)	(20)	(18)	(17)	(16)	(15)	(22)	(22)	(20)
(Foreign securities)	(–)	(–)	–	(0.1)	(3)	(8)	(9)	(15)	(13)	(8)
Real estate	11	9	9	8	6	6	6	6	6	6
Balance of total assets	192.9	752.8	5.9	12.9	26.3	39.5	53.9	116.2	130.3	167.1

Notes: **1** The Ministry of Finance lifted the foreign securities investment by life insurance companies in January 1971.
2 Totals for 1955 and 1960 are expressed in billion yen. Totals for subsequent years are expressed in trillion yen.
Source: Life Insurance Association.

age of their total assets increased from 49 per cent at the end of fiscal 1955 to 68 per cent in fiscal 1975. Meanwhile, their funds invested in equities as a percentage of their total assets decreased continuously, from 30 per cent to 18 per cent during the same period (and they dropped to as low as 15 per cent at the end of fiscal 1985).

It was around 1975 that their style of fund management, heavily dependent on long term lending, reached a turning point. As the economy plunged into a recession on account of the first oil crisis of 1973, business demand for funds shrank sharply, and to prime the economic pump, the government issued large amounts of deficit-covering bonds. As a result, life insurance companies shifted the weight of their investment from long term business loans to government bonds, and the amount of funds they invested in government bonds as a percentage of their total assets increased from 4 per cent in fiscal 1975 to 11 per cent in fiscal 1985.

Another change that occurred during this period was an increase in their investment in foreign fixed income securities as noted in Chapter 6. As the Reagan Administration pursued supply-side economic policies (Reaganomics), the difference in long term rates between Japan and the United States widened – at one point, to 6 per cent as measured in terms of yields on 10 year Treasury bonds (Fig. 7.5) – and the dollar appreciated against the yen. As a result, there arose a rush of investment in US Treasury securities by Japanese life insurance companies. Also from around 1985, life insurance companies began investing their funds in the higher yielding government securities of Canada and Australia. Their investment in American stocks – which were highly liquid and for which information was readily available – also increased sharply. In the process, their securities holdings as a percentage of their total assets jumped from less than 3 per cent at the end of fiscal 1980 to 13 per cent at the end of fiscal 1990.

Other big changes that occurred in the second half of the 1980s were the revival of investment in Japanese stocks and the start of investment in foreign real estate. The life insurance companies' investment in Japanese stocks as a percentage of their total assets picked up rapidly from a low of 15 per cent reached at the end of fiscal 1985 to 22 per cent at the end of fiscal 1989. Add to this the shares they had bought through *tokkin* trust funds, and the share of their stock investment rose to around 25 per cent (valued at the lower of cost or market). (See the next section for details of their stock investment.)

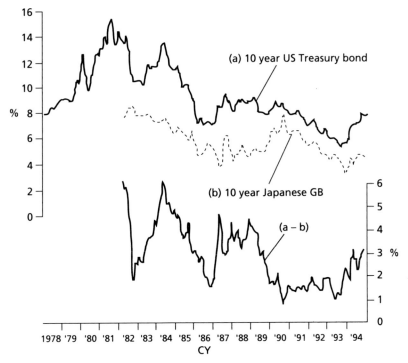

7.5 Interest rate differential between US and Japanese bonds.

Increases in their investment in foreign real estate were sparked by the much higher rates of return it generated than that available on the speculation-bloated domestic real estate market. There are no official data on foreign real estate investment of life insurance companies, but according to various private data, foreign real estate holdings of leading life insurance companies started to increase in earnest in FY 1985–6, and their estimated total value increased from about ¥1 trillion ($10 billion) at the end of FY 1988 to ¥1.5 trillion ($15 billion) at the end of FY 1989 (Table 7.10). Initially, their real estate investment converged on the United States and then spread to European countries and Australia in FY 1989. The diversification of their target markets may be explained by the facts (1) that the 'overpresence' of Japanese investors established in the US real estate market aroused resentment among the people of the United States, and (2) that they sought to position themselves on the Continent in anticipation of an integrated European Union scheduled for 1992. Most of the investments they acquired in the United States were commercial buildings bought from American banks and life insurance companies.

Table 7.10 Foreign real estate investment by Japanese life insurance companies (billion yen)

Fiscal year	1985	1986	1987	1988	1989
Nippon Life	82.5	127.9	185.4	274.6	
Dai-ichi Life	–	NA	199.8	322.3	
Sumitomo Life	–	NA	106.6	198.4	
Yasuda Life	–	3.2	43.0	68.4	
Asahi Life	–	NA	23.4	24.3	
Meiji Life	NA	NA	NA	NA	
Mitsui Life	NA	NA	NA	NA	
Total	82.5	131.1	689.3	888.0	1,500.0

Source: Nomura Research Institute.

STOCK INVESTMENT BY LIFE INSURANCE COMPANIES

One of the big changes that occurred in the investment strategy of life insurance companies in the second half of the 1980s was a pick-up in their stock investment. This was a unique development in the history of asset management of life insurance companies after the war.

They considered equities as substitute investments for business lending and bond investment in times of low interest rates (recession) when business demand for funds dried up (Fig. 7.6). Thus, stock investment took a back seat to business lending and bond investment.

Traditionally, life insurance companies invested in equities for the following reasons:

1 Until 1975, dividend yields were high (Fig. 7.7), so that they expected stock investment to generate a justifiable rate of return even when stock prices failed to rise to earn them capital gains.

2 When the economy grew continuously, stock prices rose in the long run, thereby increasing hidden (unrealised) profits.

3 By holding the shares of their corporate clients for the long haul, business relations with them strengthened, placing the life insurance companies in a better position to win business in the form of group insurance contracts and management of their corporate pension funds.

Companies which issue stocks also tend to hope the life insurance companies will behave as buy-and-hold type investors. Generally,

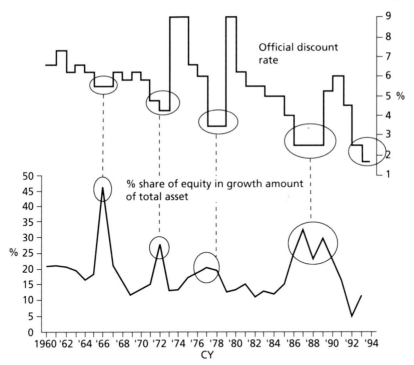

7.6 Interest rate and investment in equity by life insurance companies (sources: Bank of Japan, Life Insurance Association).

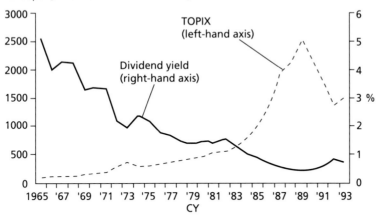

7.7 Stock price index and dividend yield (source: Tokyo Stock Exchange).
Note: TOPIX = Tokyo Stock Exchange Price Index.

life insurance companies have held the shares of their corporate clients for the reasons outlined in (3) above. So far, even when they have sold their holdings of a certain stock to take profits, they usually buy them back when the price drops, and seldom liquidate them altogether.

Since 1985 when interest rates dropped and stayed low, the rate of return on loans made to business corporations declined. Meanwhile, as stock prices rose continuously, a growing number of business corporations issued shares, convertible bonds, or bonds with warrants, and used the proceeds to repay the loans they had taken out. As a result, the lending opportunities of life insurance companies decreased, and they had to divert their funds to stock investment. To be sure, dividend yields dropped sharply in response to rises in stock prices, but they actively bought the shares of their corporate clients (1) in anticipation of capital gains and (2) to strengthen business relations with them. In addition, they also sought to make capital gains by frequently buying and selling shares through *tokkin* trust funds. In the process, the share of stock holdings in the assets of life insurance companies has increased sharply.

THE NEGATIVE LEGACY CARRIED OVER FROM THE 1980s

The consequences of the life insurance companies' asset management in the second half of the 1980s have left them with the following problems to contend with.

First, the higher discount rate adopted in the first half of the 1980s raised the cost of obligations of life insurance companies. The current level of the average cost of obligations most of the life insurance companies have to meet stands at about 5 per cent. Meanwhile, interest rates have fallen, business demand for funds has shrunk, stock prices have collapsed, and the dollar has been devalued against the yen. As a result, the rate of return on their investments has dropped and remained lower than the cost of their obligations. The rate of return on the general account assets fell from 7 per cent in FY 1989 to just 3.9 per cent in 1993.

To ameliorate the situation, the discount rate for newly sold policies was lowered three times, in fiscal 1990, fiscal 1993, and fiscal 1994, and today, the discount rate for all outstanding policies sold in and after 1994 has been lowered to 3.75 per cent irrespective of their maturities. However, as the old discount rates still apply to those issued before 1994, it may be difficult to lower the average discount rate to a level appropriate to the current economic condition until the early years of the twenty-first century. What is more, the lowered discount rate translated into a lower rate of return on insurance products, making them less competitive against other financial products. Moreover, household incomes have levelled off on account of

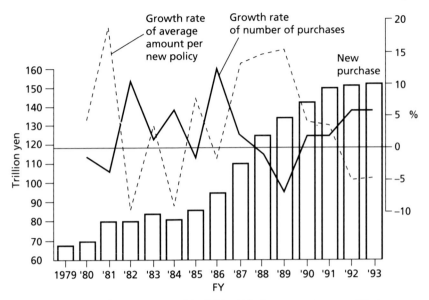

7.8 New policy purchase amount of individual life insurance (source: Life Insurance Association).

the recession, causing a slowdown in the sales of new insurance policies (Fig. 7.8). This spells the possibility of a slowdown in the growth of funds of life insurance companies in the coming years.

Worse yet, the payment of insurance is increasing year after year and should continue to grow from now on due to the ageing of the population. The pace of increase in the companies' assets has already started slowing down – from ¥19–20 trillion a year in 1989 to around ¥13 trillion in the 1990s. This trend should continue during the next several years. This is the second problem they have to contend with.

The third problem is the huge evaluation and actual losses life insurance companies have suffered in the wake of the bursting of the economic bubble. In the second half of the 1980s, life insurance companies acquired large quantities of stocks, foreign securities, and real estate at the peak of their prices, and these prices collapsed with the bursting of the speculative bubble, their losses, actual and evaluated, being magnified by a sharp rise in the yen. As shown in Table 7.11, the evaluation and actual losses the life insurance companies suffered from securities investment jumped from ¥520 billion ($5.2 billion) in the first half of the 1980s to about ¥8.4 trillion ($84 billion) in the second half to ¥11.5 trillion ($115 billion), and they continued to increase in the 1990s.

Table 7.11 Realised and unrealised profits/losses of securities held by life insurance companies (billon yen)

Fiscal year	1980–4	85–9	90–3
Losses			
Realised	187.9	3,284.1	4,809.0
Unrealised	311.0	4,343.9	6,231.6
Foreign exchange	21.0	812.3	456.1
Total	520.0	8,440.3	11,494.6
Profits			
Realised	1,046.1	11,444.4	9,278.0
Unrealised	–	–	1,188.8
Total	1,046.1	11,444.4	10,466.8

Source: Life Insurance Association.

The sharp increase in their losses that occurred in the second half of the 1980s is blamed on the appreciation of the yen against the dollar. They covered their losses by the profits (¥11.4 trillion) generated by selling old stock holdings which they carried at their book value. Those stocks sold were bought back because of the reason explained in the previous section. As the hidden (unrealised) profits on their remaining stock holdings increased with rises in stock prices, few had any concern about their risk-taking capabilities (Table 7.12). Actually, the ¥3 trillion surplus they had after making up the losses was distributed in dividends among policy holders.

However, after the collapse of stock prices early in the 1990s, their losses ballooned, and they had to sell their remaining holdings of low book valued shares to realise profits (¥10.5 trillion) to cover the new losses. As some of the life insurance companies had cleaned out their low book valued inventories, they could not cover the entire losses. As a result, some of them had to liquidate their real estate holdings to make up losses.

ASSET MANAGEMENT IN THE 1990s

Saddled with these problems, life insurance companies have been seeking to restore their business to the level that existed before the start of the economic bubble. More specifically, they will shift the weight of their investment back to business loans and fixed income securities investment, and curb investment in volatile products (dom-

Table 7.12 Hidden (unrealised) profits on stock
holdings of life insurance companies

As end of fiscal year	Book value (¥ trillion)	Hidden profits (¥ trillion)	Nikkei 225 (yen)
1988	19.6	45	32,838
1989	25.4	34	· 29,980
1990	28.8	25	26,292
1991	30.7	10	19,346
1992	31.3	10	18,591
1993	32.9	13	19,112

Source: Life Insurance Association.

estic stocks and foreign securities) for the time being. In fact, the
share of stock investment in their total assets has decreased from 22
per cent at the end of FY 1989 to 20 per cent at the end of FY 1993,
and that of foreign securities, from 15 to 8 per cent during the
same period. On the other hand, that of business loans has increased
from 35 to 38 per cent and that of bond investment, from 9 to 13 per
cent.

If stock prices do not rise from the current level, their dividend
yield will be less than 1 per cent, a far cry from the companies' cost
of obligations which stands at about 5 per cent, making it impossible
for them to justify fresh stock investment. Moreover, the advisability
of the policy of purchasing shares of their corporate clients for the
long haul in the hope of winning their insurance contracts or
managing their pension funds has been called into question. In fact,
some of the life insurance companies have liquidated the shares of
certain issues (banks' shares, for example) with low yields.

In the case of foreign securities, they are balking at purchasing
them because the difference in interest rates between Japan and
foreign countries has become much smaller than before and the
outlook for American stock prices has become murky. Moreover, as
their risk-taking capacity – the availability of hidden profits on their
stock holdings to offset exchange losses – has become sharply
limited, they no longer are in a position to take risks.

Business lending by life insurance companies has for quite some
time been in the doldrums because of the prolonged recession. The
weight of their lending has shifted to subordinated loans to banks
(which have to issue subordinated debt to meet the capital adequacy
ratio imposed by the Bank for International Settlements) and to
consumer credit companies.

All told, life insurance companies are saddled with high cost long term liabilities, assets which are prone to generate losses, and a shrinking pool of premiums. Thus, they are in for a sweeping restructuring of their operations in the second half of the 1990s. The life insurance companies of Japan will have to stick to income generating and low market risk investment (for instance, lending and fixed income securities), wait for the average discount rate to fall, and trim their payrolls through natural attrition and restrained new hiring.

The markets

The money market

This chapter surveys the movements of Japan's money market since 1985, reviews different segments of the market, and discusses challenges it faces in the coming years.

According to a report released in February 1990 by the Money Market Panel (composed of academics and executives of financial institutions and supported by a secretariat composed of officials drawn from the Ministry of Finance and the Bank of Japan), the term 'money market' is defined as a marketplace where (1) there are broad based participants, (2) financial transactions are conducted on a competitive basis, (3) interest rates change freely according to the dictate of supply and demand, and (4) short term debt instruments with a maturity of less than one year are traded. As specialised markets that meet these requirements, the panel lists six markets, namely those for call loans, bill discount, certificates of deposit (CD), commercial paper (CP), Treasury bills (TB) and financial bills (FB), and bond repos (bond repurchase agreements).

The movements of the money market since 1985

The movements of the money market since 1985 may be divided into two periods: a period of rapid expansion (1985–9), and one of mixed growth (1990 and after) (Table 8.1).

Table 8.1 Summary of the money markets in Japan (100 million yen, at year-end)

	1980	1985	1987	1989	1991	1993	1989/85 (%)	1993/89 (%)	1985 (%)	1989 (%)	1993 (%)
Call loans	41,333	51,104	160,379	244,858	353,169	447,203	47.9	16.3	17.3	29.4	45.6
Unsecured	–	8,215	29,419	100,652	234,480	339,638	87.1	35.5	2.8	12.1	34.6
Secured	41,333	42,889	130,960	144,206	118,689	107,565	35.4	–5.8	14.5	17.3	11.0
Bills	57,381	146,558	131,064	207,613	165,096	94,599	9.1	–11.5	49.8	24.9	9.6
CDs	23,574	96,572	108,328	210,860	172,983	190,449	21.6	–2.3	32.8	25.3	19.4
CP	–	–	16,982	130,659	124,004	110,506	(177.4)	–3.7	–	15.7	11.3
TBs and FBs	191	237	36,232	40,084	90,458	137,896	251.6	36.2	0.0	4.8	14.1
TBs	–	–	27,212	40,084	90,458	109,896	(21.3)	28.7	–	4.8	11.2
FBs	191	237	9,020	–	–	28,000	148.4	–	–	–	2.9
Bond *gensakis*	45,068	46,419	69,223	63,040	60,453	83,332	8.0	7.3	–	–	–

Notes:
1 The balance of yen-denominated bank acceptance stood at about ¥60 billion at the end of 1985 and about ¥8 billion at the end of 1986.
2 The balance of bond *gensakis* includes that of TB and FB *gensakis*.
3 The growth rates for CP and TB under the '1989/85' column are, in fact, those between 1985 and 1987.
4 Percentages are shares in the total that excludes bond *gensakis*.
Source: Bank of Japan.

THE PERIOD OF RAPID EXPANSION

As shown in Table 8.1, the money market expanded rapidly during the years from 1985 to 1989. Its turnover (the volume of bond repos market was excluded to prevent double counting) increased at an annual rate of 29.7 per cent in 1985–9, up from 19.2 per cent in 1980–5.

The first factor which contributed to the rapid expansion of the market was diversification of money market instruments developed during this period. Deals made on the call market are divided into those requiring collateral and those not requiring it. The market for unsecured call loans was launched in July 1985, the Ministry of Finance started the practice of auctioning off Treasury bills in February 1986 and thus paved the way for forming a TB market, and a commercial paper market came into operation in November 1987.

The second factor was the spread among dealers of the practice of combining fund raising and investment (they raised funds by selling money market instruments for the purpose of arbitrage), and a boom occurred in financial engineering. The CP market, which started in November 1987, expanded dramatically, because business corporations scrambled to issue commercial paper at a lower interest rate and invested its proceeds in higher yielding, large denomination time deposit accounts. In March 1985, the Bank of Japan countenanced such dual transactions, and in November 1988, it adopted a new monetary adjustment policy 'to facilitate efficient arbitrage transactions between markets with a view to ensuring the effectiveness of its monetary policy through active utilisation of the functions of interest rates'. Thanks to these measures, arbitrage transactions involving call money, bills, CDs, and Euro-yen increased, fuelling the expansion of the market.

The background of the rapid expansion of the money market in 1985–9 is explained by the following two points.

The first is the changes that have occurred in the political and regulatory framework. As indicated in Chapter 1, foreign pressures for further internationalisation of the Tokyo market, particularly those which the Japan–US Yen/Dollar Committee had brought to bear on the Japanese government had far-reaching impacts. Needless to say, all the changes cannot be attributed to foreign pressures, because (1) the formation of the TB market was brought about largely by the rollovers made by the government to refinance the huge amounts of 10 year government bonds it had issued since

1975, (2) the CP market came into existence in response to a mounting domestic demand for it, and (3) a new monetary adjustment mechanism was necessary for an effective implementation of the monetary policy of the Bank of Japan. However, the programme of the Ministry of Finance for the diversification of the money market referred to in its May 1984 position paper, 'The Current State and Outlook of the Liberalisation of the Financial Markets and the Internationalisation of the Yen', is a product of foreign pressure in the sense that it reflected the view of the Yen/Dollar Committee.

The second point is the changes that have occurred in the international market environment surrounding the economy and the financial markets of Japan. The pressures generated by the Plaza Accord of September 1985, the Louvre Accord of February 1987, and Black Monday of October of the same year have led the Japanese government to implement sweeping market reforms for the long haul. There is no denying the fact that a worldwide movement towards the relaxation of the financial markets, working through an expansion of arbitrage, dual transactions, and financial engineering, was behind the rapid expansion of the money market of Japan in 1985–9. It may also be said that the flattening of the yield curve during the easy money period of 1985–7 and the inversion that occurred in the yield curve during the tight money period of 1989–90 were responsible for having sparked a shift of funds within the money and securities markets, and had positive effects on the growth of the money market.

THE PERIOD OF MIXED GROWTH

As shown in Table 8.1, the five markets' annual growth rate slowed to 4.1 per cent during the period from 1989 to 1993. One of the characteristics of this period is that growth of the markets for different kinds of instruments was mixed. Those which had grown continuously in 1985 through 1989 were the markets for call money and TBs and FBs. Meanwhile, the balances of bills, CDs and CP outstanding on the market have actually decreased after peaking in 1989 and 1990. In the case of the call money market, a sharp increase in unsecured call loans boosted the call money market as a whole. As with the bill discount and CD markets, the secured call loan market peaked in 1989.

Factors behind the mixed performance of the money market may be summarised as follows. First, the factors which contributed to the sharp expansion of the money market in 1985–9 have been exhausted, and reactions thereto have slowed the forward momentum of the market. The diversification of vehicles which had fuelled its rapid expansion in 1985–9 has already run its course. If the collapse of the bank acceptance market (it evaporated in November 1989 after four years of existence) is any indication, the money market is in for a shake-out.

Foreign pressure which had led to the diversification of vehicles of the money market is still continuing. As the Structural Impediments Initiative talks initiated by the Bush Administration and the Framework Talks now being pushed by the Clinton Administration show, the focus of problems which divide Japan and the United States has become blurred and one has the impression that the opening of Japan's financial markets to foreign competition has been put on the back burner.

Since the turn of the decade, the volume of arbitrage, dual transactions, and financial engineering has decreased sharply. The discount rate was raised five times during the 15 months from May 1989 to August 1990, thanks to which land and stock prices have plummeted since 1990, generating a serious problem of bad loans. And the sharp decrease in the banks' unrealised gains from their stock holdings threatened to drive down their primary capital ratios below the BIS rule (see Chapter 7). These changes in the environment surrounding the economy and the financial markets have punctured the economic bubble and put a dampener on arbitrage, dual transactions, and financial engineering.

Second, despite the slowdown of the money market, the markets for TBs, FBs, and call loans have continued to grow rapidly for reasons stated below. The TB market played a pivotal role in boosting the TB–FB market, largely thanks to an increase in the rollover bonds issued by the government to refinance government bonds falling due. The unsecured call loan market has also grown consistently since 1990 due to the shift of funds to the call loan market that occurred for the reasons (1) that the supply of bills to the bill discount market has visibly slowed down, and (2) that an inverted yield curve has developed since the Bank of Japan cut its discount rate in July 1991. In addition, a growing amount of funds the city (large commercial) banks have been raising through unsecured call loans in recent months is attracting the attention of the market.

Movements of different segments of the money market

THE CALL MONEY MARKET

Legally, call loans are defined as loans for consumption. This practice first emerged at the turn of the century. In the wake of the Great Depression of 1929, all loans were required, in principle, to be secured and this principle had been honoured until recently. However, foreign banks operating in Japan vigorously lobbied for an exemption from this principle and in July 1985, the government decided to allow the resumption of unsecured call loans. Under the new rules, the term is set from unconditional to six days for secured call loans, and from overnight to one year for unsecured call loans. Authorised participants are city (large commercial) banks, regional banks, second-tier regional banks (formerly, mutual banks), trust banks, long term credit banks, foreign banks, the National Federation of Credit Associations, credit associations, the Central Bank for Agriculture and Forestry (Norinchukin Bank), life insurance companies, property and casualty insurance companies, part of the securities companies, and securities finance companies. The same also applies to the bill discount market, and this is why it is called the interbank market. Measured in terms of the market balance, trust banks supply close to 50 per cent of the funds available on the market. Actually, however, the bulk of the funds supplied by trust banks comes from securities investment trust management companies. In 1987–90, trust banks supplied more than 70 per cent of the market funds. Subsequently, however, their share dropped to less than 50 per cent owing to (1) decreases in the assets of *tokkin* funds and fund trusts they managed and (2) increases in the funds supplied by other financial institutions (agricultural thrift institutions, the National Federation of Credit Associations, and regional banks). As might be expected, city banks are the largest borrowers, and the amount of their borrowings as a percentage of the total market turnover has increased from less than 50 per cent in 1986–8 to about 70 per cent in 1993.

THE BILL DISCOUNT MARKET

Technically, this is a market for trading bills. It was opened in May 1971 and the Bank of Japan started to trade bills in open market operations in June 1976. Bills traded on this market are largely divided into two kinds: (1) commercial bills issued by entities other than banking institutions, industrial bills, single name bills, trade bills, and export or import usance bills, and (2) bills of exchange or drafts (issued by a banking institution against any of the bills listed in (1) as collateral, instructing the drawee (the banking institution) to pay a specified sum to a call broker (payee). The latter constitutes the bulk of those traded on the bill discount market. There are 15 kinds of maturities, ranging from one to three weeks, and one to 11 months, to one year. The same groups of financial institutions participate in this interbank market. In the past, funds were supplied by four groups of financial institutions: the Bank of Japan (through bill buying operation), the National Federation of Credit Associations, individual credit associations, and agricultural thrift institutions. In recent years, funds supplied by the three groups of private financial institutions have decreased dramatically, and the Bank of Japan alone supplies about 80 per cent of them. For several years, city banks have borrowed more than 70 per cent of the funds available on the market, but their borrowings have tended to decrease in recent months. What is more, the weight of bank lending has shifted from bill discounting to overdraft for tax reasons, with the result that the pace of supplying bills to the market has slowed down, putting a dampener on the growth of the bill discount market.

THE CD MARKET

Legally, this is a negotiable time deposit certificate, and its market was created in 1979. Because this is a market open to non-banking participants and a new money market instrument, created second after the introduction of bond repurchase agreements, and the first deposit product that carries a liberalised interest rate, the certificate of deposit (CD) was hailed as a vehicle conducive to streamlining the money market and promoting the liberalisation of interest rates. With a view, therefore, to spurring the expansion of the market, the regulatory agency reduced the minimum denomination, and raised – and in some cases, abolished – the ceilings imposed on the amount of issue. Thanks to these measures, the CD market has since expanded markedly. Although its characteristic as a high yielding instrument has somewhat weakened since the launching of large denomination time deposits in October 1985, the balance of CDs outstanding in the market ballooned to ¥19 trillion ($190 billion) at the end of 1993, helping it hold on to the leadership position as the largest open market product since 1983. Since they are negotiable, there technically exists a market for them, but as the resale of CDs involves complicated formalities, few of them are resold outright. Instead, they are used for *gensaki* (repurchase agreements). Their volume of trading (one way) peaked at ¥1,391 trillion ($13.91 trillion) in 1989 and then declined to ¥1,144 trillion ($11.44 trillion) in 1993.

THE COMMERCIAL PAPER MARKET

Legally, the commercial paper is a promissory note. The CP market was launched in November 1987. To qualify for the issuance of commercial paper, the issuer must receive a top or the second highest credit rating from two out of the nine credit rating agencies designated by the regulatory agency. Initially, securities companies, insurance companies, and non-banks were not authorised to issue commercial paper. Subsequently, however, securities companies were allowed to issue commercial paper from February 1990 and non-banks from July 1993. Unlike in the United States, issuers are not allowed to place their CP directly with their customers. Instead, they have to issue their papers through a bank or a securities company, and they can be placed only with institutional investors. Even before the system was launched in 1987, business demand for issuing commercial paper was strong. In 1990, its outstanding balance increased dramatically, largely because its issuers were able to earn a hefty spread by investing the proceeds in higher yielding large denomination time deposits. When such financial engineering became no longer profitable after the bursting of the economic bubble, the balance of its market peaked in 1990 and dropped to a level equal to two-thirds of its peak at the end of 1993. However, commercial paper is traded quite actively, mostly in the form of repurchase agreements, and its trading volume (one way) increased to ¥2,210 trillion ($22.1 trillion) in 1993, twice as large as that of the CD market. This is largely attributable to the short maturities with which it is issued.

THE TB–FB MARKET

While Treasury bills are issued to refinance government bonds falling due, financial bills are issued to fill the gap between government revenues and expenditures arising from time to time. Their legal status differs. Treasury bills have been auctioned off since February 1986, while financial bills are issued through public offering on fixed conditions (usually with a coupon rate lower than the discount rate then prevailing), and those left unsold – in most cases almost all of them remain unsold – are bought up by the Bank of Japan. Since May 1981, the central bank has been selling financial bills on the market through open market operation. At the end of 1993, ¥11 trillion ($110 billion) worth of Treasury bills and ¥2.8 trillion ($28 billion) worth of financial bills were outstanding on the market. In 1993, ¥1,442 trillion ($14.42 trillion) worth of Treasury bills and ¥61 trillion ($6.1 trillion) worth of financial bills were traded. They are mostly traded by institutional investors which are well versed in the movements of the money and capital markets, and the sale of these bills to individuals is prohibited as with commercial paper. Although they are securities for legal purposes, they are exempted from the securities transaction tax. Almost all of them are traded in the form of repurchase agreements.

THE *GENSAKI* (REPOS) MARKET

This market emerged spontaneously with the resumption of debt offering in 1949. As explained in Chapter 1, with the start of public offering of government bonds in 1965, the repos market expanded with a vengeance as the only open money market in Japan. By legally defining the repurchase agreement as a conditional trading of bonds, the Ministry of Finance officially sanctioned it. The method of making *gensaki* deals is basically the same as that employed in repos transactions effected in other countries, and it may be characterised as a loan transaction secured by bonds. However, as bond *gensaki* transactions are subject to the securities transaction tax, an overwhelming majority of repos transactions are made on the basis of other instruments which are exempted from the securities transaction tax, such as CDs, CP, TBs or FBs. Accordingly, long and medium term government bonds are mostly used for repos transactions which require relatively long maturities, and those undertaken by public agencies (government agencies and local public bodies) which are required by rules to use such government securities.

During the past eight years, their trading volume increased 1.8-fold from ¥4.6 trillion ($46 billion) to ¥8.3 trillion ($83 billion), and the bulk of the growth in their trading volume is believed to have come from increases in TB and FB repos transactions. Meanwhile, as the trading volumes of other open market products have increased, the weight carried by the repos in the money market has decreased.

Challenges lying ahead

As seen in the foregoing, the overall turnover of the money market of Japan has expanded markedly since 1985. Since 1990, however, the performance of its different segments has been mixed, largely because of the after-effects of the bursting of the economic bubble. In terms of quality, however, the money market has substantially improved – such as increased diversity of instruments, widespread use of arbitrage transactions, and growing sophistication of trading techniques. If there is room for further improvement, it is the necessity for further expanding the TB–FB market and more extensive use of repos transactions.

There has already emerged a consensus among many market leaders and regulators about the importance of expanding the TB–FB market, and many reports stress this. TBs and FBs carry lower credit risks and have the potential of high liquidity, and these short term government securities deserve a central role in the money market. The only drawback is that as Treasury bills are issued only for the purpose of refinancing government bonds falling due, their supply may eventually become unreliable. On the other hand, as financial bills are auctioned off at a rate below the discount rate, and as they are bought up by the Bank of Japan, they may not be available when the market needs them. Therefore, the system of auctioning financial bills must be improved urgently if only for the purpose of expanding the market for short term government securities.

The money market of a country of necessity reflects its history and peculiarities. Therefore, the mechanical comparison of money markets of different countries has little practical relevance. However, there is no disputing the fact that when seen from the standpoint of its functions as a place (1) for raising and investing short term funds and (2) for adjusting the flow of money of a country, the money market of the United States can serve as a model for other countries.

In the money market of the United States, repos trading carries a heavy weight and plays an important role in adjusting the flow of money. Given the heavy reliance on loans given by the Bank of

Japan as a means for adjusting the flow of money, expansion of the repos market is a viable option for remedying the situation.

Repos transactions of the US type perform the same function as that of the bond *gensaki* transaction. As noted in the foregoing, however, bonds being a security under the Securities and Exchange Law of Japan, bond *gensaki* transactions are subject to the securities transaction tax, making them costly to undertake. Although Treasury bills and financial bills are exempted from the securities transaction tax, their supply is too small to play a key role in the money market. While bonds are lent to secure cash payment in a repos transaction effected in the United States, there is a limit imposed in Japan on the interest rate payable on bonds borrowed, and there is no way of escaping the securities transaction tax. However, some argue that repos transactions can be effected in Japan by undertaking them through a foreign market to which Japan's securities transaction tax does not apply. Considering the fact that the bond *gensaki* transaction developed spontaneously in Japan, their argument is truly intriguing.

9 The bond trading market

This chapter surveys recent features of the bond market of Japan and the methods of trading employed therein. However, equity-linked debt securities (convertible bonds and warrant bonds, see Chapter 11) and money market instruments (Treasury and financial bills and banks' discount debentures, see Chapter 8) which are traded by different groups of market participants are omitted. In addition, debt issues not publicly offered and foreign bonds are excluded from the discussions.

Changes in the bond trading market

The bond trading market in Japan during the period from the second half of the 1980s to the first half of the 1990s has undergone profound changes occasioned by twice-occurred prolonged easy money periods and the advent and development of financial derivatives trading. For the purpose of reviewing these changes in the trading market centring around government bonds, the 10 year period will be divided into the following four phases (Fig. 9.1):

1 1985–7: The period of explosive growth sparked by bank dealing.

2 1988–9: The period of massive redemption of government bonds, and the appearance of the inverted yield curve.

3 1990–1: The period of high interest rates, and the disappearance of the coupon effect.

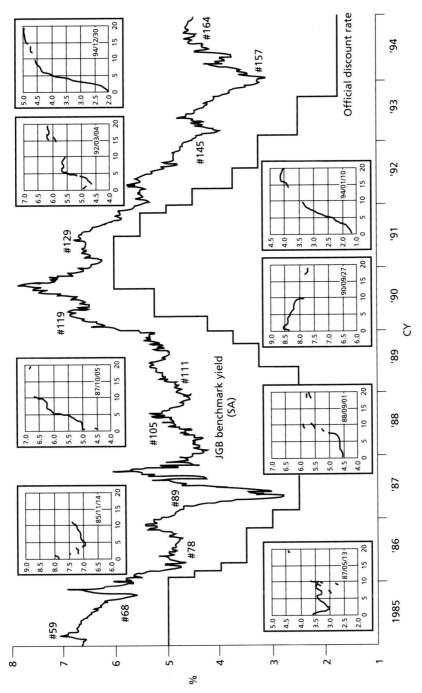

9.1 Historical changes in yields on government bonds and discount rate.

4 1992–4: The period during which yields were formed by the theory of expectations.

Figure 9.1 sums up changes in the yields on benchmark issues (based on semi-annual compound yield) and the discount rate during the 10 year period from 1985 to 1994. Except for certain periods, benchmark issues were the predominant vehicle for inter-dealer bond trading.

The figure also shows the yield curves (based on semi-annual compound yield) of 10 and 20 year government bonds at points when long term rates pivoted. The scale of the vertical axis of each graph is set to be constant (up or down 3 per cent).

THE PERIOD OF EXPLOSIVE GROWTH SPARKED BY BANK DEALING

In June 1984, banking institutions were partially authorised to deal in public bonds, and thanks to their active dealing, turnover of government bonds started to pick up. As they were fully authorised to deal in public bonds in June the following year, the bond trading market expanded sharply. Following the signing of the Plaza Accord in September 1985, the yen appreciated sharply against the dollar, and the Bank of Japan loosened its credit reins to help the economy cope with the sudden rise in the yen. Although bond prices fell temporarily in reaction to a rise in short term rates engineered by the Bank of Japan late in October of that year, long term rates have since dropped sharply to an all-time low, boosting bond yields to an overheated level. Investors and bond dealers alike scrambled to buy bonds not for the yield level but on speculation of much higher prices down the road, thereby creating what was then commonly called 'the high dealing market', and deals were concentrated on the benchmark issues. In April 1987, monthly turnover of government coupon bonds on the over the counter (OTC) market hit a peak of ¥950 trillion, of which more than ¥240 trillion worth of trades were accounted for by inter-dealer transactions. And 85 per cent of the inter-dealer trades were based on the then benchmark issue of #89 government bonds. In the process, inter-dealer prices of the benchmark issue hit a peak on 14 May.[1] Its yield was 2.55 per cent (based on simple yield) which was perilously close to the discount rate of 2.5 per cent that then prevailed. As the economic outlook brightened

---

1 The closing high is dated 13 May.

and the yen swung downwards soon thereafter, expectations for further easing on the credit reins by the Bank of Japan evaporated, and bond prices tumbled. In the process, the trading market contracted sharply, and the monthly bond turnover of the OTC market shrank to ¥120 trillion, about one-eighth of the peak. On 4 October 1987, shortly before Black Monday, #89 government bonds were traded among dealers at a yield as high as 6.4 per cent (based on simple yield), heralding the end of the unprecedentedly high dealing market.

The violently fluctuating bond prices left deep scars on the market. When the debacle of Tateho Chemical Industry (which had lost its shirt in the bond futures market) came to light on 2 September 1987, investor confidence in the bond market was badly shaken, driving the bond market to the brink of a rout. For good or for evil, the bond market recovered its calmness thanks to the funds fleeing from the equity market after Black Monday, but the image of a money-spinning bond market whipped up by high dealing has become a thing of the past. Thereafter, the market has gradually changed into one based on rationally formed bond prices which reflect the relative strength of supply against demand of investors.

THE PERIOD OF MASSIVE REDEMPTION OF GOVERNMENT BONDS AND THE APPEARANCE OF THE INVERTED YIELD CURVE

With a view to rehabilitating public finances, the government had decided to cut down on the amount of deficit-covering government bonds starting in FY 1980, and finally stopped issuing them in FY 1990[2] (see Chapter 4). In the process, the issuing amount of outstanding government bonds itself has decreased, and in FY 1989, the issuing amount of publicly offered long term (10 year) and super-long term (20 year) government bonds decreased to less than ¥9 trillion. Moreover, the government started redeeming large amounts of high coupon (7–8 per cent) bonds in 1988, with the result that investors had to rebuild their portfolios. Although long term rates did rise, they still hovered around 5 per cent after Black Monday, and investors found it difficult to manage their bond portfolios.

Under such circumstances, investors sought to replace maturing bonds by higher coupon issues. Therefore, low coupon bonds (carrying a coupon rate of 3–4.5 per cent) issued in 1987 were traded

---

2 The government restarted issuing deficit-covering bonds in FY 1994.

below par and were perennially used as instruments for delivery under futures contracts. In addition, yields on short and medium term issues with high coupon rates were relatively low, producing a distorted yield curve.

Come 1989, short term rates began to rise slowly on expectations of a tightening of credit conditions, pushing up the yields on short and medium term securities. On or around 31 May when the Bank of Japan effected the first round of discount rate hikes, the yield curve was almost flat, and the sense of overvaluation of short and medium term securities was erased. And in the remaining months to the year-end, the discount rate was raised three times, to 4.25 per cent. Although these rises generated upward pressure on the yields on short and medium term securities, yields on long term securities rose only marginally partly because of the strong demand for them. As a result, an inverted yield curve reflecting the distorted relationship between supply and demand had seemed to become a semi-permanent phenomenon.

THE PERIOD OF HIGH INTEREST RATES AND THE DISAPPEARANCE OF THE COUPON EFFECT

Owing to persistent expectations of an interest rate hike from the turn of the year, a weakening yen, and the instability of the political situation, long term rates shot up in 1990. To make the situation worse, the Bank of Japan raised the discount rate twice, by 1 per cent on 20 March and 0.75 per cent on 29 August. With the BIS regulation of banks' primary capital ratio looming ahead, and the tension in the Middle East turning for the worse, yields on the benchmark #119 government bonds traded among dealers rose to a 1990 high of 8.735 per cent on 26 September. Although short term rates hung high thereafter on fears of a resurgence of inflation, long term rates began to edge downwards in reaction to a prospect for an economic slowdown. And by the time the Bank of Japan effected the first round of discount rate cuts on 1 July 1991, short term rates also began to fall, and the yield curve of government bonds all but flattened. With the third round of discount rate cuts on 30 December, the inverted curve of long and short term yields almost disappeared.

In the course of this rise in long term rates, most of the long term bonds were traded below par. And with the introduction of a new accounting standard by the banks, the pronounced investors' consciousness of current yields – the excessive preference for high coupon issues and aversion against low coupon ones – died down.

A majority of investors have now come to select their investments on the basis of compound yield, rather than simple yield which had been fashionable among Japanese investors. What is more, since the bond trading market expanded – helped by a continuous rise in interest rates which took place for the first time – there has emerged a tendency of bond prices being formed on the basis of the futures prices. In other words, prices of futures which typify the long term bonds as a whole are formed according to the relative strength of supply and demand, and yields on cash bonds eligible for delivery under futures contracts seem to be formed at a level where the net basis is equal to zero.[3]

THE PERIOD DURING WHICH YIELDS WERE FORMED ACCORDING TO THE THEORY OF EXPECTATIONS

As the economy had shown distinct signs of a slowdown since 1992, the market discounted in measured steps an easing on the credit reins by the Bank of Japan. The yield curve of government bonds has gradually become less susceptible to the disparity of yields among bonds with different coupon rates, and has become smoother. Furthermore, the strictly arbitraged relationship with futures has disappeared. This appears to have been brought about by the fact that the market has come to form long term rates by anticipating future movements of short term rates by adding a risk premium. By the time the Bank of Japan cut the discount rate for the fifth time on 27 July 1992, yields on deliverable bonds with a remaining life of close to 10 years had fallen several basis points below the level on which the net basis is equal to zero with futures, suggesting that yields had begun to be formed on the basis of cash bonds not driven by futures. Delivered issues of futures which had been relatively scattered have gradually been narrowed down to a few issues beginning with December 1992 contracts.[4] This suggests that the deliverable issues which are arbitraged with futures have been narrowed down to issues with certain maturities.

---

3 The net basis is defined as the difference between the actual cash price and the theoretical cash price implied by the futures price.

4 The number of delivered issues of ¥10 billion or more for the June 1992 contracts stood at 15. Those for the September 1992 contracts and those for the December 1992 contracts stood at 9 issues each, while those for the December 1993 contracts decreased to 3.

With the recession continuing to bite deeper, the yield curve moved slowly downwards. Meanwhile, the discount rate was cut for the sixth time on 4 February 1993 to 2.5 per cent, level with the past record low. Unlike in the days of the high dealing market created by banks' dealing in 1987, in the bull market the yield curve was steepened by rationally discounting expected movements of short term rates down the road. As the discount rate was cut for the seventh time to a new all-time low of 1.75 per cent on 21 September, the market discounted further easing on the credit reins by the central bank. In reaction, bond prices continued to rise without creating the sense of overheating, and early in 1994, yields on 10 year government bonds dropped to as low as 3.4 per cent, thus ushering in an unprecedented low interest period.

Current state of the bond trading market

TYPES OF BONDS AND THE SCALE OF THE MARKET

Straight coupon bonds with a maturity of one year or longer publicly offered in Japan include:

1 Government securities (6, 10, or 20 year government bonds, and 2 or 4 year government notes);

2 Publicly offered municipal bonds;

3 Government-guaranteed bonds;

4 Banks' coupon debentures;

5 Corporate bonds (including broadcasting debentures and Tokyo traffic debentures); and

6 Yen-denominated foreign bonds (*samurai* bonds).

At the end of 1994, a total of more than ¥420 trillion ($4.2 trillion at the rate of ¥100 to the dollar) worth of bonds were outstanding on the market. Of these, about ¥180 trillion were accounted for by publicly offered coupon bonds with a remaining life of one year or longer.[5] An overwhelming majority of them are government bonds,

5 They cover issues included in Nomura Research Institute's bond performance index (NRI–BPI).

and they are followed by – and in the order of – banks' coupon debentures and government-guaranteed bonds. As a percentage of coupon bonds with a maturity of one year or longer, government bonds outstanding at the end of 1994 stood at about 53 per cent, banks' coupon debentures at about 22 per cent, government-guaranteed bonds at about 10 per cent, corporate bonds at about 9 per cent, and publicly offered municipal bonds at about 5 per cent (Fig. 9.2).

The NRI–BPI is an index designed to show the performance of the Japanese bond market. Most of the publicly offered domestic coupon bonds which have a remaining life of one year or longer are included in the index. As it stands now, more than one-half of the total par value of the bonds included in the NRI–BPI is accounted for by government bonds, and together with banks' coupon debentures, they account for about 75 per cent of the total par value.

Although publicly offered municipal bonds were available in a large variety, individual issues were offered in small amounts, and the total of outstanding municipals was relatively small. Both the primary market and the secondary market of corporate bonds still remain underdeveloped, and are expected to grow in coming years.

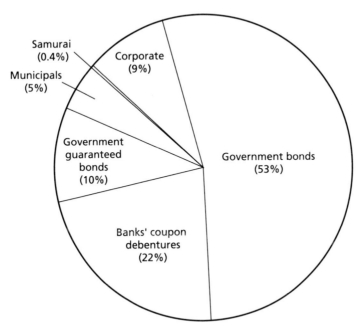

9.2 Ratios of par values of bonds included in NRI–BPI.

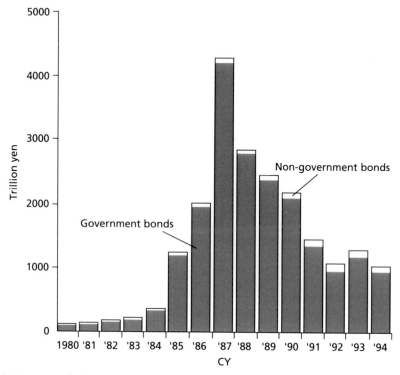

9.3 Turnover of the OTC domestic bond market.

As shown in Fig. 9.3, annual turnover of domestic bonds on the OTC market (includes only publicly offered coupon bonds and excludes those traded under repurchase agreements) peaked in 1987 (when their trading was boosted by banks' dealing) and has since been on the decline. In 1993, however, annual turnover of publicly offered coupon bonds edged higher thanks in part to a decline in long term rates and rose to about ¥1,200 trillion. More than 90 per cent of them were accounted for by government coupon bonds, and the dominance of government bonds in the secondary market is thus markedly stronger than in the primary market. However, their share of the market has decreased compared with the 98.5 per cent share they had in 1987, and this suggests that investors' interest has shifted, if moderately, to non-government bonds. Particularly, turnover of bank debentures increased to about ¥64 trillion in 1993, three times that of 1987. Although their absolute turnover is still small, it is to be noted that turnover of corporate bonds also increased sharply in 1993.

The declining tendency of turnover of the bond market as a whole has been brought about primarily by the flagging interest of investors in high dealing. At the same time, however, the shift of funds to derivatives trading – long term government bond futures (listed in November 1985), futures options (listed in May 1990), and OTC options (the ban on them was lifted in April 1989) – has had an effect on it. One way turnover of these derivatives amounted to about ¥1,300 trillion, ¥170 trillion, and ¥145 trillion, respectively, in 1994. With investors growing increasingly conscious of risk management, the shift to relatively less costly trading techniques may be the way of the future (see Chapter 10 for details).

TRADING PRACTICE AND DELIVERY AND SETTLEMENT

Under the established practice of the bond trading market of Japan, contracts are written on the basis of simple yield, and dealers rarely indicate bond prices. Simple yields and prices have the following relationship and are closely related with one another on the basis of a detailed rule of calculation.

$$\text{Simple yield} = \frac{\text{(coupon rate} + (100 - \text{price})/\text{remaining life})}{\text{price}} \times 100$$

Simple yield is generally higher than the semi-annual compound yield of the US type when the bond price is under par and lower when the bond price is over par. Japanese dealers have long been using simple yield because it is simpler to calculate and coincides with the rate of return shown on the books. Aside from the question as to whether it is appropriate as a basis for making investment decisions, it is a fact that simple yield has an important bearing on the formation of bond yields. Lately, the number of investors using compound yield of the US type as a basis for making investment decisions has been on the rise, and prices of relatively liquid bonds such as government bonds are rationally formed on the basis of compound yield.

Bonds traded between dealers are delivered and settled on every fifth day of the month, and those traded between a dealer and a customer over the counter are also settled likewise.[6] Under the

6 Trades in bonds are settled on the 5th, 10th, 15th, 20th, 25th, and last days of each month, and when any of these days falls on a holiday, they are, in principle, settled on the next following business day. In the case of bonds other than government bonds, trades are usually settled on the 10th, 20th, and last days of each month. Prior to July 1987, trades in government bonds were also settled on

existing rules, it usually takes up to half a month to settle trades in government bonds largely to allow dealers enough time to secure necessary bonds and funds. While trades in government bonds are delivered and settled at the same time through the network of the Bank of Japan, those in other bonds are settled through their respective trustee banks. Some blame this cumbersome system of settlement as a factor impeding the growth of the trading market for non-government bonds.

LISTING OF BONDS ON THE STOCK EXCHANGE

In Japan, bonds are primarily traded over the counter, and only a small number of bond issues are listed and traded on the stock exchange. Ten and 20 year government bonds, and yen-denominated foreign bonds, in principle, must be listed on the stock exchange.[7] In addition, several issues of government-guaranteed bonds, publicly offered municipal bonds, and banks' coupon debentures are also listed on the stock exchange to establish and disclose their prices.[8] As a matter of principle, these issues are listed on the Tokyo Stock Exchange, the Osaka Securities Exchange, or the Nagoya Stock Exchange two months after they are issued. The purchase or the sale of government bonds (worth ¥1 million or more and less than ¥10 million), and yen-denominated foreign bonds (worth ¥100,000 or more and less than ¥10 million) must be effected on the stock exchange. As mentioned, the amount of bonds traded on the exchange is far smaller than those traded over the counter.

DISCLOSURE OF PRICES OF NON-LISTED BONDS

Until recently, prices of non-listed bonds have not been adequately available to the market participants because of their large number. Until 1991, prices of about 30 issues were published daily, and those of about 200 issues published weekly, as OTC reference quotations.

the 10th, 20th, and last days of each month, but as trades in them had increased sharply to a level making their yields distorted, additional settlement days were established.

7 Lately, trades in non-listed yen-denominated foreign bonds have also increased.

8 As of the end of December 1994, one each of government guaranteed bonds and publicly offered municipal bonds, five issues of banks' coupon debentures and seven issues of corporate bonds are listed on the stock exchange.

These quotations were average prices quoted by several securities companies on these issues. Given the number of issues covered and the frequency of publication of these quotations, it can hardly be said that they were adequate. As the 1991 stock market scandals brought to light that business firms had traded bonds at prices far removed from market price to settle their accounts, and that securities companies compensated their favoured customers for trading losses on the basis of bond prices which were removed from their actual market value, Japan Securities Dealers Association started publishing daily OTC reference quotations covering about 300 issues, on the basis of which the Association formulated a rule for computing market prices of non-listed bonds. In addition, the Association adopted a self-regulatory rule limiting price changes within a certain band from the base prices established the day before.[9] Thanks to these rules, the practice of trading bonds at prices far removed from market price has almost disappeared.

TAXES ON BOND TRADING

Taxes levied on bond trading are divided into (1) those on interest income (coupon income) accruing from coupon bonds, (2) those on redemption gains made from discount bonds, and (3) those on securities transactions. In the case of coupon income, 20 per cent of it is withheld in taxes at the time of its payment, and in the case of redemption gains, 18 per cent of them are initially withheld in income tax at the time of issuance from corporate (other than designated financial institutions) and individual recipients. In the case of designated financial institutions, also, 18 per cent of their redemption gains are withheld in income tax but refunded in proportion to the period of their holding at the time of redemption. Securities transaction tax is levied at the time of the sale of bonds at a rate of 1/10,000 of the trading value for securities companies and

---

9 Under this rule, trading in government bonds, government-guaranteed bonds and bank debentures at prices 2 per cent higher or lower – and other publicly offered bonds at prices 3 per cent higher or lower – than their base prices formed the day before are not allowed. The limitation on price swing is relaxed when the price of the main contract month for long term government bond futures formed on the Tokyo Stock Exchange or the price of the benchmark issue traded between dealers changes by the equivalent of 1 per cent or more from their closing price of the day before.

bond-dealing banks (intermediaries) and 3/10,000 of the trading value for corporations and individuals (investors). There is a body of opinion which holds that the securities transaction tax is hampering the growth of the bond trading market, and pressure is growing for its abolition.

MARKET PARTICIPANTS

Major participants in the trading market other than bond dealers include (1) city (commercial) banks, (2) regional banks, (3) long term credit banks, (4) trust banks, (5) agricultural thrift institutions, (6) insurance companies (life, and property and casualty), (7) investment trusts, and (8) foreign investors. The banking institutions listed under (1) through (3) hold bonds in their asset portfolios as a substitute for lending, and the net value of their bond trading changes depending on changes in interest rates and the balance of their outstanding loans. However, when bonds they have underwritten and spot issues of debentures by long term credit banks are included, they often end up a net seller. By contrast, investors listed under (4) through (8) perennially tend to be net buyers by injecting fresh funds. Particularly in recent years, the ratio of purchases of Japanese bonds by foreign investors (mostly, the central banks of different countries) has been on the rise owing to a fall in interest rates in Japan and a rising yen.

Characteristics of the formation of yields

Characteristics of the formation of yields on the bond market of Japan include the preference for current yields, the formation of yields primarily on the basis of benchmark issues, and more recently, changes occurring in yields under the leadership of bond futures. This section surveys the characteristics of yields on government bonds and non-government bonds especially the disparity of yields among bonds with different coupon rates and the formation of premiums of benchmark issues.

DISPARITY OF YIELDS AMONG BONDS WITH DIFFERENT COUPON RATES

Generally, Japanese investors have had a strong preference for high coupon issues which tend to generate lower yields than others with the same remaining life. This tendency was particularly pronounced in the years before 1990 largely because of their peculiar accounting methods. More specifically, while banks included income gains from bonds in their operating income, they were not allowed to include capital gains in it. Accordingly, when they were keenly conscious of competition with other banks, many banks invested in high coupon bonds even at the expense of yields to maturity in order to increase their net operating income. Life insurance companies also were not allowed to divert their capital gains to the distribution of profits to their policy holders, with the result that they had to invest in high coupon issues to stay ahead of their competition in the distribution of profits (see Chapter 7).

As large amounts of government bonds fell due while new issues declined in 1988 and 1989, these institutional investors had to scramble to secure high coupon issues, intensifying competition among them to a degree not experienced before. However, when the banks introduced a new accounting standard, and when the life insurance companies revised the accounting principle of income distribution in FY 1990, their preference for high coupon issues (preference for current yields) weakened.

Figure 9.4 shows semi-annual compound yields (the scale on the left) of #95 government bonds (maturing in June 1997 with a coupon rate of 5.3 per cent) and #100 government bonds (maturing in June 1997 with a coupon rate of 4 per cent), and their difference (the scale on the right). While these two issues mature on the same date, there is a difference of 1.3 per cent in their coupon rates. More recently, the preference for current yields has died down, and investors are shying away from excessively over-par (high coupon) issues. In the process, only the tendency to prefer near-par (current coupon) issues has survived, and the disparity of yields among bonds with different coupon rates created by the preference for current yield is no longer pronounced.

CHARACTERISTICS OF YIELDS ON BENCHMARK ISSUES

On the bond trading market of Japan, trades are concentrated on one long term government bond issue called the 'benchmark issue'. Its role is to help dealers adjust their positions and serve as a benchmark of bond yields. The benchmark issue is selected on the basis of requirements (1) that its remaining life is sufficiently long (close to 10 years), (2) that its yield is close to the current coupon (its price is

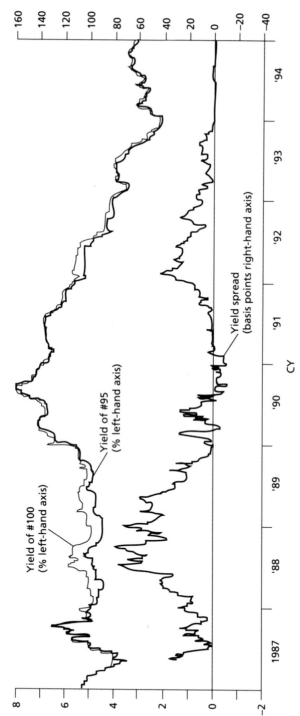

Yield of #100
(% left-hand axis)

Yield of #95
(% left-hand axis)

Yield spread
(basis points right-hand axis)

9.4 Disparity of yields between bonds with different coupon rates.

close to par), and (3) that it has plenty of supply and is highly liquid. It is selected on the basis of a tacit consensus of the market and changed roughly once a year. Therefore, speculative trading occurs sometimes when a benchmark issue is about to be replaced by another one.

Because it is highly liquid, it is traded at a premium and at a price higher than other kindred issues. In recent months, it has been traded at a yield of zero to 20 basis points under other issues. However, until 1988 when banks and securities companies dealt heavily in the benchmark issue, it was traded at a high premium for liquidity. During the years from 1986 to 1987, benchmark #78 and #89 government bonds were sometimes traded at a yield as low as 70 basis points, as shown in Fig. 9.5. This figure shows the difference in semi-annual compound yields between benchmark (the scale on the left) and non-benchmark issues (which have a remaining life almost the same as benchmark issues and coupon rates close to those of the benchmark issues) (the scale on the right). While the benchmark commanded a very high premium in 1986–8 when the market boomed on account of high dealing by banks and securities companies, the difference in compound interest yields between them has narrowed in step with changes in the market.

Until 1991, turnover of the benchmark issues traded among dealers accounted for more than 90 per cent of the aggregate turnover of government coupon bonds. Particularly, in 1987 when bank dealing in government bonds reached its peak, the market excessively discounted expectations for an easy money period, and #89 benchmark government bonds became a target of speculation. Daily turnover of the benchmark issue traded among dealers sometimes exceeded ¥10 trillion, and given the day-to-day swing in yields and the difference in yields from other issues, there is no denying that the heavy concentration of trading on benchmark issues has produced a distortion of the bond trading market.

The tendency to form bond prices mainly on the basis of benchmark issues has declined since 1992, with the result that the volume of benchmark issues as a percentage of the total turnover of government bonds has shrunk to about 80 per cent, and its share in the total turnover of domestic bonds has also dropped sharply. This tendency is expected to continue in coming years for the reasons (1) that a growing number of bond dealers have come to use bond futures for adjusting their positions, (2) that the liquidity of other non-benchmark government bonds and non-government bonds has

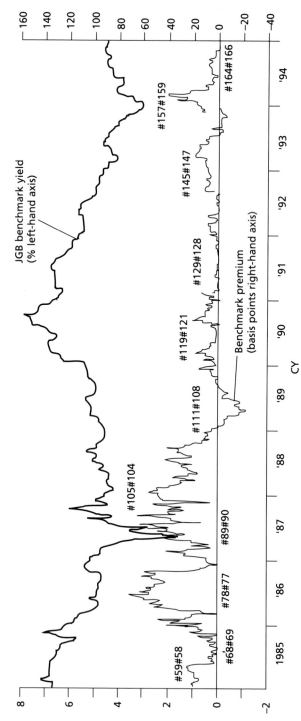

9.5 Disparity of yields between benchmark and non-benchmark issues.

since increased, and (3) that speculative trading of bonds also has been declining.

FORMATION OF YIELDS LED BY FUTURES

Since the second half of 1989, the tendency to form yields under the leadership of futures has become pronounced. When viewed in terms of trading costs, liquidity, and the transparency of price formation, the use of futures for risk management and dealing made sense. Accordingly, there has emerged a tendency of making market on issues of low liquidity on the basis of futures prices which are used for hedging against risks. This tendency was particularly strong in the case of government bonds. As a result, the net basis between government bonds and futures has been relatively stable. As bond trading was largely effected in their futures, the margin of changes in yields of issues belonging to a zone cheapest to deliver for futures (those with a remaining life of around seven years in recent low interest years) was the largest. By contrast, those of non-deliverable bonds (with a remaining life of less than seven years), deliverable bonds other than the cheapest to deliver ones, and 20 year government bonds were smaller than the former. This was due to the fact that when bond prices rose (or fell), futures were bought (or sold) first, and cash bonds were bought (or sold) thereafter. Figure 9.6 shows the standard deviations of day-to-day changes in semi-annual compound interest yields of 10 and 20 year government bonds during the three month periods from January to March and from April to June 1994.

FORMATION OF YIELDS OF GOVERNMENT-GUARANTEED BONDS AND PUBLICLY OFFERED MUNICIPAL BONDS

Issuing terms of government-guaranteed bonds and publicly-offered municipal bonds are uniformly decided on the basis of those of government bonds issued during the month, not by their issuers. Reflecting this practice, current issues of these bonds immediately after their issuance are traded at a yield corresponding to the difference in issuing yields from those of government bonds. Such difference in yields is about 10 basis points in the case of the government-guaranteed bonds issued by Japan Finance Corporation and about 20 basis points in the case of publicly offered municipal bonds such as Tokyo municipal bonds. On the secondary market, however, yields on government-guaranteed bonds and publicly offered municipal bonds generally vary from one issuer to another. The difference in yields on bonds issued by other issuers from those issued by Japan Finance Corporation and Tokyo municipal bonds generally ranges from 10 to 20 basis points. And as shown in Fig. 9.7, yield spread between government bonds and other non-current government-guaranteed issues tends to be larger than that of current ones. The graphs shown in the upper half of the figure are the yield curves (the scale on the left) of government bonds, government-guaranteed bonds, and IBJ's coupon debentures as of 31 March 1994. Those in the lower half are estimated yield spreads to government bonds (the scale on the right), government-guaranteed bonds and IBJ's coupon debentures. The yield spread of current issues is about 10 basis points, and as the issues move away from the current issue, the spread widens.

The practice of lump sum redemption at maturity started with the April 1987 issue (redeemable in April 1997) in the case of government-guaranteed bonds and with the April 1992 issue (redeemable in April 2002) in the case of publicly offered municipal bonds. Redemption of those issued prior to these dates was frozen for three years and then an amount equivalent to 6 per cent of the issue was

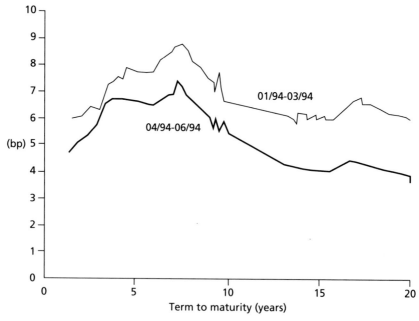

9.6 Standard deviations of margin of swing in yields.

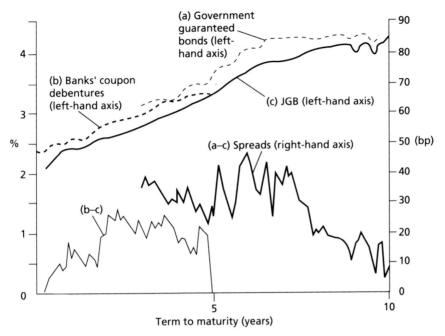

9.7 Yield spreads to government bonds, government-guaranteed bonds and banks' coupon debentures.

redeemed each year from the fourth year by drawing on the day of interest payment (twice a year). Therefore, their yield to maturity cannot be mechanically compared with those of government bonds.

FORMATION OF YIELDS OF BANKS' COUPON DEBENTURES

Trading in government bonds is concentrated on those eligible for delivery under futures contracts (those with a remaining life of 7 to 11 years), and the liquidity of those outside this zone normally declines. Therefore, it appears that market yields on debt securities with a remaining life of around five years are formed on the basis of banks' coupon debentures,[10] rather than government bonds. The yield spreads between government bonds and banks' coupon debentures correspond primarily to the difference in their credit standing, and yields of government bonds are generally lower than the latter. In the past, yields on government bonds with a remaining life of five years could not be mechanically compared with banks'

10 Although the maturities have diversified in recent years, most of the banks' coupon debentures are still issued with a maturity of five years.

coupon debenture, because their liquidity and coupon rates were different. Since the second half of 1990, however, the effect of disparity of coupons on the formation of yields has weakened, making it possible quantitatively to grasp the disparity of yields between bank debentures and government bonds.

In the case of the coupon debentures issued by the Industrial Bank of Japan (IBJ) which were issued in large amount and enjoyed relatively high credit standing, the difference in their compound yields from those of government bonds normally ranged from zero to 20 basis points and sometimes reversed. Ordinarily, the yield spreads between banks' coupon debentures and government bonds with a same maturity should be larger than the actual value, but the relative smallness of their spread seems to reflect the difference in their liquidity. While the credit standing of banks' coupon debentures is lower than that of government bonds, the liquidity of the former is generally higher because the term from their issuance is short.[11]

Until around 1992, the reputation of issuers of coupon debentures had no effect on their trading,[12] owing to the practice that only the coupon rate and the maturity of a debenture issue are decided at the time of its trading[13] and that the issue to deliver is decided only at the time of its delivery. The liquidity of banks' coupon debentures is thus ensured. However, as the magnitude of bad loans besetting debenture issuing banks came to light in the wake of the bursting of the economic bubble, the market began to be concerned about the credit standing of debenture issuing banks in 1992. Investors have since become increasingly selective in investing in bank debentures, and yields on them have come to vary from one issuer to another depending on their creditworthiness and liquidity of their debentures. Figure 9.8 shows the trading volume and contracted yields (based on simple yield) of different debentures traded among deal-

---

11 While the Industrial Bank of Japan issues ¥100 billion to ¥200 billion worth of coupon debentures each month, the value of long term government bonds effectively traded in the market is estimated at an amount less than those of IBJ.
12 At present seven banking institutions are authorised to issue coupon debentures and they are the Industrial Bank of Japan (IBJ), Long Term Credit Bank of Japan (LTCB), Nippon Credit Bank (NCB), Bank of Tokyo (BOT), Central Bank for Agriculture and Forestry (CBAF), Central Bank for Commerce and Industry (CBCI), and Zenshinren Bank.
13 When their coupon rates and dates of maturity are the same, they are often traded in the mass omitting to identify their issuers.

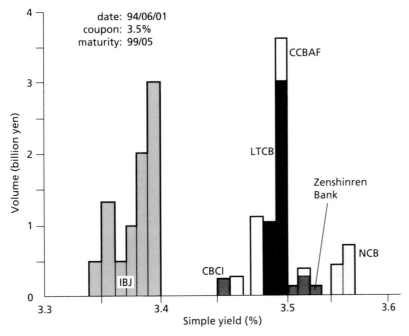

9.8 Disparity of yield of banks' coupon debentures with various issuers.

ers. This figure shows the volume of current issues issued in May 1994 traded among dealers through Japan Mutual Securities on 1 June 1994 listed in the order of their yields (based on simple yield).

Yields on the debentures of IBJ which enjoy the highest liquidity and creditworthiness among the investors are the lowest, and those on current coupon issues issued by Japan Long Term Credit Bank (LTCB) are 10 to 20 basis points higher than the IBJ's and those of Nippon Credit Bank (NCB) 20 to 30 basis points higher than the IBJ's. Debentures issued by the Central Bank for Agriculture and Forestry (CBAF: Norinchukin) and the Central Bank for Commerce and Industry (CBCI: Shokochukin) are usually traded at a yield zero to 10 basis points higher than the IBJ's.

GROWTH OF THE CORPORATE BOND MARKET AND FORMATION OF YIELDS

Prior to the bursting of the economic bubble in 1990, a growing number of business corporations had raised funds through offering equity-linked securities (convertibles and bonds with warrants) by taking advantage of high prices of their stocks. The bulk of straight bonds outstanding on the domestic market was accounted for by utility bonds (electric companies' bonds) with a maturity of 12 years and NTT bonds with a maturity of 10 years, while many business corporations raised funds through debt financing on foreign markets including the Euro market. As a result, except for those utility and NTT bonds that were traded immediately after their issuance, the volume of bonds traded on the domestic market was negligibly small. However, as businesses' equity-linked financing ground to a halt in the aftermath of the stock market collapse early in 1990, demand for fostering the corporate bond market became increasingly vocal. In response, the utility companies and NTT sought to diversify the maturity of their debt issues. Meanwhile, the needs of other business corporations for issuing straight bonds – and the amounts of their issues – have mounted since around 1992. As it happened at such a critical juncture, long and short term rates continued to fall, and the issuance of corporate bonds with terms of issue that matched the needs of investors increased rapidly. Since the eligibility standards for issuing bonds were relaxed, and since the issuance of dual currency bonds and variable rate notes was authorised early in 1994, the market has become far more liberalised.

With the market thus expanding, pressure for streamlining the trading market has mounted. Owing to the lack of bond dealers willing to make market on corporate bonds, price information has not been adequately disseminated to investors. Since 1993, however, the number of bond dealers making market on corporate bonds through computer terminals has increased. More recently, yields are being formed in a manner more transparent to investors on the basis of the yield spread between corporate bonds and government bonds, the creditworthiness of issuers, and the liquidity of their issues.

Repurchase agreements and bond lending

As noted in Chapter 8, trading in bonds may be largely divided into ordinary trading (simple purchase and sale of bonds) and trading under a repurchase agreement (repo or *gensaki*), an agreement whereby the seller agrees to repurchase the bonds at an agreed price and, usually, at a stated time. Under a repurchase agreement, the buyer of bonds can park his funds with a fixed rate for the period of the agreement (reverse repurchase agreements), and the seller can raise funds he needs (repurchase agreements). Securities companies often use repurchase agreements as a vehicle for financing their bond inventories, and this is called 'self-repurchase agreements'). Business corporations sometimes enter into a repurchase agreement with another business corporation through the intermediary of a securities company.

The share of government securities in the debt securities used for repurchase agreements is predominantly large, and they accounted for more than 99 per cent of the total turnover in 1994. However, almost all of the government securities used for repurchase agreements are Treasury bills (TB) and financial bills (FB), and the ratio of repurchase agreements to government coupon bonds is about 3 per cent.

In Japan, repurchase agreements are subject to securities transaction tax except for TB and FB, and this is a characteristic which makes them markedly different from the repos of the United States. Because of the effect of the securities transaction tax, interest rates charged on repurchase agreements are generally lower than those of negotiable certificates of deposit (CDs) and commercial paper.

In Japan, short sales of bonds (selling bonds not owned by the seller) have been severely restricted, and they had to unwind their short positions before the delivery day. To enhance the liquidity of bonds and help the market form fair prices of bonds in keeping with the expansion of the trading market, the ban on lending bonds was lifted at the end of May 1989 for the first time in its history. This has opened the way, in principle, for selling bonds short not owned on the delivery day. Since then, arbitrage transactions between issues with different yields have been effected, and yield curves of bonds, except those hampered with a special factor, have become smoother.

Bond lending is an arrangement under which a bond dealer borrows bonds from an institutional investor at a stated rent for a fixed period.[14] The dealer sells the borrowed bonds on the market to facilitate the bond trading. The dealer buys back the borrowed bonds from the market and returns them by the last day of the contract together with the interest and rent accrued for the period. Bond dealers borrow bonds either through brokers such as Japan Securities Finance or directly from investors over the counter through

---

14 At the end of 1994, the going rent for ordinary issues stood at about 0.3 per cent per annum.

negotiations. In Japan, the amount of bonds borrowed through negotiations with institutional investors is predominantly large. In 1994, while the value of bonds borrowed through brokers amounted to about ¥30 trillion, the value of those negotiated over the counter was more than 10 times those borrowed through brokers. More recently, the scale of bond borrowing, particularly by foreign securities companies and large domestic securities companies, has expanded rapidly.

Rate of return on domestic bonds

As the market has become increasingly dominated by institutional investors (such as pension funds), their behaviour has come to carry large weight on the market. In the process, there has developed a strong tendency to measure the performance of their bond investment not in terms of the absolute rate of return but in terms of their rate of return relative to that of the benchmark index. With a view to meeting such needs, Nomura Research Institute (NRI) compiled an NRI–BPI (bond performance index) which shows the movement of publicly offered domestic bonds as a whole. This index is designed to serve as an indicator of an average rate of return of almost all of the publicly offered coupon bonds with a remaining life of one year or longer.[15]

Figure 9.9 shows the historical performances of the NRI–BPI (an authoritative index of bond performance) and TOPIX (Tokyo stock price index) during the 10 years from 1985 to 1994. The average and the standard deviation of monthly rate of return of these indices are as follows, provided that the figures given below represent their annualised equivalents.

	Average rate of return	Standard deviation
NRI–BPI	6.3 %	3.9 %
TOPIX	5.4 %	22.6 %

As stock prices collapsed in the aftermath of the bursting of the economic bubble during the period, the performance of bonds was

15 Government notes and yen-denominated foreign bonds other than those rated AAA at the time of their issuance are excluded.

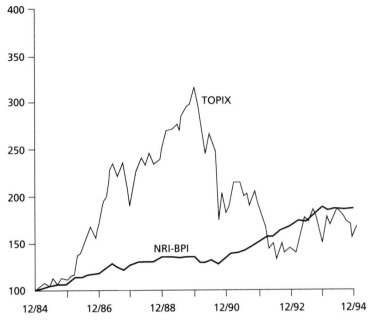

9.9 Performance of bond and stock investment.

higher than that of stocks. In terms of subdivided periods, the rate of return on bonds during the years of easy money was markedly higher and topped 10 per cent in each of the three years from 1991 to 1993. Considering the much lower risks of bond investment than those of stock investment, it was obvious that bonds were much more attractive than stocks during the period.

Conclusions and future challenges

One of the events that has characterised the bond market of Japan since the second half of the 1980s has been the introduction of derivatives of government bonds including their futures. Although the market experienced confusion during the initial period, derivatives trading on the exchange and the over the counter markets has taken hold. The scale of derivatives trading is expected to grow larger with the years, and the variety of derivative instruments is also expected to become increasingly diversified in coming years. Their impact on the cash market will also grow larger, making it essential for both bond dealers and investors to pay closer attention to risk management including that involved in derivatives trading.

Another change has been the fact that investors have weaned themselves from their heavy reliance on government bonds, particularly benchmark issues. Thanks to this development, the distortion of yield formation has been corrected, and the process of price formation has become increasingly transparent. More recently, the market for debt securities other than government bonds has expanded, and particularly, the growth in the turnover of banks' coupon debentures has stood out. In addition, the market for corporate bonds, which had been impeded by various government regulations and institutional problems, has expanded thanks to the progress made in deregulation, and its turnover has picked up sharply in recent years. With business demand for debt financing on the rise, the market for corporate bonds will expand further in coming years.

Challenges facing the bond market of Japan are to step up the effort for market making by bond dealers and create a system for broader disclosure of marker prices of bonds.

10 The fixed income derivatives markets

Swaps

With the financial markets increasingly liberalised, corporate financing internationalised, and the scale of institutional investors enlarged, the yen swap market has been expanding rapidly since 1984. Figure 10.1 shows changes in the semi-annual turnover of swap transactions published by the International Swap Dealers' Association (ISDA). Increases in them were particularly pronounced in the past few years, and the total value of interest rate swap transactions effected in the first half of 1993 topped ¥39 trillion ($390 billion at the rate of ¥100 to the dollar). Moreover, it is said that their actual total value was larger than that published by ISDA. While the volume of on balance sheet transactions is stable, off balance sheet transactions have been increasing lately in major financial markets across the world, and the use of interest rate swaps is expected to catch on in Japan, also. In the following pages, we would like to survey the growth of swap transactions, analyse the present market, and look at its possible future development.

CHANGES IN THE SWAP MARKET

The advent of new types of debt securities

The abolition of the principle of real demand (a principle allowing only such forward exchange contracts which are intended to cover the payment of import bills), effected pursuant to the April 1984 amendment of the Foreign Exchange Control Law, was largely responsible for having boosted the swap market in Japan. Following

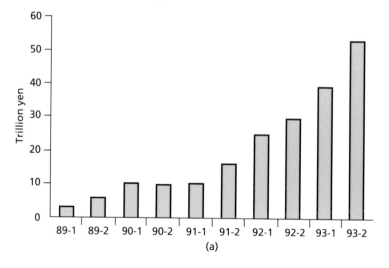

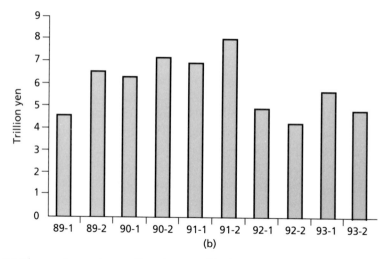

10.1 Volume of swap transactions (source: ISDA).
(a) Yen interest rate swap.
(b) Currency swap.

the enforcement of the amended Foreign Exchange Control Law, the ban on the issuance of foreign bonds by residents and currency swaps to hedge currency risks on yen-denominated bonds issued by non-residents was lifted, opening the way for Japanese firms to issue foreign currency-denominated bonds on overseas markets. As these bonds can be swapped for yen-denominated bonds immediately after their issuance, turnover in the yen currency swap market has increased sharply. It was around that time that the *harakiri* (suicide) swap by main banks of Japanese issuers became the talk of the market. A *harakiri* swap means a transaction in which, as explained in Chapter 5, the main bank – a system unique to Japan strongly binding the main bank to its clients, come rain or shine – has to swap a yen-denominated bond issue, often at an absurd rate, for a foreign currency-denominated bond issue of its clients, and has often made the headlines.

In 1985, restrictions on the types of Euro-yen bonds issued by non-residents were eased, and a large number of dual currency bonds have since been issued. (Issuers of dual currency bonds pay interest on them in yen and redeem their principal in dollars. To make them attractive, they carry a coupon higher than yen-denominated straight bonds to offset exchange risks inherent in them.) It was also in 1985 that index currency option notes and exchange index bonds ('heaven-or-hell' bonds) made their debut. While their redeemable principal changes, up or down, with the exchange rates, these bonds carry a coupon higher than straight bonds. These bonds were developed to attract Japanese institutional investors who preferred higher yields for accounting purposes, and later they changed into stock price-linked bonds. Swaps were frequently used as a tool for changing the cash flow of bonds, and the variety of the transactions has increased rapidly.

Since the ban on the importation of warrants detached from cum-warrant bonds issued by Japanese firms on overseas markets was lifted in 1986, the volume of foreign currency-denominated bonds issued on the Euro market has increased sharply, reflecting rising prices of their underlying stocks. Issuers prefer to swap their *ponkasu* (ex-warrant foreign currency-denominated) bonds into yen, because that offers cheaper costs on an Internal Rate of Return (IRR) basis.

Around 1986, foreign banks operating in Japan began to offer a market-making service for yen–yen swaps. At that time, Japanese banks contented themselves with acting as agents or retailing by merely covering their position risks arising from transactions with their clients with deals made with foreign banks. However, they were gearing up to participate in the swap market in earnest by establishing swap subsidiaries in overseas markets.

High tech loans and swap dealing

In 1989, the 'koala' loan made its debut. This is an arrangement under which a firm takes a yen loan at a long term prime rate from a bank and at the same time has a swap contract to receive Australian dollars and pay yen with the aim of reducing interest liabilities in exchange for a currency risk. It was a simple loan transaction to which the idea underlying dual currency bonds was applied. However, as it caught on rapidly in the market, it helped change the market participants' perception of swaps. Until then, the conventional wisdom had been that swaps are special transactions applicable only to large debt offerings made on the Euro market, but the koala loan has changed that, and the market came to perceive it as a vehicle that can be effectively employed for arranging small denomination loan transactions by businesses at large. It has also been instrumental in spurring the development of small denomination derivatives as a new type of debt financing and at the same time has helped boost the liquidity of the market.

In 1989, short term yen futures, Euro-dollar interest futures, and yen-denominated futures were listed on the Tokyo International Financial Futures Exchange (TIFFE). The volume of yen short term interest rate futures has since increased steadily and rose, in a matter of one year after its listing, to a level second only to that of Euro-dollar interest rate futures traded on the Chicago Mercantile Exchange (CME). By using financial futures and bond futures (listed in 1985) as tools for hedging positions against risks, management of risks on swap positions has become easier, helping the market boost its trading in swaps.

Since the collapse of the stock market in 1990, the conventional idea of designing swap products has changed gradually. During the speculative bubble years, products were generally designed to realise high returns at high risks. However, as stock prices tumbled, and as corporate financial officers came keenly to realise the necessity for hedging against interest rate risks under the much tighter monetary conditions enforced by the monetary authorities from 1989, their preference has shifted from one for higher returns to one for lower risks and costs.

After the introduction of the BIS primary capital ratio regulation (see Chapter 7), swap assets, while having an economic effect identical to that of other assets listed on the balance sheet, were given only a low risk weighting. As a result, long term credit banks and city banks have come to utilise swap transactions as an alternative vehicle for conventional fund dealing. This was responsible for sparking an explosive growth in swap transactions. As generic swaps became increasingly liquid, new wrinkles such as cap, floor, and swaption have been introduced to the market. Meanwhile, with stock prices remaining depressed, vehicles employed by corporations have shifted sharply from equity and equity-linked financing to debt financing, creating the necessity for devoting greater attention to debt management. And this has created a larger demand for swap transactions.

Thus, swaps were initially used by large corporations as a tool for exchanging the cash flow raised on the capital markets. More recently, however, swaps have become widely used by banks for making high tech loans to businesses or as a dealing instrument.

MARKET PLAYERS

Initially, foreign banks played a pioneering role in developing the swap market in Japan. However, as long term credit banks and city banks have worked out a system for developing swap products and for marketing them, the clout of foreign banks wielded in the market has waned gradually. Nevertheless, their presence in the market – in terms of their know-how of managing risks involved in highly volatile products and developing new products – is still felt strongly.

City banks carry an important weight in the swap market as main players. Although city banks are not authorised to issue debentures as long term credit banks are, they sometimes make fixed rate long term loans with short term funds raised at variable rates. Therefore, they often swap their short term debts for fixed rate long term ones to adjust mismatches between borrowing and lending.

By contrast, the principal vehicles for raising funds of the long term credit banks, another important swap player along with the city banks, are limited to fixed rate long term (five year) debentures, so that they generally end up with receiving fixed rate instruments in the swap market.

Among life and property–casualty insurance companies, swap transactions have traditionally been treated as grey area transactions. More recently, however, they have come to participate actively in swap transactions. In addition, business corporations are also utilising swap transactions to make adjustments between their fixed rate loans and variable rate ones. And with the authorisation of securities companies to participate in swap transactions, the market's players have been increasing consistently in recent years.

FORMATION OF YIELDS

In the dollar interest rate swap market, the swap rate is generally decided by adding a certain number of basis points to the yield of

Treasury securities then prevailing. In the yen interest rate swap market, however, the swap rate is not always decided on the basis of the yields of government bonds.

In the medium maturity zone where swap transactions are actively made, swap rates are decided at a level between the high end of the long term prime rate and the low end of yields on bank debentures. This is because for city and regional banks, a swap rate higher than the long term prime rate means an investment with a yield below the London Interbank Offered Rate (LIBOR), and for long term credit banks which raise funds by selling debentures, a swap rate lower than the yields on their debentures means a funding at a cost above LIBOR. Therefore, when the pressure on debenture issuing banks to accept a swap is stronger than that on city and regional banks to pay, the swap rate is decided at a level closer to the long term prime rate, and when the situation is reversed, it is decided at a level closer to the yield on a newly issued debenture. On the other hand, swaps between securities with a remaining life of seven to 10 years have their rates pegged to the yields on government bonds with similar maturities, because there are not many swap transactions in that zone, while yields on those of the short term zone are decided through an arbitrage with Euro-yen interest rate futures.

In Western countries, the longer the term of a swap contract, the larger the spread between the yields on government bonds and the swap rate is. In Japan, however, the spread between government bond yields and swap rates of those with a medium zone maturity widens most as shown in Fig. 10.2. This suggests that the swap market and bond market are not always integrated. In some cases, yields that make no investment sense have been formed.

However, improvements are gradually on the way. Following the liberalisation of interest rates, both long term credit banks and city banks have strengthened their system of asset liability management. They have established an organisation charged with the responsibility for centrally managing interest rate risks inherent in off and on balance sheet transactions by appointing a chief financial officer on the model of their Western counterparts. These banks are utilising in earnest highly liquid bond futures as a hedge instrument to control price fluctuation risks arising from their growing swap positions. They have also started making transactions aimed at taking advantage of the spread between bonds and swap deals. Moreover, the number of investors who use the swap spread as a reference for making investment decisions has been increasing in recent months.

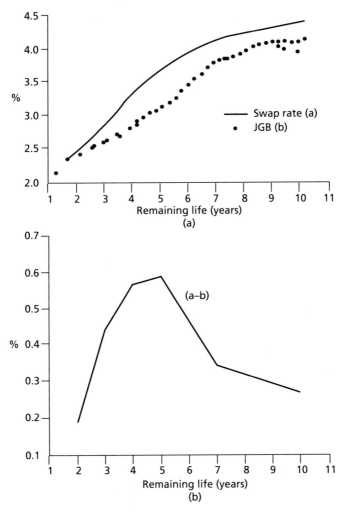

10.2 Spread between yields on government bonds and swap rate.
(a) Yield curve (swap, JGB; as at the end of March 1994).
(b) Spread (swap − JGB; as at the end of March 1994).

All these developments suggest that the bond and swap markets in Japan are being integrated in terms of formation of yields, and that the system of forming yields will gradually shift to one of the Western type in coming years.

OUTLOOK FOR THE SWAP MARKET

The development of the yen–yen swap market has brought on a sweeping change in both the direct (bond and equity) and indirect (bank borrowing) financing markets. Now, corporate financial officers can use spreads over LIBOR as a measure to evaluate interest rates charged by lending institutions and readily compare the costs of raising funds among different modes of financing including bond issuing. What is more, they can readily convert the least costly mode of fund raising into one that offers cash flow most suitable to their company. This has raised the possibility that the typical forms of lending based on long term, short term, and new short term prime rates will gradually outlive their relevance and usefulness.

As swaps are transacted off the balance sheet, they are not entered into the balance sheet, and corporate financial officers are thus free from the constraints of the main bank system. At the same time, swap trading has blurred the division between long and short term banking (that between city bank and long term credit bank), and this has set the stage for full scale competition among the banks for business involved in interest rate swaps.

Until recently, the vehicle of swap transactions was used by business corporations mostly for financing or for the purpose of managing liabilities, but lately, the financing techniques have developed to such an extent that the usefulness of swap transactions for the purpose of managing assets cannot be ignored. Simple asset swaps such as those for converting fixed rate assets to variable rate ones or vice versa, or the yields on repackaged bonds from illiquid outstanding bonds are decided on the basis of the swap rate. Life and property–casualty insurance companies are actively utilising swap transactions as part of the management of their assets, and for the purpose of investing their assets, also, swap transactions have become an indispensable tool.

What is more, the swap rate has become an important basis of reference in managing cash bond portfolios. For example, investors who seek to earn a rate of return higher than LIBOR are buying bonds with swaps. And many investors closely follow the relative value of L-spread as a basis for judging a given price of bonds. Previously, yields on 10 year government bonds served as the only and absolute benchmark for selecting cash bonds. Now, there is no doubt that the swap rate has been widely accepted as an important reference, along with the yields on government bonds, for selecting bond issues.

One thing over which the growing swap market is concerned is the credit ratings assigned to Japanese banks. Prior to the bursting of the economic bubble in 1990, many Japanese banks enjoyed the highest credit ratings, but their credit ratings have been downgraded for reasons of bad loans developed in their loan portfolios. As a result, while the yen–yen swap market is expanding, its leading players have been narrowed down to a few blue chip banking institutions which still maintain high credit ratings. This tendency has become pronounced among foreign players, and the limited number of Japanese players preferred by foreign players could turn out to be a barrier.

Another development over which the swap market is concerned is the move of the regulatory agencies to toughen the regulation of derivatives trading. Alarmed by the fact that a growing number of corporations have suffered losses in derivatives trading, regulators of many industrial nations are keeping their eyes on the swap market. Although the regulators in Japan have not yet stirred to institute new regulations, there are signs that the Ministry of Finance is seeking to curb a sharp increase in derivatives trading by requiring market players to disclose their off balance derivatives transactions.

Swap transactions have been increasing sharply year after year in Japan, but the share of its derivatives trading in the world's total is much smaller than that of its cash bond trading in the world's total. While the total amount of notional principal of derivatives of many US banks outstanding at the end of 1993 was 10 to 20 times their gross assets, it was only three times gross assets for Japanese banks. Japanese financial institutions are bent on adding value to their financial transactions by combining them with derivatives, and their derivatives trading is expected to increase by double digit percentage points per year for some time to come.

One has the feeling that swap transactions which had been considered an arrangement of swapping liabilities are being treated as a vehicle for swapping cash flow that has the same present value. It is believed that swap transactions will continue to contribute to improving the efficiency of the financial markets of Japan by creating diverse and flexible cash flow in coming years.

Government bond futures

Bond futures currently traded in Japan are those of 10 and 20 year government bonds, and US Treasury bonds, and they are all listed on the Tokyo Stock Exchange. Of these, the 10 year government bond futures contract, which is the oldest as well as the biggest, is the most important and it has the largest influence on the bond market as a whole. In the following pages, we will review the history of the development of this market and its current state.

THE WORLD'S LARGEST BOND FUTURES MARKET

Trading in government bond futures contracts started on the Tokyo Stock Exchange on 19 October 1985 – the first futures market in Japan to emerge since the war. The market has since expanded, and its annual turnover rose to ¥1,295 trillion in 1994, the largest in the world – compared with ¥1,000 trillion worth of Treasury bond futures traded on Chicago Board of Trade (CBOT) and ¥580 trillion worth of BUNDs futures on London International Financial Futures Exchange (LIFFE).

Today, government bond futures play a pivotal role in the bond market of Japan and it is one of the most successful exchange traded products the world over. However, this is not to say that all of its functions were effectively utilised from the start. The ups and downs it went through after its launch in 1985 reflect the vicissitudes that the bond market of Japan have undergone, and the structural changes that occurred in the latter half of the 1980s caused marked changes in the use of bond futures.

THE INCREASING POPULARITY OF BOND FUTURES

The liberalisation of the financial markets and low interest rates spurred dealing in bonds, sharply boosting the bond market in terms of both turnover and the number of participants. In the process, bond futures have caught on among traders as a leading product for trading. During the growth period of the market that started in 1985, short term dealing in benchmark issues of government bonds and bond futures by bond dealers (proprietary trading departments of securities companies and city banks) accounted for the bulk of the market's turnover. During the period from 1985 to 1994, as is shown Fig. 10.3, the turnover of government bonds increased sharply and futures proved to be a suitable vehicle to meet the need for liquidity of the market participants. And thanks to the convenience they offered, the turnover of the market grew to a scale surpassing that of the Treasury bond futures market of the United States in a span of two short years.

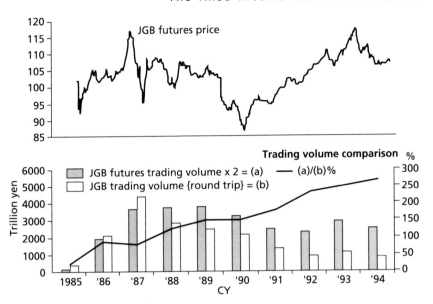

10.3 Market history of JGB futures.

BOND FUTURES AND THE SPECULATIVE BUBBLE

The investment behaviour of bond market participants during the second half of the 1980s was such that the investments they were after did not have to be bonds (as long as volatility enabled them to make sufficient capital gains during the short period of their holding). As a result, yields on the benchmark government bond dropped perilously close to the discount rate then prevailing. Such a low level of long term interest rates, which was not justifiable by the fundamentals, was a telltale sign of the nearing of a speculative bubble. To all intents and purposes, bond futures offered another benchmark product which pumped up the bond market bubble.

Basically, futures were intended to be a catalyst for setting up an efficient secondary market and for meeting investors' needs to hedge their positions against the risks which the market saw coming following the massive offerings of government bonds and the liberalisation of the financial markets. And the opening of the futures market as it did at such a juncture could not have come at a better time.

However, the liquidity generated by futures at that time had, as it turned out, converged on futures trading and had not spread to the cash bond market. One has the suspicion that it did not even occur to players in the futures market that the real function of the futures was to serve as a tool for enhancing the efficiency of the cash bond market and for hedging their positions against risks.

For instance, the bond futures price dropped more than ¥20 in October 1987 from the peak it had reached in May the same year. In the process, holders of cash bonds and futures contracts had to scramble to bail out of their holdings and commitments, undercutting one another's prices, because many of them had committed themselves to one and the same direction. This is further evidence showing that investors lacked the basic understanding of the role of futures as a hedging tool.

In September the same year, the news of a crippling loss suffered by Tateho Chemicals from speculation in bond futures hit the headlines. Shocked by the Tateho fiasco, futures contracts traded by business corporations and individuals shrank dramatically from a peak of 9 per cent of the market in 1987 to less than 1 per cent, and this low level was still the case even in 1994. This serves to underscore the painful realisation on the part of investors about the folly of their blind pursuit of capital gains and their imperviousness to the risks involved in highly leveraged speculation – a pattern of behaviour typical of investors during the period of speculative boom and bust. At the same time, it betrays the deep-rooted misperception of futures as a tool of speculation.

IMPROVED EFFICIENCY ATTRACTS INVESTOR INTEREST IN FUTURES TRADING

The volume of trading in 10 year government bonds has sharply decreased since the Bank of Japan tightened its credit reins hard in 1989. Conversely, that of bond futures has increased owing to a sharp increase in futures trading by bank traders. On balance, however, the combined turnover of the two markets decreased, and the bursting of the speculative bubble thinned the ranks of participants in the bond market. At the same time, this suggests that investors were shifting the weight of their activities from the cash market to the futures market.

The mechanism of trading of government bond futures is as follows:

  ▪ Standard contracts (10 year government bonds carrying a coupon rate of 6 per cent) are written for delivery on the 20th day of March, June, September, and December. Issues that are eligible for futures contracts are government bonds that have a remaining life of seven to 11 years.

▪ The minimum trading unit of par value is ¥100 million, and a margin equivalent to 3 per cent of the total par value (1 per cent of which is in cash) has to be deposited, and the minimum amount of margins is ¥6 million.

▪ Swings in the price of futures are limited to ¥2, up or down from the previous closing prices.

As such, the trading mechanism of bond futures in Japan is not much different from those of other countries. However, when compared with that of cash bonds, it has the following characteristics:

1 *Low cost*: Direct costs of trading in futures (brokerage commission and exchange tax, etc) are far lower than those for trading in cash bonds (securities transaction tax, etc). In addition, the trading system has been streamlined (see below), and indirect costs (those for obtaining information, etc) are also cheaper than those for trading in cash bonds.

2 *Efficiency of the trading system*: With a view to improving the efficiency of executing orders, an on-line system was introduced in the exchange in April 1988, thanks to which the number of contracts priced per unit of time has increased dramatically. As futures contracts are based on standard issues and traded centrally on stock exchanges, their prices are immediately publicised, and their trading is far more transparent than the over the counter trading of cash bonds. And the settlement of futures transactions, made through the clearing house, is highly trustworthy and dependable.

The convenience of futures trading, thus demonstrated, may have persuaded investors to shift the weight of their investment to the futures market. However, the cost advantage counts only to those who have a high turnover rate, which is why traders keep dealing in future contracts.

SIGNS OF STRUCTURAL CHANGE AND DIVERSIFICATION OF THE USE OF FUTURES CONTRACTS

The price of government bond futures dropped to a low in September 1990 owing to five hikes in the discount rate. Although the central bank eased its credit controls about a year later, the trading volume of bonds kept decreasing, and that of bond futures also started decreasing. Although signs of increases in the volume of futures trading began to surface at long last in 1993, a visible pickup in their trading volume failed to materialise despite the fact that the discount rate was at an all-time low of 1.75 per cent and that the market cycle, historically, was on a sharp upslope – a far cry from the frenzied dealing witnessed during the market bubble.

With recession-battered business demand for funds shrinking, and bank lending continuing flat, bond investors have become more sensitive to risks and their behaviour has become definitely portfolio-oriented seeking higher rates of return.

In the course of such structural changes, the ratio of turnovers of futures to those of cash bonds has increased consistently (Fig. 10.3). Meanwhile, the volume of futures traded by banks' dealers as a percentage of the total has levelled off after peaking at 80 per cent plus, and the pace of increase in the market shares of financial institutions other than banks, foreign investors, and investment trusts has stood out in recent years. During the first half of the period 1991–3, the inverted yield curve between long and short term rates remained unchanged, and owing in part to this cyclically higher cost environment of carrying cash bonds, the utilisation of futures continued unabated even after speculative dealing wound down.

In fact, given the high reliability of bond futures as a benchmark for bond trading, futures have become indispensable not merely as a substitute investment vehicle for cash bonds but also as a tool for hedging dealers' inventories and investors' portfolios against risks. Bond futures also serve as a major risk-controlling tool for swaps and more sophisticated derivatives of yen and interest rates, both in the development of them and the management of long term interest rate risks.

The utilisation of bond futures as a link between those yen interest rate-related products will thus become diversified and continue to play an important role.

TASKS OF THE CASH BOND MARKET SEEN FROM THE STANDPOINT OF FUTURES

For all the diversification of the use of futures, however, the tendency among the market participants towards opting for futures when investment in cash bonds makes sense has not disappeared. In the following pages, we will review some of the problems relating to cash bonds inherent not only in the attitude of investors but also in the market infrastructure.

First, theoretically, the price of futures is determined from the 'cheapest to deliver' bond price through an arbitrage process, known as a cash-and-carry strategy. However, as the futures market is far more liquid and their price formation is far more transparent than cash bonds other than the benchmark issue, that theoretical process is actually reversed, and prices of eligible bonds other than the benchmark issue tend to be determined in reference to the prices of futures. By the very nature of their trading, the futures market takes precedence to others as the place for discovering prices, but a sound cash market should develop a price forming mechanism on its own.

Second, amid rising expectations that a public auctioning of 20 year government bonds would spur the development of the new issue and trading markets of bonds, this market was launched in July 1988. However, the volume of trading in 20 year government bonds did not increase as much as had been expected and the volume of their futures trading kept decreasing year after year, to less than 0.1 per cent of the total trading volume of bond futures. In many overseas markets, also, there is a plural number of futures on the yield curve, and they are quite useful for hedging issues with different remaining lives and for yield curve plays. However, no matter how effective futures may be as a trading tool, they cannot be sustained in the absence of the underlying cash bond market on a certain scale.

Third, London International Financial Futures Exchange (LIFFE) started trading Japanese government bond futures in July 1987, but their trading volume did not come to much. Until the convenience of trading for Japanese investors improved through the adoption of an automatic settlement system at the opening price of the Tokyo Stock Exchange in 1991, only a limited number of investors utilised the futures trading. This underscores the importance of establishing a linkage between exchanges operating in different time zones and of involving investors of their main market. At the same time, it has brought to light the inadequacy of the overseas secondary market for Japanese bonds. In this connection, complaints were often directed against the onerous practice of withholding taxes from the interest incomes of non-resident investors. This discourages the participation of foreign as well as Japanese corporate and individual investors, and it also impedes the growth of the bond market.

LIFFE takes over business where it is left off by the Tokyo Stock Exchange for the day and carries on ongoing inter-dealer businesses, thus enhancing the linkage and continuity of transactions of the futures markets of different countries. It has therefore taken on growing importance as a marketplace where prices are formed or discovered after the closing of the Tokyo Stock Exchange. The listing of Japanese government bond futures on the Singapore International Monetary Exchange (SIMEX) in 1993 may be characterised as a logical development that was sparked by the success of LIFFE in bringing bond futures to international markets. Faced with such developments, the cash bond market of Japan will have to be further streamlined to fill the gap between itself and the increasingly sophisticated international markets of its government bond futures.

Bond options

Aware that bond options are an integral part of international markets for cash bond and futures trading and necessary for the development of an efficient bond trading market, the market was mulling over the introduction of bond options from 1987 and they were introduced on the Euro market in the form of warrants of government bonds in April 1988. Since then, they have been introduced in the domestic market in the form of over the counter (OTC) options and government bond futures options.

OTC OPTIONS (BONDS WITH OPTION RIGHTS)

Even today, the Securities and Exchange Law has no provisions for dealing with OTC options which are traded off the floor. This is why they had to be traded in the form of warrants at first. To sidestep the possible conflict with the law, bond options trading takes the form of a contract for the cash bond transaction, and by entitling their holders to exercise their right at a certain price (the exercising price) on a certain date, it has in effect become a transaction in OTC options.

They are traded in units of ¥100 million on the basis of bonds other than convertible and warrant bonds with a maximum maturity of one year and three months (one year until 1993). Terms and conditions are decided through negotiations between the option writer and the buyer. Currently, securities companies make market by displaying on the screen quotations of options with a standardised maturity (one week to three months) and exercise prices of the benchmark government bonds.

Monthly turnovers doubled in the half year that followed the launching of the market in April 1989 and rose past the ¥25 trillion mark in November. In the ensuing years, however, the monthly turnovers have more than halved owing to sluggish trading of cash bonds and they plunged to about ¥10 trillion in 1991 and 1992. Then they picked up again in step with increases in the turnover of cash bonds and rose back to ¥21 trillion in December 1993.

The bulk of trades were accounted for by inter-dealer trading, and more than 90 per cent of their trades converged on government bonds, especially the benchmark issues. Trading in issues other than government bonds concentrated on options of banks' coupon debentures issued during the year. Other issues traded sporadically mostly related to the bonds held in each investor's portfolio, and as they are negotiated individually, their liquidity is not very high. Trading in these issues tends to converge on those with a remaining life of less than three months.

GOVERNMENT BOND FUTURES OPTIONS

Options based on government bond futures were listed on 11 May 1990. Futures options are of the American type in that they are written for delivery in two nearby futures contracts, renewable up to six months, and exercisable in units of one point of the underlying futures price. And they are traded through the computer system as is the case with government bond futures. Margins are put together with those on government bond futures, and their trading mechanism is thus closely related to that of government bond futures trading.

The turnover of futures options swelled rapidly during the initial months to a level equivalent to 30 per cent of futures volume, and then diminished, in part because of the introduction of the exchange tax (0.01 per cent of the premium) in October 1990, and settled down to a monthly average of ¥10 trillion to ¥15 trillion, or 10–15 per cent of the futures volume (Fig. 10.4).

Securities companies and banks actively participated in trading futures options. Banks, in particular, accounted for half the futures options traded in mid-1992. However, as is the case with the futures

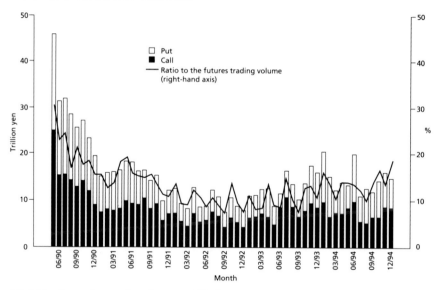

10.4 Trading volume of options on JGB futures contracts.

market, dealers' share has since dwindled, and the shares of the banks and securities companies fell to about 40 per cent of the market, respectively.

As the options are based on futures, their prices are formed more efficiently than the less liquid OTC options. But the difference in volatility between ATM (at-the-money) put and call is relatively larger than the listed futures options of other countries, suggesting the lagging efficiency of the market. There is still room for expansion (active trading in distant issues) by streamlining the market.

TYPICAL SELLING STRATEGY OF OTC INVESTORS

An analysis of monthly turnovers of OTC options shows that most of the dealers are net buyers of put and call options (and investors are net sellers) (Fig. 10.5 and 10.6). If an options buyer gives up his right, he loses the premium he has paid, an undesirable accounting result for the investor (the premium is recorded as loss), so most of them simply sell options, or, if they buy options, they offset their purchase costs by selling them.

Most of the investors sell options continuously despite the fact that such actions would add to the risk of running unlimited losses. This is because they could limit the risk to the extent tolerable to investors by combining options with cash bonds. Typical option selling strategy includes the following:

220

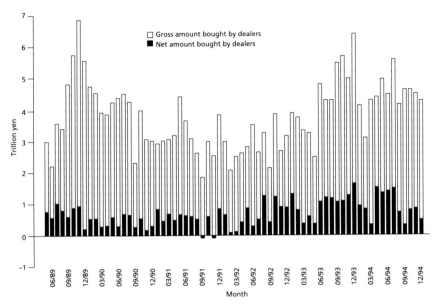

10.5 OTC call – amount bought by dealers.

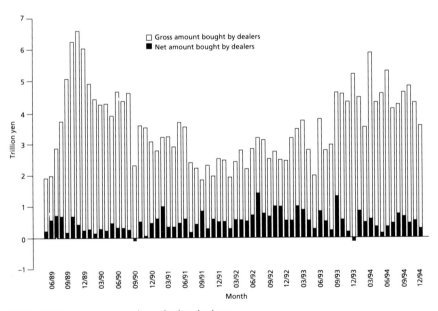

10.6 OTC put – amount bought by dealers.

1 *Target buying* (the sale of an OTM (out-of-the-money) put): When the market rallies, the premium income can be fixed as a gain. If the market sells off and the put is exercised, it results in the purchase of bonds at a low limit price.

2 *Buy and write* (the purchase of cash bonds and the sale of OTM call options): The investor receives the premium income from the call options, and the current yield becomes fixed when the option is exercised.

3 *Covered call* (the sale of call options against a long position): This is used to hedge the investor's position against a drop in bond price or to cash the hidden profits of bonds with a low liquidity. If the option is exercised, it results in the sale of bonds at a high limit price that includes the premium.

In fact, the sale of put options increased during the initial phase of a bull market that occurred in 1992 through 1993, while the sale of call options increased during the subsequent market corrections. This pattern is a typical strategy for option selling that combines cash bonds as outlined above. Also synthetic short, based on the sale of put options and the purchase of call options, is often used as a means of short sale of cash bonds rather than options.

As the position is apt to become a net option long (or a gamma long as dealers call it), dealers arrange a delta hedge, a contrarian operation in which cash bonds or futures are sold when the market rises or bought when the market drops. When dealers conduct a contrarian operation all at once in response to a large sale of options, such an operation sometimes performs the role of mitigating the price swings of cash bonds.

DIVISION OF ROLES BETWEEN THE OTC AND LISTED MARKETS

The main characteristic of OTC options is that they provide tailor-made tools for hedging individual positions. As such, they have a definite role to play in facilitating bond trading. However, not many investors use them as an independent trading tool. As happened during the first half of 1991 when the volatility dropped below 3 per cent, 'volatility sales' sometimes increase, but not much trading taking advantage of the specific price behaviour of options themselves has taken place.

On the other hand, government bond futures options have the attraction of liquidity because of their standardised trading on the exchange, and carry a large weight in options trading for the main players of the futures market (securities companies and banks). In other words, they are important as a complement not only to futures but also to the liquidity of OTC options.

In expanding the bond options market, steps should be taken to discourage the selling-tilted behaviour of investors. And it is desirable to improve the efficiency of the market as a whole by effectively taking advantage of the complementary relationship between the OTC and listed markets.

11 The equity trading market

Overview

This section surveys the present state of the equity market of Japan with a focus on the secondary market as it relates to trading in derivatives.

At the end of December 1984 when a stock market bubble was in the making, the Nikkei 225 index stood at ¥11,542.60. Although it temporarily dropped in the wake of Black Monday in October 1987, the Nikkei 225 rose consistently and hit an all-time high of ¥38,915.87 at the end of December 1989 (Fig. 11.1). This represents a 3.37-fold increase in five years or an increase at a steep annual rate of 27.5 per cent at a time when yields on 10 year government bonds hovered within the range of 4–7 per cent.

As a large number of corporations offered during the period new shares at market price to take advantage of rising prices of their stocks, market capitalisation of the firms listed on the First Section of the Tokyo Stock Exchange (TSE) swelled 3.8 times in a matter of five short years (1984 to 1989) from ¥155 trillion ($1.55 trillion) to ¥591 trillion ($5.91 trillion). In addition, these listed firms raised huge sums of money by issuing convertible bonds on the domestic market and bonds with warrants on overseas markets. Some of the funds they raised through equity-linked financing were invested, as discussed in Chapter 7, in *tokkin* trust funds (a specified money trust managed by a trust bank in accordance with instructions given by the investor) and fund trusts (non-designated money in trust), or were used to buy shares of their banks or other associated firms under cross-shareholding arrangements.

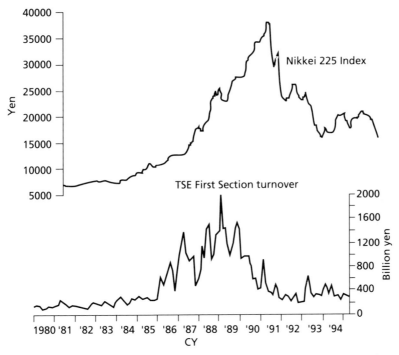

11.1 The Nikkei average and turnover of the First Section of the Tokyo Stock Exchange.

Turnover of shares listed on the First Section of the TSE also ballooned at an unprecedented rate and grew 4.2 times during the same five year period, from ¥66.6 trillion ($666 billion) in FY 1984 to ¥282.6 trillion ($2.82 trillion) in FY 1989. The sharp increase in stock market turnover is explained by explosive increases in share trading not only by these *tokkin* trust funds and fund trusts but also by corporate and individual investors who scrambled to get a piece of the action in what was then called '*Zaitech*' (financial engineering).

After hitting an all-time high in December 1989, the Nikkei 225 began to slip and on 18 August 1992, it nose-dived to as low as ¥14,309.41, a 63 per cent drop in two and a half years. Thereafter, the Nikkei 225 see-sawed and climbed back to around ¥20,000. What helped to arrest the fall was the purchase of shares by publicly run pension funds (in what were sarcastically called 'price-keeping operations' or PKO, a paraphrase of the United Nations peace-keeping operations) and foreign investors. As the months wore on into 1994, signs of life began to crop up in the stock market, largely buoyed by the gathering pace of the economy.

However, these developments do not necessarily mean that the stock market is out of the woods. For one thing, the stock market has become less liquid, because large chunks of shares have been locked up in corporate vaults through cross-shareholding. Now faced with decreasing earnings under the pressure of a super-strong yen and recession, a growing number of corporations are dumping their low yielding shares that they acquired through cross-shareholding arrangements. What is more, a large number of Japanese investors who had their fingers burnt in the aftermath of the bursting of the stock market bubble are simply not in the mood to touch shares again – at least until they have recouped the large evaluation losses they have suffered. And the banks have been writing off their bad loans with the proceeds of their shareholdings. Such being the situation, the after-effects of the economic bubble are likely to persist into the second half of the 1990s.

In the following sections, we will take a look at the characteristics of the Japanese stock market from three angles: (1) the mechanism of trading and the present state of trading in cash shares and stock derivatives as they compare with those of Western countries, (2) whether Japanese stocks are overvalued in terms of PER and other valuations, and lastly (3) the behaviour of Japanese investors exhibited during and after the stock market bubble.

The mechanism of trading and the present state of trading

THE MECHANISM OF TRADING

The secondary market of Japan may be divided into the market opened by the securities exchanges and the over the counter (OTC) market. The exchange market is highly organised and plays the leading role in transacting the purchase and sale of equity shares. More recently, however, OTC shares have become increasingly popular among investors, and their turnover is on the rise, increasing from ¥0.19 trillion ($1.9 billion) in 1985 briefly to ¥6.04 trillion ($60.4 billion) in 1990 (soon after TSE's First Section stock prices collapsed). In 1992, it stood at ¥1.08 trillion ($10.8 billion). In the following pages, cash transaction, margin trading, and futures and options trading on the stock exchange will be reviewed.

CASH TRANSACTION

The trading system of stock exchanges in Japan is based on the principle of concentrating stock trading on the stock exchange (the concentration principle) and the principle of competitive trading. Pursuant to the concentration principle, shares of all listed companies are traded on the nation's eight stock exchanges, and the great bulk of them are traded on the Tokyo Stock Exchange. Of the nation's 2,155 companies listed on stock exchanges as of the end of 1993, 1,667 companies are listed on the Tokyo Stock Exchange (of which 1,234 companies are on its First Section). On each of these stock exchanges, stock prices are decided according to the principle of competitive trading. In other words, they are decided on the basis of the highest bid on an issue made ahead of others through auctions between sellers and buyers. Under the separate auction system such as the one adopted in Japan, securities companies which have a seat on the exchange present orders received from their customers and their own orders to the exchange, and when a highest bid price is matched by a lowest asked price, a deal is struck. This system differs from those employed in the United Kingdom and the United States. In London, the market-maker system is adopted, under which the market-maker, a member of the stock exchange, maintains firm bid and offer prices in a given security by standing ready to buy or sell round lots at publicly quoted prices for its own account. The New York Stock Exchange adopts the specialist system, which is designed to play a role intermediate between the two systems mentioned above. The specialist performs the function of matching buy and sell orders converging on the market in accordance with a certain priority rule and buying or selling for the specialist's own account to counteract temporary imbalance in supply and demand and thus prevent wide swings in stock prices.

When deals cannot be struck through auctions of individual issues, *saitori* members (arbitrage brokers) of the exchange are supposed to offer a quotation on a given issue, but their primary role is to match buy and sell orders, and actual market-making is performed by securities companies for their own account.

Under the individual auction system, all stock transactions are carried out by one of two methods: the *itayose* method and the *zaraba* method. All orders reaching the floor before the opening and the close of a session are processed by the *itayose* (auction) method. Under the *itayose* method, each buy order is compared with sell orders till its quantity and price are matched by a sell order and the

227

price is treated as a single price for the consummation of the transaction. Under the *zaraba* (continuous day trading) method, transactions other than those processed by the *itayose* method are consummated under the principle of auction conducted on the basis of the following two priorities: (1) price priority, in that the sell (buy) order with the lowest (highest) price takes precedence over other orders, and (2) time priority, in that an order placed earlier than others takes precedence over other orders if at the same price.

Issues that can be traded on the stock exchanges in Japan are divided into floor-traded issues and system-traded issues. Floor-traded issues consist mainly of the first 150 most actively traded issues that are eligible for loan transactions or margin trading, and the remainders (system-traded issues) are traded automatically through computers. Futures and options are included in the system-traded issues.

MARGIN TRADING

With a view to facilitating stock trading and formation of fair stock prices by creating speculative demand, Japan introduced in June 1951 the system of margin trading crafted on the model of the margin trading system of the United States. Under this system, a customer makes a good faith deposit with a securities company, borrows from the securities company a certain amount of money to buy shares or shares to sell, and repays the loan or returns the borrowed shares within a stated period.

At the time the margin trading system was launched, a system of loan transactions was established. Under this system, a 'securities finance company' lends to a securities company through the settlement mechanism of the stock exchange funds or share certificates that are necessary for the securities company to settle a margin trading contract. Issues which can be used for loan transactions are called 'eligible issues', which consist mainly of those listed on the First Section of the Tokyo Stock Exchange, each with more than 60 million outstanding shares. As of the end of February 1994, there were 864 such issues listed on the Tokyo Stock Exchange. The balance of outstanding margin buying had tended to increase since the second half of the 1980s and briefly topped ¥10 trillion ($100 billion) during the second 10 day period of March 1990. However, as stock prices remained depressed thereafter, the balance of margin buying dropped steeply to ¥2.28 trillion ($22.8 billion) in May 1994. And the balance of margin selling stood at around ¥500 billion ($5 billion) in each of the eight years from 1986 to 1994 and fell to ¥464.8 billion ($4.64 billion) in May 1994. The number of shares traded on margin accounted for 16.8 per cent, and their market value 15.1 per cent, respectively, of the regular trading effected in 1993. Individual investors have actively participated in margin trading and accounted for 49.7 per cent of the total value of margin-traded shares in 1992.

As securities companies did not have sufficient funds at the time the margin trading system was introduced in 1951, securities finance companies (one each in Tokyo, Osaka, and Nagoya) played a pivotal role in creating speculative demand. More recently, in an effort to increase yields on their share holdings, life insurance companies and other institutional investors loaded with Japanese shares have been lending their holdings to foreign share lenders. While lending shares through competitive negotiations is commonplace in Western countries, they can only be lent through a securities finance company in Japan. Borrowing shares on foreign markets through competitive negotiations is generally less costly than borrowing them in Japan through a securities finance company. Some foreign securities companies are short selling Japanese shares they have borrowed on foreign markets. Short selling of Japanese shares (particularly, bank shares) by, for example, a foreign hedge fund came as a surprise to many Japanese investors, because it poignantly reminded them of the backwardness of Japan's loan transactions market.

MAJOR STOCK PRICE INDEXES OF JAPAN AND PROBLEMS CONFRONTING THEM

There are two representative stock price indexes: the Nikkei 225 and TOPIX (the TSE stock price index). The Nikkei 225 is known not only in Japan but also the world over. More recently, a number of stock indexes have been published including the Nikkei 300 (which has served as a base of futures and options trading since 14 February 1994). They are used for a number of purposes, and a growing number of institutional investors have come to use them as a benchmark for measuring the performance of their portfolios.

Meanwhile, lively debate has been going on over the validity or serviceability of stock indexes – what issues they cover, and how they are computed – as a vehicle for derivatives trading since futures trading became active in 1990. The Nikkei 225 is an index of weighted prices of stocks incorporated in it (arrived at by dividing the total of the 50 yen par value equivalents of the 225 issues by a divisor). However, some have been complaining since around 1989 that as the index includes many issues with low liquidity (their prices are prone to change sharply because their turnover is relatively small), they have often become a target of manipulation.

In response, the *Nihon Keizai Shimbun* (Nikkei for short), a leading economic daily which authors the index, decided regularly to replace issues (six issues at the most each time) with a low turnover with other issues with a larger turnover. And the situation has been getting better.

An index which is purportedly designed to correct such distorting effects is the Nikkei 300. As with the TOPIX, this new index is computed by weighting 300 stocks with market capitalisation of the TSE issues. According to an analysis, however, while changes caused in the index itself by index trading are muted, impacts of certain issues included in the index (financial issues whose liquidity does not rise in step with changes in the total market capitalisation) are disproportionately larger than those of other index issues. Of the 33 industry groups represented on the Tokyo Stock Exchange, the bank sector accounts for 7.7 per cent of the total market capitalisation of Nikkei 225 stocks, while it accounts for more than 20 per cent of that of the Nikkei 300 stocks or TOPIX. The Nikkei 300 includes 10 bank issues (or 3.3 per cent), and the total market capitalisation of these 10 banks accounts for more than 20 per cent of that of the 300 issues.

FUTURES AND OPTIONS TRADING

Major stock index futures and options listed on Japanese stock exchanges include (1) TOPIX futures and options, (2) Nikkei 225 futures and options, and (3) Nikkei 300 futures and options.

When stock prices started to fall after 1990 (following the stock market collapse), many market watchers blamed the collapse and volatility of stock prices on derivatives-linked arbitrage transactions. And sudden increases in the volume of derivatives trading which far outpaced that of the cash market provided weapons to those critical of derivatives trading.

These criticisms may or may not be valid, but in any case the regulators introduced from August 1990 various measures aimed at regulating derivatives trading (particularly, stock index futures). And these measures have added hugely to futures trading costs. Particularly, the hike of cash margin requirements (to 13 per cent) effective from December 1991 and the rise in brokerage commission effected on 23 March 1992 had a devastating effect on derivatives trading, as witnessed by a sharp decrease in the turnover of the Nikkei 225 futures traded on the Osaka Securities Exchange. More recently, however, deregulatory measures have been taken in steps. Since the launching of Nikkei 300 futures and options trading in February 1994, the cash margin requirements and the good faith deposits have been lowered in stages, and the margin of price swings was widened with the introduction of a circuit breaker.

However, securities companies have become increasingly disenchanted with trading in derivatives on the Japanese stock market on account of the stifling overregulation, and a growing number of them have shifted their derivatives trading from the Osaka Securities Exchange to SIMEX (Singapore International Monetary Exchange).

One of the factors which has boosted the turnover of futures trading far above that of the cash market is the large difference in brokerage commission. While trading in a basket of Nikkei 225 issues costs ¥1.7 million to ¥1.8 million in brokerage commission, a contract for the Nikkei 225 futures of an amount identical to the cost of a basket of Nikkei's cash stocks costs a mere ¥0.14 million, or less than one-tenth.

Over the long term, the current fixed brokerage commission is expected to be liberalised to a certain degree. The first salvo of liberalisation was fired on 1 April 1994 by allowing investors placing an order to buy or sell over ¥1 billion worth of a security to negotiate the brokerage commission with their broker for the difference. However, when investors place a buy or sell order worth ¥1 billion involving more than one issue, they are not yet free to negotiate the brokerage commission. Therefore, this deregulation measure will not narrow the difference in brokerage commission between cash and futures trading.

CONVERTIBLE AND WARRANT BONDS AND NIKKEI-LINKED BONDS

As huge amounts of convertible and warrant bonds were issued during the speculative bubble years, their exercise prices turned out to be far higher than the prices of their underlying stocks by the time the rights became exercisable, with the result that many of them remained unexercised, and their redemptions surged to a peak in 1993. However, there is little likelihood that their issuers will be hard pressed to raise fresh funds to meet the redemptions for any extended period.

The Nikkei-linked bonds are one of the debt packages whose amount of redemptions or coupon rate is linked to the Nikkei 225. One of the Nikkei-linked bonds is called the 'bear hell bond' and these were issued in 1988 and 1989 when expectations for still higher stock prices were widespread. However, owing to the bursting of the speculative bubble, the amount of redemption of many of the bear hell bonds went down to zero. As these bonds fell due after the bubble burst, and as the hedge positions of option writers were liquidated, it was feared that their redemptions would have serious impacts on bond prices. However, according to a Nomura Research Institute (NRI) survey, Nikkei-linked bonds which were to be redeemed in large amounts and could thus have dealt a serious blow to the market had almost disappeared by mid-1994.

Are Japanese stocks overvalued?

PERs OF JAPANESE STOCKS

Price–earnings ratios (PERs) are generally used as a yardstick to determine whether the price of a stock is overvalued or undervalued. Depending on the base – reported earnings of the preceding term or an analyst's forecast of next year's earnings – used for the purpose of computing the PER, they are called a trailing P/E or a forward P/E. Changes in PERs are summarised in Fig. 11.2. The analyses cover the NRI-350, which excludes financial service and utilities groups from the NRI-400.

During the 1970s, PERs ranged between a high of 30.5 (registered in February 1977) and a low of 9.8 (registered in December 1970), averaging at about 20. This pattern has changed since the beginning of the 1980s. At the end of December 1983, the trailing P/E stood at 32.0 and the forward P/E at 30.6. Since then, the multiples have never dropped back to the area of 20 and have increased continually, rising to 40.3 (trailing) in April 1986 and 42.8 (forward) in August the same year and then to 79.9 (trailing) in March 1989. As stock prices collapsed after 1990, the multiples ranged in the area of 30–40, and then turned upwards again in 1993 and climbed back to 59.8 (trailing) and 78.9 (forward) in February 1994.

Are the multiples of 60 or 80 justifiable? For example, some argue that Japanese stocks are overvalued when compared with American stocks in terms of their PERs. True, the forward P/E of S&P 500 rarely

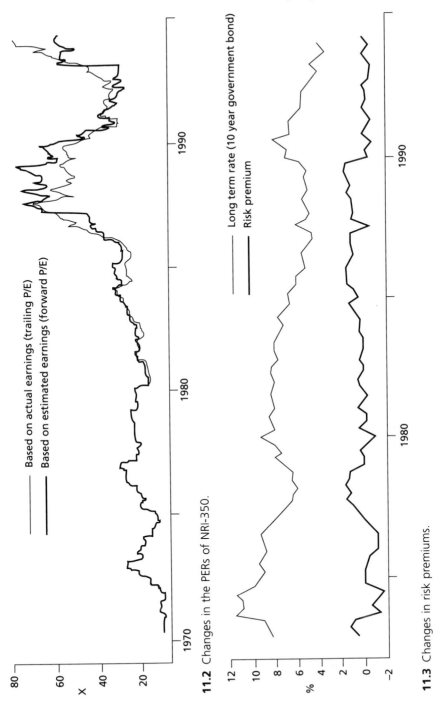

11.2 Changes in the PERs of NRI-350.

11.3 Changes in risk premiums.

rises to 20 at the highest, and when compared in terms of multiples, Japanese stocks are overvalued. However, this simplistic comparison does not take into account the difference in trading system and market practices unique to Japan. A mechanical comparison which does not take into account the difference in underlying factors can be misleading. Therefore, we will review the market systems and practices unique to Japan in the following pages.

AN ACCOUNTING SYSTEM THAT AFFECTS PROFITS

The accounting system of Japan is different from that of the United States in many respects. The largest difference lies in the fact that while US firms calculate their profits on a consolidated basis, their Japanese counterparts do so on a parent-only basis. While US firms use the straight line method in depreciating their fixed assets, Japanese firms follow the declining balance method. In addition, the methods of evaluating investments, pension liabilities, construction in progress, and leases, etc are different between the two countries. The difference in these accounting methods also varies from one industry group to another or from one company to another. The profit of a Japanese company calculated according to the Japanese accounting method tends to be smaller than that calculated according to that of the United States. If the market discounts such difference in accounting methods between the two countries, a higher PER to a certain degree compared with that of US stocks does not pose any problem.

The difference in accounting methods can be corrected to a certain extent. Take the method of depreciating fixed assets, for example. As the amount of depreciation charges set aside each year and the book value of depreciated assets are disclosed, the average useful life of a piece of fixed asset and depreciation charges calculated according to the straight line method can be estimated. Other items are excluded from the correction because they are either not disclosed or have little impact one way or another. As a result, the corrected forward P/E calculated on a parent-only basis of NRI-350 for the March 1993 term dropped from pre-correction 75.1 to 72.2. Corrections of PERs made at several points of time reduced the PERs by an average of about five points. Corrections made in 1992 and 1993 when depreciation charges surged on account of huge capital investment made in the second half of the 1980s reduced the multiples by eight to 10 points.

The taxation system of Japan also considerably influences earnings reported by Japanese firms. In Japan, incomes calculated for tax purposes accord, as a rule, with those reported to shareholders. Under the system, corporations can reduce their tax liabilities by compressing their earnings by taking advantage of authorised accounting gimmicks. In the United States, by contrast, earnings reported for tax purposes do not have to be the same as those reported to shareholders. Actually, US firms seem to be encouraged to inflate their reported earnings within the limits allowed by authorised accounting techniques. So, there is a good possibility that the taxation system pushes up the PERs of Japanese stocks.

A SHAREHOLDING STRUCTURE UNIQUE TO JAPAN

In addition to the difference in the accounting system, another practice which directly pushes up the PERs of Japanese stocks is cross-shareholding, a practice of holding shares of one another prevalent among many companies (see also Chapter 2). The practice helps companies secure shareholders loyal to them and allows them a large scope of discretion in the management of their corporate affairs.

Some argue that cross-shareholding pushes down earnings per share (EPS) and pushes up PER. Although it is difficult to distinguish shares held in cross-shareholding from those held for investment purposes, findings of a survey conducted by NRI suggest the possibility that the shareholding structure of Japanese firms dominated by cross-shareholding does push up their PERs.

As the recession has continued to squeeze their earnings since 1990, businesses have been shedding their assets, and shares they hold in cross-shareholding with other companies are not an exception. Some of them have gone so far as to disengage themselves from cross-shareholding altogether.

ASSET VALUE AND Q RATIO

In discussing stock prices of Japanese firms, the evaluation of their worth and assets cannot be ignored. For example, there is a concept called 'hidden (or unrealised) assets'. Many Japanese firms hold land or marketable securities worth billions of yen but recorded at their costs, and it is said that profits hidden in these assets are discounted in their management. In the case of companies with a long history behind them, they are loaded with huge sums of unrealised profits, hidden in the form of difference between the book value of their assets (particularly land) and their market value.

Until around 1990, land prices in Japan rose almost uninterrupted. Most of the old firms hold tracts of land of considerable size in urban areas. As their book value is far smaller than their market value, they carry large sums of unrealised profits in their books. The same is true of their shareholdings. As the market value of shares they have been holding for many years has risen far higher than their book value, they have generated large sums of unrealised profits. According to the latest White Paper on the economy, Japanese firms as a group held ¥452 trillion ($4.52 trillion) worth of land and ¥259 trillion ($2.59 trillion) worth of equities at the end of 1989. These compare with the nation's gross domestic product worth slightly less than ¥400 trillion ($4 trillion) reported at the end of 1989.

When unrealised profits are small, it is technically correct to ignore them, but when they are as large as those reported in 1989, something should be done to account for them in order not to mislead the market about the true worth of Japanese firms. To remedy the situation, analysts came up with the idea of evaluating the worth of Japanese firms in terms of their Q ratio, a sort of price book-value ratio (PBR) based on market price, arrived at by dividing the market capitalisation of a firm by net assets evaluated at market price.

As hidden profits are, basically, the difference between the market value and the book value of net assets, evaluation of such hidden profits is the key to the calculation of the Q ratio. According to a calculation made by Japan Stock Price Research Group, the Q ratio of Japanese firms was 0.7 in 1988. This suggests that Japanese stocks are undervalued when viewed in terms of the market value of their net assets. And this helped boost the stock prices in 1988 and 1989. Incidentally, unrealised profits from land and stock holdings as of the end of 1992 dropped to as low as ¥380 trillion ($3.8 trillion) and ¥70 trillion ($700 billion) respectively.

CONCLUSIONS

The foregoing suggests that to claim that Japanese stocks are overvalued compared with US stocks merely on the basis of PERs is misleading. However, it is also true that the high PER of Japanese stocks which have stuck on a high plateau cannot be explained away merely by the difference in accounting systems and cross-shareholding. On the other hand, evaluating the worth of a firm on the basis of unrealised profits, such as the Q ratio, which are difficult to measure is also problematic.

In the next section, we will therefore review the process of formation of stock prices in Japan and changes that have occurred in this process by applying a dividend discount model to Japanese stocks.

Structure of Japanese stock prices seen from the standpoint of a dividend discount model

Dividend discount models provide important clues to determining fair prices for Japanese stocks. By substituting a stock price in the dividend discount model, a discount rate incorporated into the stock price can be computed. The discount rate thus computed is an expected rate of return which balances the current price of a stock and the projected growth rate of the company.

In using the dividend discount model, the question of how the growth in dividends and changes in the payout ratio that will occur in the future are assumed is important. If these assumptions are changed, not only will the results change but they could also mislead the reading of stock prices. Various assumptions are possible, but in this analysis, it is assumed (1) that profits will grow in two stages, (2) that during the first stage, profits will grow for five consecutive years with the ratio projected by NRI analysts, (3) that during the second stage, profit will grow at a rate of internal growth, and (4) that for the payout ratio, the average of the past five years will not change. The analysis covered NRI-350 firms, and collective data computed from those of individual firms are used to represent the market. The analysts covered only the NRI-350 firms, and excluded financial service companies, because the process of formation of their stock prices, being not always the same as that of other industry groups, may distort the overall picture. In addition, as analysts' five year projections are available only from September 1987, a single stage model built on the basis of internal growth rate was used for the periods prior to that month.

Actual stock prices and other data effective at that point in time were factored into the dividend discount model thus established to calculate the discount rate inherent in stock prices. As the discount rate represents an expected rate of return based on current earnings forecast and stock prices, the higher the rate of interest, the higher the discount rate rises, or vice versa. So, we estimated an expected rate of excess return by deducting long term rates from the discount rate to see how factors unique to the stock market will change. In the sense that an expected rate of return is composed of a risk-free rate and a risk premium, the expected rate of excess return corresponds to risk premium.

There are several characteristics in the pattern of change in risk premium (Fig. 11.3). Prior to 1980, the risk premium kept moving up and down between a high of 1.68 per cent (December 1977) and a low of minus 1.62 per cent (September 1974). Long term rates also moved up and down during the same period. However, the discount rate stayed relatively steady between 8 per cent and 9 per cent. In the first half of the 1980s, the risk premium increased steadily from 0 per cent to 1 per cent, hitting a low of minus 1.04 per cent in March 1980 and a high of 1.25 per cent in December 1984. During the same period, interest rates fell at a pace faster than the risk premium, and the expected rate of return was on the decline. In the second half of the 1980s, the risk premium held steady between a high of 0.80 per cent (March 1986) and 1.73 per cent (September 1989), while interest rates continued to fall during the period from 1985 to 1987 and then steadied in the remaining years to 1990. After 1990, the risk premium dropped sharply and hovered below 0 per cent. Interest rates declined consistently after briefly rising sharply early in 1990, and the expected rate of return declined.

One development of particular interest was the fact that despite the steep rises in stock prices during the bubble years of the second half of the 1980s, both risk premiums and expected rate of return have remained steady. As the discount rate derived from the model is calculated in such a way as to make projected rate of growth of a company match the current price of its stock, the stability of the discount rate observed during this period suggests that the market expected the rate of growth of the earnings of the company to be high enough to justify the high price of its stock. In other words, many market participants were optimistic about the future of the market, and this optimism has supported the high stock prices.

Since 1990, however, the discount rate has continued to decline, although the premium rate has remained steady. As the economy was bogged down in a recession in this period, projected corporate earnings declined continuously. Despite the fall in stock prices, the discount rate also declined, and this means that the rate of fall in stock prices was smaller than that of projected profits. As the negative risk premium means that the expected rate of return on stock investment was lower than long term rates then prevailing, this is unthinkable. In fact, in the 1980s, when the risk premium turned negative, it was corrected within a short period. From this, it may be concluded that stocks were overvalued relative to their projected rate of return.

Stock market players

Main players who invest their funds in Japanese stocks on the stock market of Japan are (1) individual and corporate investors who invest their own money, (2) institutional investors who run the trusted money, such as investment trusts, life insurance, postal savings and postal insurance, publicly run and private pension funds, funds of agricultural thrifts, *tokkin* trust funds and fund trusts, and (3) foreign investors.

PRIVATE INVESTORS

The clout wielded by private investors in the stock market has diminished considerably since the second half of the 1980s. More specifically, first, as explained in Chapter 2, their shareholdings as a percentage of the total shares outstanding on the market have decreased, and second, their share in the turnover of the stock market has also declined. While the number of shares held by private investors has not decreased, those held by financial institutions and business corporations have increased markedly, with the result that the ratio of private holdings to the total number of shares outstanding on the market dropped from 69.1 per cent in fiscal 1949 to 23.9 per cent in fiscal 1992. This compares with the 45.8 per cent share of private investors in the United States (FRB, *Flow of Funds*, 1993). The shrinking share of private investors in Japan is attributable to the fact that Japanese firms have relied heavily on bank borrowing since the war, that individuals have lacked understanding of the role played by the stock market, and that a huge number of shares have been locked up in corporate vaults through cross-shareholding. More recently, however, the decline in the number of private shareholders has been arrested thanks to the incentives – stock splits and the lowering of trading units – provided to private investors.

CORPORATE INVESTORS

It is said that the practice of cross-shareholding between a firm and its main bank and among business firms has triggered a sharp increase in corporate investment in shares. According to a survey of distribution of share ownership, the ratio of shares held by financial institutions (excluding investment trusts) jumped from 9.9 per cent in fiscal 1949 to 41.3 per cent in fiscal 1992. The ratio of shareholdings of business corporations also increased sharply to 24.4 per cent in fiscal 1992. However, the structure of cross-shareholding has begun to change in recent years, because as the dividend yields have fallen below 1 per cent, and their holders have suffered huge evaluation losses on account of the recent collapse of stock prices, cross-shareholding no longer makes economic sense. With corporations relying less and less on bank borrowing, cross-shareholding between banks and their corporate clients is expected to go out of fashion. And the shares liquidated by these banks and corporations are expected to be taken up by individual investors and pension funds.

In addition, the number of shares bought by business corporations for *Zaitech* purposes, or managing surplus cash, during the bubble years has been decreasing since the stock market collapse in 1990.

INVESTMENT TRUSTS

Assets of an investment trust are managed by an investment trust management company and administered by a trust bank. Investment trusts are divided into two categories: those of the unit type which do not accept additional investment from subscribers once established, and those of the open-end type which accept additional investment. They are also divided into bond investment trusts which do not invest their assets in equities and those that incorporate equities in their portfolios.

Net assets of stock investment trusts as a group multiplied more than 10 times thanks to sharp rises in stock price during the speculative bubble years in the second half of the 1980s, from ¥4 trillion ($40 billion) at the end of 1980 to ¥45.5 trillion ($455 billion) at the end of 1989. However, owing to sharp falls in their asset values in the wake of the bursting of the stock market bubble early in 1990, massive cancellations of contracts immediately after the expiration of the closed period, and sharp decreases in the launching of new investment trusts for lack of investor demand, their net assets contracted sharply to about ¥22 trillion ($220 billion) as of April 1994. It is to be noted, however, that stock investment trusts do not invest 100 per cent of their funds in equities, and their exposure to equities stood at about ¥12 trillion ($120 billion). Certificates of investment trusts can be purchased over the counter of securities companies or through monthly deductions from salaries (such as private annuity plans). Their assets are invested in diverse forms, such as the index type, the sector-specific type, the blue chip type, the growth stock type, and the small capitalisation type.

Compared with other institutional investor groups of Japan, investment trusts have the characteristics (1) that they are devoted exclusively to pure investment, (2) that the investment period they offer is, in effect, relatively short, (3) that the rate of turnover of their investment is high, and (4) that the published value of their portfolio assets is based on market prices.

Investment trusts are also large futures traders. It was in the second half of 1990 that investment trusts began trading in futures in earnest. Their futures position reached a peak in August 1992 and accounted for 12.5 per cent of the outstanding Nikkei 225 futures contracts. It is believed that they have consistently been net buyers of the Nikkei 225 futures commitments since 1990.

POSTAL SAVINGS AND POSTAL INSURANCE

Since FY 1989, part of the postal savings collected by the nation's post offices has been channelled through the Postal Insurance Welfare Corporation to, and managed by, trust banks under *shiteitan* trust account (independently run designated money trust). Under the *shiteitan* trust account, the trust banks are authorised to invest up to 30 per cent of the funds in stocks. In FY 1992, a new *shiteitan* trust account was launched for which the restrictions on the amount of funds that can be invested in stocks were lifted.

Likewise, part of the funds post offices raise through the sale of postal life insurance policies has been channelled through the Postal Insurance Welfare Corporation to, and managed by, trust banks, which are authorised to invest up to 80 per cent of the funds in Japanese equities (see also Chapter 2 and Chapter 7).

LIFE INSURANCE

In FY 1991, life insurance companies held 13.2 per cent of the shares then outstanding on the market, the largest share for a single sector. Funds raised through the sale of life insurance policies are normally invested through a commingled account called 'general account' which includes funds provided by other sources such as pension funds. By their very nature, only up to 30 per cent of these funds are authorised to be invested in Japanese equities. Moreover, as the rate of return on the insurance account is computed on the basis of interest distribution incomes and realised gains or losses, major thrusts of investment of its funds tend to be directed towards investments yielding greater realised incomes. The total hidden (unrealised) gains from the stock holdings of the nation's eight largest insurance companies dropped from about ¥37 trillion ($370 billion) at the end of fiscal 1988 (March 1989) to about ¥10 trillion ($100 billion) owing to the stock market collapse in 1990 and profit taking (to increase realised gains by liquidating appreciated stocks). Meanwhile, the regulators authorised life insurance companies to establish a special account for investing the proceeds of variable life insurance policies launched recently (See Chapter 7 for details).

PUBLIC AND PRIVATE PENSION FUNDS

Publicly run pension funds include the national pension (the basic pension), the employees' welfare pension insurance (covering salaried workers), and the mutual aid pension (covering public service personnel). Part of the funds of the national pension and the employees' welfare pension insurance is channelled through the Pension Welfare Corporation to, and managed by, trust banks and life insurance companies.

Private pension funds include the employees' welfare pension funds and eligible retirement annuities (eligible for deductions from taxable income). Particularly, the employees' welfare pension funds are expected to grow rapidly in coming years and will grow into a major player in the securities market. All of these private pension funds are authorised to invest up to 30 per cent of their assets in Japanese equities, but the regulators are moving to ease the restrictions. Until recently, trust banks and life insurance companies had a monopoly over the management of these funds, but since 1989, investment advisory service companies are authorised to manage their 'new money' (premiums received after 1989). Meanwhile, it has been decided to abolish the distinction between 'old' and 'new' moneys in due course. As the pension fund market will be deregulated at a rapid pace in coming months, competition among investment advisory service companies including those from other countries is about to heat up, and their management style is likely to undergo a sweeping change from one tilted towards the balanced type to one inclined to embrace more imaginative ideas.

TOKKIN TRUST FUNDS AND FUND TRUSTS

Tokkin trust funds (a specified money trust managed by a trust bank in accordance with instructions given by the investor) and fund trusts were authorised in December 1980 by virtue of an amendment to the tax laws. Advantages offered by *tokkin* trust funds and fund trusts may be summed up as follows:

1 As the shares acquired under the account of *tokkin* trust funds are allowed to be treated separately from those previously acquired at different book values, they can be traded without regard to the hidden profits of previously acquired shares.

2 As investment incomes accrue nominally to the trust bank, its investor can trade shares without regard to the impact they may have on relationships with other companies.

3 Investment incomes, together with capital gains, can be treated as income gains of the trust.

Investment of assets under a *tokkin* account can be made by the management company at its own discretion or in compliance with instructions given by an investment advisory service company. Most of the institutional investors (banks and life insurance companies) invest the assets of the account on their own, while business corporations and small to medium-size financial institutions rely on the advice of investment advisory service companies.

These funds settle their accounts on a yearly basis. Their managers use the time deposit rates of commercial banks as a benchmark and strive to generate yields certain basis points higher than the time deposit rates then prevailing. Therefore, their trading tends to be aimed for a short term horizon.

Since March 1988, business corporations have been given a choice between the cost method and the method of stating the lower of cost or market for the purpose of accounting their assets in a *tokkin* or fund trust account, with the result that the number of shares they have acquired under these accounts has increased sharply, and the combined total value of shares they held under these accounts increased four-fold in a matter of four short years, from ¥10.7 trillion ($107 billion) at the end of March 1986 to ¥43 trillion ($430 billion) in December 1989. About 30–40 per cent of these funds were invested in equities. However, as stock prices continued to plunge for several years from early 1990, their performance soured sharply, with the result that the outstanding balance of *tokkin* trust funds and fund trusts decreased sharply by as much as ¥19 trillion ($190 billion), from ¥43 trillion ($430 billion) in December 1989 to ¥24 trillion ($240 billion) in March 1994. Worse yet, as these figures are based on their book value, their market value has fallen far more (see also Chapter 7).

FOREIGN INVESTORS

The turnover rate of Japanese shares traded by foreign investors during the three years from 1989 to 1991 averaged at a relatively high 96 per cent, and the shares traded by foreign investors during the same three years as a percentage of the total turnover of the Tokyo Stock Exchange rose to 8.8 per cent. Except for isolated cases involving oil stocks, the great bulk of Japanese shares they have traded have been purely for portfolio investment purposes.

As their investment is more value-oriented than Japanese institutional investors, issues foreign investors pick have often become price leaders. And many of them are fund managers and draw their funds mostly from foreign pension funds and investment trusts.

When Japanese stock prices surged in the second half of the 1980s, foreign investors were consistently bearish on Japanese stocks and net sold as much as ¥17.6 trillion ($176 billion) during the seven years from 1984 to 1990. However, when Japanese stock prices tumbled, they turned into net buyers from the end of 1990. In FY 1993, Japanese business corporations net sold ¥2.46 trillion ($24.6 billion) worth of equities, far exceeding the past high of about ¥1 trillion ($10 billion) reached in fiscal 1991, and individual investors also net sold ¥1.4 trillion ($14 billion) worth of their share holdings. By contrast, foreign investors net bought ¥4.83 trillion ($48.3 billion) worth of shares in fiscal 1993, virtually taking up the shares liquidated by Japanese corporate and individual investors.

PART IV Reforms

CHAPTER 12
Financial system reforms

Liberalisation and internationalisation of the market

As described in Chapter 1, the Securities and Exchange Law which defined the institutional framework of the securities market of Japan after World War II was drawn up on the model of the US Securities Act of 1933 and Securities Exchange Act of 1934. Although it apparently adopted many systems – the disclosure requirements and self-regulation of the market by stock exchanges and securities dealers associations, etc – which are similar to those of the United States, it may hardly be said that a free and efficient market, a given underlying the US securities market system, took root in Japan. Rather, as betrayed by restrictive practices – such as the licensing system introduced in 1965 which virtually precluded the entry of new participants into the broker–dealership business, the (corporate bond offering) eligibility standards, and restrictions of the offering of new shares, etc – exclusive and stiflingly stringent regulation became a permanent fixture, restraining the participants from engaging in free competition.

Since the 1970s, however, the market environment has undergone profound changes. Helped by the liberalisation of capital transactions, foreign investment in Japanese securities expanded, a massive issuance of government bonds helped create the government bond trading market, interest rates were liberalised in stages, the world's financial and capital markets have become increasingly integrated, and securitisation of financial assets spread. And under these changes, the regulators have come under growing pressure to overhaul the financial system.

Particularly, since the Japan–US Yen/Dollar Committee made public its recommendations, 'Steps to be Taken for Liberalisation and Internationalisation', the government came up with a series of regulatory reform measures. They covered wide-ranging areas, but when we focus on capital market issues, they may be largely divided into (1) the creation of markets for new products including financial derivatives, (2) the opening of the securities market to international competition including membership of stock exchanges to foreign securities companies, and (3) a revision of the system imposing uniform rules such as the eligibility standards.

THE CREATION OF MARKETS FOR NEW PRODUCTS

Thanks to this measure, the markets for financial derivatives (futures and options) have expanded dramatically. In October 1985, the Tokyo Stock Exchange (TSE) started trading in government bond futures, and by 1990, major futures and options products had made their debut (see Chapter 10 and Chapter 11). Their trading has since caught on rapidly among institutional investors. Meanwhile, there has emerged a body of opinion blaming the excessive trading in stock index futures for the collapse of the stock market and the confusion of the cash stock market that occurred in and after 1990. In addition to financial derivatives, the Ministry of Finance (MOF) authorised in June 1987 the private placement of large denomination bond issues worth more than ¥2 billion ($20 million at the rate of ¥100 to the dollar), and liberalised the issuance of commercial paper on the domestic market. Moreover, the MOF sought to diversify vehicles for debt financing by allowing diversity of maturities of corporate bonds and by lifting the ban on the issuance of variable rate notes.

INTERNATIONALISATION

Since the opening of membership of the TSE to foreign firms, the number of foreign securities companies opening offices in Tokyo has increased sharply. Following the enactment of the Law Concerning Foreign Securities Firms in 1971, they have technically been allowed to engage in the securities business in Japan, but only a smattering of them (10) had opened their branches in Tokyo by the end of 1984. However, after the Japanese government authorised European universal banking firms to engage in the securities business through their less than 50 per cent owned overseas affiliates, and thanks to mounting foreign interest in the Tokyo market, a spate of foreign securities companies flocked to Tokyo, and by the end of June 1990, their number had risen to 52. Meanwhile, the policy of the Japanese stock exchanges barring foreign securities firms was taken up by the Japan–US Yen/Dollar Committee and came under fire from many countries. In response, the Tokyo Stock Exchange, for the first time in its history, granted seats to six foreign securities companies in November 1985, and its foreign membership increased to 25 by the end of 1990. Ironically enough, however, as stock prices and stock market turnover have remained depressed after the bursting of the speculative bubble, a number of foreign securities firms have returned their membership, while others have closed their branches in Japan.

REVISION OF UNIFORM RULES

Another way of saying this is to give full play to the market mechanism. Until recently, there were a number of regulatory juggernauts steamrollering with uniform standards what could be left to the discretion of investors to exercise at their own risk, such as the eligibility standards restricting the issuance of corporate bonds, administrative rules curtailing the issuance of new shares, and official guidelines imposing ceilings on holding different kinds of securities by institutional investors. Towards the second half of the 1980s, however, the government began to ease its regulatory reins. Among other things, the Bond Flotation Committee composed of underwriting securities companies decided to phase out the eligibility standards (which require bond offering companies to have a certain amount of net assets and a certain payout ratio) and introduce a system of allowing corporate borrowers with a certain minimum credit rating to offer debt securities on the market.

Revision of the system of segregating commercial banking from investment banking

In parallel with these measures for the liberalisation and internationalisation of the financial markets, debates over the system of segregating commercial banking from investment banking went on in earnest. On the model of the system of the United States, the Securities and Exchange Law of Japan banned, in principle, banking and other financial institutions from engaging in securities business. However, as the government had issued massive amounts of bonds, banks' dealing in government bonds increased, while securities companies began to sell medium-term government securities funds, a Japanese version of Money Market Mutual Funds (MMMF), which, in effect, competed with bank deposits. And the demand of banks calling for a revision of the system segregating commercial banking from investment banking became increasingly vocal from the beginning of the 1980s. Meanwhile, Japanese banks established in foreign countries locally incorporated subsidiaries through which they engaged in securities business, and this gave an added fillip to the debate.

The segregation of commercial banking and investment banking was a system established by the Securities and Exchange Law (Article 65), but the institution which started official debate over the revision of the system was not the Securities and Exchange Council, an advisory body to the Minister of Finance dealing in matters that are under the jurisdiction of the Securities Bureau, but the Financial System Research Council, a body dealing in matters that are under the jurisdiction of the Banking Bureau. In September 1989, the Financial System Research Council appointed a panel on financial systems to look into the relevance of the existing system of compartmentalising the money lending business into long and short term credits and the system of segregating commercial banking from trust banking. In its final report submitted in December 1987, the panel indicated the necessity for a sweeping overhaul of the financial system, including the dismantling of the system of segregating commercial banking from investment banking. In response, the Second Subcommittee of the Financial System Research Council, appointed in February 1988, debated the advisability of allowing banking institutions to enter into other financial service markets. Meanwhile, the Securities and Exchange Council, which had not started public debate on the matter until then, concerned that the policy debate had been dominated by the banking industry, started in September 1989 a debate on problems which the proposed entry of banking institutions into the securities business was likely to pose to the securities industry.

Both the Financial System Research Council and the Securities and Exchange Council examined from various angles measures to be taken to improve the efficiency and convenience of the financial system, effects which the entry of different financial service groups into one another's markets were likely to have on promoting competition, the compatibility of Japan's market systems and practices with those of other major countries, and abuses which the combination of commercial and investment banking may give rise to. After lengthy debates, these two advisory bodies released their final reports in May and June 1991, respectively. And both of them were united in their view that while it remained necessary to ensure the protection of investors and depositors by regulating financial service institutions to a certain degree, steps should be taken to revitalise the banking and securities markets by introducing the principles of competition – such as the lowering of the existing barriers blocking the entry of one financial service group into the markets of other groups. In response, the MOF started drawing up amendment bills, and in June 1992 the Parliament passed a total of 16 financial system reform bills which included amendments to the Banking Law and the Securities and Exchange Law and the repeal of other related laws.

Under the reform laws, banks, trust banks, and securities companies are authorised to participate in one another's markets through service-specific subsidiaries. More specifically, the MOF granted licenses for engaging in securities, banking or trust banking business to banks, trust banks, and securities companies, as the case may be, through purpose-specific subsidiaries 100 per cent owned by them. In the course of the debate, the ideas of adopting a universal banking system of the German type and the system of bank holding company of the US type were considered, but they were rejected. In the ensuing months, Cabinet orders and Ministerial ordinances were drawn up, laying down rules and regulations which called for the establishment of a so-called 'fire wall' to shield subsidiaries from the influence of their parent banks or securities companies and to define in great detail the scope of services the subsidiaries of different groups could provide. These rules and regulations having been instituted, the reform laws were enacted in April 1993.

Entry of new participants into the securities markets and their impacts

The authorisation of securities subsidiaries of banking institutions granted under the financial system reform laws has touched off a dramatic change in the securities market system since the market shifted from the registration system to a licensing system following the securities market crash in 1965 – in that it marked the beginning of an end to the vertically integrated compartmentalisation of financial services that had reigned over the financial markets of Japan since World War II. With the opening of securities subsidiaries of Industrial Bank of Japan (IBJ), Japan Long Term Credit Bank, and the Central Bank for Agriculture and Forestry (Norinchukin Bank) for business in July 1993, banks' securities business started in earnest. Two months later, they were followed by Mitsubishi Trust and Banking Corp and Sumitomo Trust and Banking Co, Ltd. Pursuant to the licensing policy of the MOF, these subsidiaries were wholly owned by their parent banks, and their scope of business was restricted to narrowly defined areas.

The supplementary provisions of the financial system reform laws authorise the MOF to bar these securities subsidiaries of the banks 'for the time being' from engaging in stock brokerage business. This reflects the concern of the regulators that as the banks already hold large chunks of shares of their corporate clients, their entry into stock brokerage business could seriously erode the revenue bases of small to medium-size securities companies. In addition to such statutory restrictions, the MOF announced its policy not to allow banks' securities subsidiaries to engage in the business of underwriting stock issues or dealing in shares and stock index futures.

Meanwhile, an illegal stock parking scandal which drove Cosmo Securities to the brink of insolvency came to light in August 1993, and Daiwa Bank in effect took over Cosmo Securities as its subsidiary by bailing it out in the form of a private placement of its new shares. The bail-out was treated as an exceptional case authorised for the purpose of maintaining order in the financial markets. Cosmo Securities survived the crisis as a listed company, not as a wholly owned subsidiary of Daiwa Bank, and was allowed to continue providing a full range of securities services as before. (A similar rescue was made for Nippon Trust Bank Ltd by Mitsubishi Bank in November 1994.)

As their scale of operation is not large, and as they are allowed only a limited scope of operation, banks' securities subsidiaries have posed no serious threat to the existing securities companies, at least not yet. However, some of them have already won the lead managership underwriting corporate straight bond issues and have thus contributed, though in a limited way, to spurring competition in the securities market and improving the quality of financial services.

The financial system reforms have already had certain positive impacts on the activities of Japanese banking institutions and securities companies, domestic as well as overseas. One of them is a planned phase-out of what is known as the Three Bureau Administrative Guidance jointly enforced by the Banking Bureau, the Securities Bureau, and the International Finance Bureau of the MOF since August 1975. The Three Bureau Administrative Guidance gives priority to overseas subsidiaries of Japanese securities companies over overseas securities subsidiaries of Japanese banks in acting as lead manager of a debt issue offered or placed by a Japanese firm on an overseas market when they are in direct competition with each other. And these three Bureaux justified their decision by citing the spirit of the Securities and Exchange Law (Article 65) which provides for the segregation of commercial banking and investment banking. However, once the reciprocal entry of one another's markets had taken effect on the domestic market, restricting banks from underwriting bond issues on overseas markets no longer made any sense, so it was decided to phase out the Three Bureau Administrative Guidance gradually by March 1998. In ensuing months, some of the overseas securities subsidiaries of Japanese banks have won the lead managership of underwriting straight Eurobond issues of Japanese firms offered on overseas markets.

The advent of securities subsidiaries of banking institutions has thus brought on certain changes in the securities market of Japan. However, the process of such change had exhibited characteristics unique to Japan. In the United Kingdom and the United States, also, their governments pursued deregulation of their securities markets and financial system reforms from the second half of the 1970s, but their regulators contented themselves with limiting their role to creating an institutional framework, and the drastic structural changes that occurred in these markets were the result of free competition waged by diverse players of their own volition. A case in point is the UK's Big Bang of 27 October 1986. With the enforcement of Big Bang, the trading floor of the Stock Exchange was abolished altogether, the system of market-making was introduced, membership of the Stock Exchange was opened to all interested parties, the brokerage commission was liberalised at a stroke, and most of the securities brokers were absorbed into British merchant banks, securities companies and banking institutions of the United States and Continental countries – thus completely changing the landscape of the securities industry. By contrast, the activities of Japanese banking institutions and securities companies are strictly controlled by the MOF pursuant to a labyrinthine web of laws, regulations, and administrative guidance. As the regulators ostensibly sought to reform the financial system while maintaining the basic regulatory framework aimed at protecting the post-war banking system, reform measures they have taken had necessarily to be measured ones.

For example, with a view to averting confusion of the market that could be caused by allowing too many banks to establish their securities subsidiaries all at once, the MOF put off the licensing of commercial banks' securities subsidiaries till the second half of 1994, and the amounts of capitalisation of securities subsidiaries that the MOF did license were more or less the same, reflecting the MOF's preference for producing no winners or losers. What is more, the various restrictions imposed on their securities subsidiaries by virtue of a position paper 'Guidelines for the Implementation of the Financial System Reforms' made public by the MOF in December 1992, which further reinforced the statutory regulation banning the securities subsidiaries from engaging in stock broking, have left the banking institutions with little elbow room for strategic manoeuvring. Some market watchers commented that while such a cautious approach may prove to be effective in averting confusion of the market (meaning possible bankruptcy of certain brokerage firms which are not equipped with sufficient resources to survive the overheated competition these securities subsidiaries might bring), it could run counter to the very ideal of the reform, i.e. promotion of the convenience and efficiency of the securities market and international compatibility.

Stock market scandals and the financial system reforms

The major thrust of the financial system reforms surveyed in the foregoing has primarily been directed towards gearing up the securities market of Japan for the worldwide current of liberalisation and internationalisation of the capital markets, including the overhaul of the system of segregation of commercial banking and investment banking. However, the securities market must be a free, internationally compatible, and fair market. Indeed, it may be said that fairness of trading is the most basic requirement a securities market has to deliver in order to protect investors.

The second half of the 1980s was not exactly barren of reforms. For example, a provision making insider trading a criminal offence was instituted in May 1988. Another provision requiring investors who have acquired a large number of shares – 5 per cent or more of the outstanding shares – in a company to report to the Minister of Finance was introduced in June 1990, and the tender offer (or takeover bid (TOB)) system was also revised. However, only a few investors have been convicted of insider trading during the six years that followed the institution of the provision. And no tender offer, to speak of, has been made. Therefore, one cannot escape the suspicion that these reform measures have not done much to enhance the fairness of the securities market of Japan.

Come 1991, a series of irregularities involving securities companies – unfair compensation of favoured customers by securities companies for their trading losses, shady deals with known crime syndicates, and overzealous solicitations of customers for the purchase of selected equity issues – came to light, poignantly reminding the investing public of the unfairness and lack of transparency of the securities market, and the lack of sense of responsibility of investors for their own investment decisions. In response to a mounting chorus of popular demand for the prevention of stock market scandals, provisions banning compensation for investment losses and acceptance of discretionary investment accounts by securities brokers were instituted in the Securities and Exchange Law in September 1991. In May the next year, the Securities and Exchange Law was amended to establish the Securities and Exchange Surveillance Commission, a new watchdog of the securities market, and delegate certain regulatory power to self-regulatory organisations such as stock exchanges and securities dealers associations. Additional provisions were also instituted to replace the administrative circular notices issued by regulators with formal orders and regulations based on specific statutory provisions.

The Securities and Exchange Surveillance Commission launched in July 1992 was technically attached to the MOF, but unlike other bureaux of the Ministry, the Commission is a collegiate body composed of the chairman and two commissioners who are appointed by the Minister of Finance with the approval of both chambers of the Parliament and is empowered to exercise its authority independently from the Minister of Finance. And by picking a former public prosecutor as its chairman, the Minister sought to impress the independence of the Commission on the public. In addition to monitoring the day-to-day trading activities of the securities companies and banks' securities subsidiaries, the Commission is charged with the responsibility for investigating illegal securities trading, bringing charges against violators of the Securities and Exchange Law and related rules and regulations, and recommending administrative disciplinary actions or policy measures to the Minister.

The Surveillance Commission is often called the Japanese version of, and compared with, the Securities and Exchange Commission (SEC) of the United States. However, compared with the SEC which performs wide-ranging regulatory functions – registration of broker–dealers and new security issues, and writing rules and regulations of the securities market – the roles played by the Surveillance Commission and the number of its staffers are limited. This is not to say that its function and power are inadequate. Rather, as far as its surveillance of the securities market and its power to prosecute offenders are concerned, it has more powerful authority than the SEC.

Some have commented that the securities companies have become so used to relying on regulatory controls that they have developed a culture impervious to free competition, and the Securities and Exchange Council drew up in January 1992 a report urging the government to take steps spurring competition in the securities market. This has prompted the regulators to relax the licensing standards for securities companies and investment trust management companies and liberalise part of the stock brokerage commission. Until then, only those investment trust management companies affiliated with Japanese securities companies and foreign-affiliated investment trust companies had been licensed to launch and manage investment trusts. Since April 1992, however, companies established by investment advisory service companies which are authorised to handle discretionary investment accounts have been licensed for managing investment trusts. In October 1993, investment advisory service subsidiaries of four commercial banks and the Central Bank for Agriculture and Forestry established investment advisory service companies. In the area of stock brokerage commission, the MOF decided to liberalise it in stages, and in April 1994, brokerage commission on large trades involving ¥1 billion or more was unfixed for the difference (the trading value and ¥1 billion).

In fairness, it must be recognised that since the Japan–US Yen/Dollar Committee urged the Japanese government to liberalise and internationalise its financial markets in May 1984, Japan has made headway – to a point where it has reaffirmed its commitment to achieving the fairness of its securities market. However, even today several years after the revelation of stock market scandals, the MOF is still reportedly meddling in the choice of top executives of self-regulation organisations and individual securities companies – suggesting that the penchant of the regulators for directly controlling the affairs of the securities market down to its details has not changed. Whether the Japanese government can – indeed, will – establish a regulatory system genuinely respecting the independence of the market bears a close watch in coming years.

CHAPTER 13

Looking towards the twenty-first century

Costs of gradualism

As seen in Chapter 1, the Japanese economy, buoyed by sustained robust growth and increases in cross-border capital transactions, has come under mounting pressure to change its financial system, from the one which has been based on the policy-dictated allocation of funds since World War II to one which is driven mainly by market forces. Although the change gathered pace somewhat after the Japan–US Yen/Dollar Committee made public in 1984 its recommendations urging the Japanese government to take steps to liberalise and internationalise the financial markets of Japan, the steps it has taken have been marked by a gradualist approach. True, the regulators have eased their stance on the segregation of commercial and investment banking (see Chapter 12), and banks and securities companies have entered into one another's markets through their subsidiaries, but the activities of these new entrants are restricted to narrowly defined areas ostensibly to cushion their jolting impacts on the existing players. And the initial restrictions are supposed to be reviewed once every two to three years. For all the talk of liberalisation and deregulation, the gradualist adjustments are still largely dominated by the policy thinking of the regulators.

In areas other than those touched on in the foregoing chapters, there are signs galore indicating overzealous gradualist government intervention in the market. Given the thrust of liberalisation efforts, government intervention should be limited to maintaining the consistency of reform measures, but the regulators are preoccupied with sustaining the continuity of the existing institutional interests and have failed to take transitory measures designed to make the market system congruous with developing a freer market beneficial to its users. The net effect of such gradualist interventionism has been disorganised reform. In the following pages, we will examine some of the victims of this gradualist approach.

DIVERSIFICATION OF SECURITIES

The Securities and Exchange Law defines securities by listing their specific categories and thus precludes the development of innovative products. Particularly, mortgage-backed securities (MBS) and asset-backed securities (ABS), which emerged in the United States in the course of securitisation of financial assets, were not recognised as a security – and therefore, have not been traded in Japan. From 1989, the Securities and Exchange Council studied measures for streamlining the securities-related laws to accommodate the securitisation of financial assets. Although an amendment to the Securities and Exchange Law enacted on the recommendations of the Council did add commercial paper and mortgage-backed investment trusts to its list of securities, the restrictive approach of listing specific categories of securities was left intact, making it necessary to promulgate a new Cabinet order and a Ministerial ordinance whenever a new product is developed to include it in the list of the Securities and Exchange Law. Furthermore, owing to the turf battle among the Ministries and government agencies, a new law has to be enacted to give legal status to such products as commodity fund shares and lease-backed and real estate-backed certificates, with the result that their trading on the market has been strictly limited (because the Securities and Exchange Law is not applicable to them). Naturally, investors who have access to such products are limited, and their markets have become stunted.

The problem is not confined to regulation and goes even deeper. For example, the procedure for issuing preferred stocks was simplified by virtue of an amendment to the Commercial Code in 1990. As of September 1994, however, only one bank among the listed companies has issued preferred stocks and only a few of them have actually amended their articles of incorporation authorising them to issue preferred stocks. Japanese firms are supposed to be wary of increasing the number of voting shares. Why are they shy of issuing preferred stocks which do not carry voting rights? Some argue that it is because Japanese firms are worried that their preferred shares may not command a good price on the market. But the validity of their argument is doubtful, and there is no demonstrable evidence to support it. Investors' attitude is also to be blamed for it; there is not much preference among them for a greater variety of investment vehicles. A similar situation existed with respect to corporate bonds. Bond issuing companies had long been bound by a straitjacket of regulation, that is until the ceiling on the amount of debt securities they could issue was removed, the role of the trustee company was clearly defined, and the eligibility standards were lowered by virtue of an amendment to the Corporate Bond Law enacted in 1993. The regulation that limited the variety of maturities has been relaxed, but the domestic bond new issue market has not yet shown signs of life because many restrictive regulations (such as the bond registration system) still remain unchanged, with the result that many Japanese firms go to the Euro market to offer their debt securities.

DIVERSIFICATION OF TRADING METHODS

Along with the broadening of the definition of securities, the amended Securities and Exchange Law has also defined private placement of debt securities for the first time. More specifically, when a bond issue is intended for private placement with eligible institutional investors or a small number (less than 50) of investors, the issuer is not required to register the issuance of such bonds. In form, the former is akin to Rule 144a of the SEC, but few have taken advantage of this method of private placement in Japan.

In 1994, stock companies were authorised to repurchase their shares outstanding on the market by virtue of an amendment to the Commercial Code. Thanks to this amendment, corporations can acquire their own outstanding shares for the purpose of retiring them as long as they can finance such repurchases with their profits distributable as dividends, and they can hold such repurchased shares for a certain period when they are intended for transfer to their employees (employee stock ownership plans). Apparently, this was a measure to help corporations soak up the large number of shares they had to issue in conversion of the convertible or warrant bonds they had issued during the bubble years. However, under the existing tax laws, shareholders who do not sell their holdings in response to a repurchase offer of the company are subject to a tax on the increase of book value per share as dividend. Deterred by this problem, no company has so far taken the plunge and repurchased its outstanding shares.

It is tempting to dismiss the lack of such trading as marginal, but the need to diversify trading techniques, such as trading in a basket of listed shares, has been growing. However, the existing rules and systems of trading and the taxation system are impeding the diversification of trading methods. While the capital markets across the industrial world are being increasingly integrated and are fiercely vying for business, Japan alone, oblivious to the shifting economic winds outside, has been going about tinkering with the domestic market to preserve its order, making it all the more inaccessible and unwieldy.

Outlook for the financial markets in the remaining years to 2000

There has arisen not just from the financial markets but also from many other sectors of the economy a chorus of demand for deregulation as a lever to help them climb out of the prolonged recession that visited Japan in the aftermath of the bursting of the economic bubble. In response, a consensus has emerged among the leaders in and out of the government that the economy has to be deregulated, but it ends on general principles, and does not extend to specifics. Meanwhile, the gradualist approach – with which the regulators act as a mediator adjusting conflicting interests of different groups – still grinds on, and there is not even a hint of genuine liberalisation.

If the financial markets of Japan are left to their own devices, they are bound to encounter knotty problems down the road. Of particular importance are the following three.

THE GREYING POPULATION AND AN EXPANDING PENSION MARKET

The proportion of elderly people in Japan will rise rapidly during the next 20 years. According to an estimate made by the Ministry of Health and Welfare in 1992, given the prospects for continuing improvement of life expectancy and a decline in birth rate (owing to the growing tendency of late marriage among women and increases in the ratio of single women, the birth rate is expected to hover around 1.5–1.8), the ratio of those aged 65 and older will increase from 17.33 per cent in 1990 to 25.13 per cent in 2000 to 34.13 per cent in 2010 and to as high as 43.20 per cent in 2020.

While it obviously is necessary to provide against the growing aged population, the present public pension system is funded not with premiums paid by the current beneficiaries but with those paid by the present working population. (It is to be noted that the public pension funds have a surplus of ¥84 trillion at the last counting.) Therefore, the present working population is sharing a very heavy burden of pension insurance. Computed on the basis of the estimate of the Health and Welfare Ministry cited above, when the public pension fund starts paying benefits at the age of 60, the ratio of insurance premium to the average worker's income will increase

Table 13.1 Japan's pensions and the balance of their assets

	Assets (trillion yen)		
	31.03.92	31.03.93	31.03.2000 (projection)
Pensions			
Public pensions			
Welfare pension insurance	84.0	–	138.4
National pension	4.4	–	12.0
Mutual aid societies			
Government Officials Mutual Benefit Association	6.1	–	44.6
Local Officials Mutual Benefit Associations	22.2	–	44.6
Private School Teachers Mutual Benefit Associations	1.9	–	44.6
Mutual Benefit Associations of Employees of Agricultural, Forestry, and Fisheries Organisations	1.6	–	44.6
Subtotal (A)	120.2	(estimate) 128.0	195.0
Private pensions			
Business annuities			
Welfare annuity funds	28.3	32.2	69.5
Eligible retirement pensions	14.4	15.0	33.7
Non-eligible retirement pensions	(42.7)	(47.2)	(103.2)
(including pension insurance of the contribution type)	12.2	13.9	30.0
Note: Only those managed by life issuance companies			
Subtotal (B)	54.9	61.1	133.2
Total (A) + (B)	174.9	(estimate) 190.0	328.2

Table 13.1 *Continued*

	Assets (trillion yen)		
	31.03.92	31.03.93	31.03.2000 (projection)
National pension fund	(¥100m)	(¥100m)	
Trust banks	168	622	–
Life insurance companies (including those of the National Federation)	319	953	–
Subtotal	487	1,575	–
Private pensions[1]	(¥100m)	(¥100m)	
Private pension insurance (life insurance cos)[2]	97,471	110,945	–
Postal annuity (postal offices)[2]	(estimate) 1,100	(estimate) 1,500	–
Annuity mutual aid (agricultural co-operatives)	9,833	–	–
Annuity mutual aid (life co-operatives)	2,212	–	–
Casualty insurance of instalment annuity (property and casualty insurance companies)	–	–	–
Individual pension trust ('My Route', trust banks)	658	–	–
Asset formation annuity savings (handled by all financial institutions)	34,637	36,678	
Subtotal[3]	¥14–15tr	¥15–16tr	–

Notes: **1** The balances of private pensions represent liability reserves in the case of private pension insurance, estimates in the case of postal annuity, reported amount of annuity mutual aid associations and asset formation pensions.
2 At 31 March 1992, life insurance companies had a balance of ¥65.33 trillion, and postal annuity ¥760.1 billion.
3 The subtotal includes estimated balance of pension mutual benefit associations whose data are not available.
Source: Nomura Research Institute.

from the current 14.5 per cent to 30 per cent in 2020, and even if it starts paying them at age 65 as currently proposed, the ratio will rise to 27.7 per cent.

As the outlook for the public pension funds is quite bleak, expectations for private pension funds to bolster the nation's sagging pension system have mounted. True, corporate pension funds are expected to grow rapidly in coming years (Table 13.1). The problem is, their investment performance has not always been good (Table 13.2). Of course, the depressed stock market is largely to blame for their poor performance. However, compared with US pension funds, their manoeuvring elbow room is far more limited on account of the tight regulation imposed on them. More specifically, (1) there are too

Table 13.2 Returns on pension assets (%)

Fiscal year	1984	1985	1986	1987	1988	1989	1990	1991	1992	1993
Trust banks	9.50	9.54	10.18	9.65	8.58	6.93	6.45	5.38	3.36	–
(only pension trusts)	–	12.98	12.72	4.52	7.62	1.26	1.12	−0.49	5.06	–
Life insurance companies	8.97	8.95	9.11	8.86	8.52	8.53	7.60	6.31	5.48	–
Total	9.32	9.33	9.83	9.39	8.56	7.46	6.85	5.71	4.16	–
NRI-BPI	7.60	13.70	9.97	3.86	2.85	−4.19	8.56	−6.51	2.85	−4.19
NRI-400	14.60	29.60	51.10	14.00	16.60	−14.60	−8.70	−26.60	4.30	10.60

Notes: **1** NRI-BPI represents the market's average rate of return on bonds, and NRI-400 that on stocks.
    2 Figures for life insurance companies represent the rate of return of general account.
Source: Compiled by Nomura Research Institute on the basis of data drawn from the Welfare Pension Fund.

few kinds of investment vehicles for Japanese pension funds to choose from; (2) only a limited number of asset management companies are authorised to administer their trusted funds; and (3) the administration of trusted funds by trustee companies is uniformly regulated. Indeed, it must be said that improvement of the management system of pension funds is the highest priority for the pension system of Japan.

INTERNATIONAL COMPETITIVE POSITION

In the 1980s when an economic bubble was in the making, the Tokyo market was counted as one of the world's largest money centres along with New York and London. As the years wore on into the 1990s, however, its image as an unwieldy market has come to stand out. For all the huge surplus savings it has on call, the Tokyo market has proved incapable of tapping them to the good. On the contrary, it has failed to attract foreign demand for Japanese funds, one foreign firm after another has pulled up stakes by delisting their stocks from the Tokyo Stock Exchange, and even Japanese firms are taking their capital transactions to foreign markets.

Factors hampering the growth of the Tokyo market are the high trading costs, the inconsistency of its rules of trading with those of other markets which are being increasingly standardised across the world, the lack of transparency of regulations, and the lack of diversity of investment vehicles. Even more important, despite the growing intensity of competition for business among the players of the Western and other markets, those of the Tokyo market are not sufficiently aware of the necessity for competition, and the lack of initiatives on the part of the regulators or intermediaries to improve the situation. Market participants may feel that they can cope with the changing situation of the world markets by internationalising their operations on their own – sell their debts on the Euro market and trade in Japanese shares through the Securities Exchange Automated Quotations International (SEAQI) of London – but venture businesses and individual investors have no access to such international markets. When seen from the perspectives of market intermediaries who operate in an uncompetitive domestic market, it is extremely doubtful that they can compete on the world markets with their counterparts of highly competitive markets which are armed with an array of innovative new products.

REORGANISATION OF THE FINANCIAL SERVICE INDUSTRY

The aftermath of the economic bubble continues to plague the financial service industry in the form of soured asset portfolios and an increase in overheads caused by a sharp decrease in business. Worse yet, there is no sign of the bleak market environment improving any time soon. According to a survey of the securities market conducted by Japan Securities Dealers Association in June 1994, for example, the stock price index and the value of stock market turnover will still hover around 85 per cent and 70 per cent, respectively, of the peak reached at the end of the economic bubble, as late as the year 2000 (Table 13.3). Weighed down with the capital investment made to cope with a market scale swollen by the speculative bubble, many securities companies saw their break-even point rise sharply, making them prone to running deficits.

Already, one medium-standing securities company and one trust bank, no longer able to meet obligations on their own, have become subsidiaries of city banks. In addition, some of the credit associations have been merged, and the funds of the deposit insurance agency had to be used to bail out others. So far, these mergers have been treated as special cases outside the new policy of reciprocal entry of one another's market, and no new restrictions have been imposed on the business activities of these acquired subsidiaries. However, similar problems are likely to crop up down the road, making reorganisation of the financial service industry inevitable.

For all the reform efforts and despite cries for an immediate attention to these problems, no visible moves for their resolution have been taken, at least not for now. One cannot escape the feeling that the gradualist approach to the financial system reforms now on

265

Table 13.3 Market scales (in trillion yen, yen, and companies)

Fiscal year	1991	1992	1993	1995 (proj.)	2000 (proj.)	1995/ 93	2000/ 93
1 Equity financing (excluding banks and insurance companies)							
Total	6.3	2.6	5.0	4.4	10.5	0.9	2.1
Of which, domestic	2.0	0.7	2.3	2.4	7.7	1.0	3.7
Issuance of paid-for shares	0.3	0.1	0.3	0.7	3.6	3.0	14.5
Overseas	4.3	1.9	2.7	2.0	2.7	0.7	1.0
2 Stock market							
Market capitalisation of the First Section of the TSE	303.7	308.0	340.6	407.2	604.1	1.2	1.8
Turnover	84.2	60.8	93.6	146.2	233.2	1.4	2.3
The Nikkei average	23,380	17,183	19,640	22,469	33,339	1.1	1.7
Market capitalisation of the OTC market	10.4	9.3	13.7	20.2	39.7	1.5	2.9
Turnover	4.6	1.1	3.7	5.5	13.2	1.5	3.6
No. of companies registered	429	438	489	634	1,026	1.3	2.1
3 Domestic bond market							
Total value of bonds issued	99.4	114.8	117.2	128.9	150.0	1.1	1.3
Of which, government securities	37.3	46.1	54.8	58.0	56.1	1.1	1.0
Straight corporate bonds	4.1	4.7	3.4	4.0	12.8	1.2	3.8
CB, bonds with warrants	1.7	0.6	2.0	1.7	4.1	0.9	2.1
Total turnover	2,634.2	3,281.6	3,286.0	3,950.0	5,960.0	1.2	1.8
Of which, government securities	2,481.8	3,112.8	3,101.7	3,680.0	5,360.0	1.2	1.7
4 Investment trusts and derivatives							
Investment trusts launched	17.8	35.1	55.6	60.8	91.4	1.1	1.6
Of which, stock investment trusts	8.5	7.8	13.7	13.9	20.9	1.0	1.5

Table 13.3 *Continued*

Fiscal year	1991	1992	1993	1995 (proj.)	2000 (proj.)	1995/ 93	2000/ 93
Outstanding balance of principals of investment trusts	45.6	49.6	50.5	64.7	113.5	1.3	2.2
Of which, that of stock investment trusts	32.4	26.8	24.0	26.5	45.4	1.1	1.9
Turnover of stock futures	482.2	205.3	192.5	350.9	443.1	1.8	2.3
Turnover of options	280.5	147.7	117.3	204.7	279.8	1.7	2.4

Notes: 1 The Nikkei average represents the year's average for the Nikkei 225 index.
2 The value of bonds issues represents the total of bonds publicly offered and privately placed.
3 The turnover of bonds is based on their par value, and represents two way trading effected on the OTC market of Tokyo and the nation's eight stock exchanges.
4 Figures for stock futures and options represent the total of TOPIX, Nikkei 225 stock average, Nikkei 300 stock average and Option 25.
Source: Japan Securities Dealers Association.

the official agenda may prove ineffective for curing the ills now plaguing the financial markets of Japan.

Remaining tasks

If the gradualist approach reaches a dead end, Japan will face at a certain point down the road the necessity for making a sweeping overhaul (a Japanese version of Big Bang), and in fashioning such an overhaul, policymakers must keep the following points in mind.

First, they have to create a framework explicitly based on the principle of *caveat emptor*, self-responsibility (investors are responsible for their own investment decisions). The rule of payout ratio requiring firms to pay dividends at or above a certain level for a certain number of years in order to qualify for issuing equity-linked debt securities, and the regulation of the management of assets by life insurance companies and private pension funds (restricting their investment in stocks to 30 per cent of their assets) tend to encourage the feeling among fund managers that they have fulfilled their duties when they meet these requirements. Under the framework of unrestrained management, managers have to make every decision on their own, and this freedom leads to diversity of their investment activities. The restrictive policies, such as the three year-long suspension of issuance of new shares at market price and the insistence on the eligibility standards for issuing corporate bonds, are incongruous with the idea of letting investors make investment decisions on their own and at their risk under an appropriate disclosure system. And such regulations which have outlived their relevance to changed reality should be abolished resolutely.

The second point is the tax system. As the experience the market has had with commercial paper and repurchases of one's own outstanding shares by corporations demonstrates, taxes have impeded the development of these markets. Especially, the lack of development of new financial products is blamed on the hindrance posed by the tax system. The securities transaction tax has proved to be a serious hurdle hampering the growth in bond trading and the development of the money market which is essential for the growth of the Tokyo market as an international financial centre. A comprehensive overhaul of the tax system including taxes on dividends and capital gains has to be undertaken in earnest.

THE IMPORTANCE OF DISCIPLINED INVESTORS

The problems are so complex and wide-ranging that they defy simple solutions. But one policy that is particularly in need of rethinking is that for the protection of investors based on the assumption of an ignorant investor which has cut across the post-war framework of the financial system.

In order for the market to function effectively not just in theory but in practice, selective choice of securities by investors with varying investment objectives is essential. If the regulators seek an easy way out by holding the players of the market on a tight leash, oblivious to the stifling effect of the uniform rule for investor protection, they will court moral hazards by denying the investors the opportunity to develop a sense of responsibility for their own investment decisions and by robbing securities issuers of incentives for developing new and innovative financial products.

For example, Fig. 13.1 compares the relationship between return on equity (ROE) and price/book value ratios (PBR) of large corporations of Japan with that of their US counterparts. While there is a positive relationship between projected ROE and projected PBR of US firms (projection by Value Line), no such relationship can be

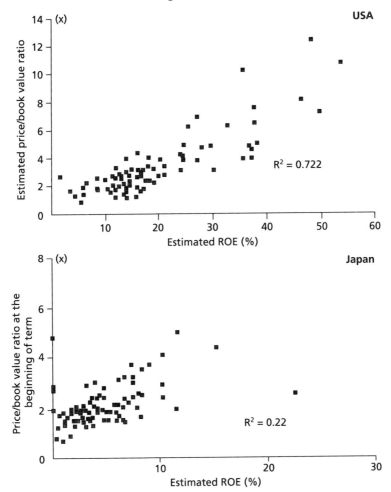

13.1 Return on equity and share price valuation (source: Nomura Research Institute).
Notes: 1) US data for 87 companies selected from Fortune 100 (excluding unlisted companies and other special situations), estimates are from Value Line.
2) Japanese data for 91 companies selected from 100 companies with the largest annual sales in the NRI 400 (excluding special situations), estimates from Toyo Keizai, *Japan Company Handbook*. Stock prices are closing prices on 19 November 1993.

observed in the case of Japanese stocks. While it is important for business corporations to increase their returns on equity, as long as improved returns on equity are reflected in the market prices of their stocks, they do not offer incentives to their managers.

In Japan, also, institutional investors have increasingly become dominant in the market, but their market dominance has been undermined by the spread of cross-shareholding through which large chunks of shares have been locked away from the market. In the next section, we will weigh various options necessary to encourage active participation of the investing public in the stock market.

POLICY MEASURES TO BE TAKEN

Institutional investors

To look askance at institutional domination is barking up the wrong tree. The presence of institutional investors will grow stronger, not weaker, as the financial markets become more sophisticated. It is desirable to have institutional investors play the same important role in Japan as in other developed countries, and the following measures should be taken.

An increase in the number of institutional investors
The number of institutional investors in operation in Japan is too small: 16 trust banks, 27 life insurance companies, and 19 investment trusts. There are 308 investment advisory service companies, but only a handful of them really count in terms of the scale of their operations and impacts. Only trust banks and life insurance companies are authorised to handle 'old money' (funds pooled before the pension system shifted to one based on contributions), and their number is too small to provide diversity in the methods of investment management. Investment trust management companies established as subsidiaries of investment advisory service companies are scheduled to participate in the market, but broader based participation of specialised companies should be encouraged.

Clarification of fiduciary duties
Generally, trustees owe fiduciary duties to trustors, but when an institutional investor uses its investment service for its own gain, the possibility of a conflict of interest cannot be completely ruled out. In the United Kingdom, which authored the concept of trust, the idea of enacting a pension law is being debated in reaction to a misappropriation of corporate pension funds by Robert Maxwell which came to light in 1991.

Fortunately, no such scandalous irregularities have happened in Japan. However, in order to ensure that institutional investors are restricted to pure investment (exclusive of relationship-oriented investment), Japan will have to enact the like of the Employee Retirement Income Security Act (ERISA) of the United States.

If such statutory rules are enforced, the existing individual rules which uniformly regulate the acquisition of various types of securities should be abolished. (While certain rules may be necessary to ensure the safety of the financial system, there is no need for doubly regulating the operation of the trustees of pension funds, namely, life insurance companies and trust banks.) More specifically, it is desirable to enforce certain regulations designed to reduce the risks for portfolios as a whole as does the Prudent-Man Rule adopted by some US states in order to encourage trustee institutions to exercise innovative and selective discretion as professional investors.

Establishment of performance evaluation agencies

It is necessary to make full and timely information concerning the business performance, not only of securities issuers but also of institutional investors, available to the investing public, and for this purpose, there must be some third party institutions similar to credit rating agencies whose duty it is to analyse and evaluate their business performance according to scientific methods.

Corporate investors

During the bubble years, many business corporations dabbled in securities investment after the fashion of institutional investors as part of their financial engineering. However, when stock prices dropped and remain depressed, their activities of this kind have died down. What the shareholders want their companies to do is invest their resources not in financial products but in capital goods and inventories, and corporate governance will not tolerate too long such deviation from their core business.

The remaining task to be addressed is the acquisition of shares of other companies in a cross-shareholding arrangement which is motivated by designs that have nothing to do with improving their core business.

This is not to say that the participation of corporate investors in the securities market with different motives should be rejected. However, the practice of cross-shareholding which deviates from the original mandate as a business corporation should be checked. Instead, they should be encouraged to issue preferred stocks and the obstacles (mainly taxes) regarding the repurchase of their own outstanding shares should be lifted.

Private investors

Along with criticisms against institutional domination of the market, demand for fostering active participation of private investors in the securities market has been vocal, more particularly, for lowering the trading unit (stock split and repackaging trading unit), a revision of the dividend policy, the abolition of double taxation on dividends, the strengthening of investor relations, and a fuller and more timely disclosure of corporate information.

In response, the comprehensive fiscal stimulus package announced by the government in August 1992 called for the promotion of the development of stock investment trusts suitable for long term holding, flexibility of the operation of employee stock ownership plans to spur their further growth, the lowering of stock investment units, the encouragement of cumulative stock investment system, tax exemption of investment trusts acquired by workers for asset formation purposes, and an increase in the payout ratios of publicly traded companies. Of these, LLF (for Long Life Fund) (trust period seven years, and non-distribution period four years) and the cumulative stock investment plans have already been introduced. While these measures represent a big step towards reform, many of the proposed measures for fostering private investors tend to be technical tokenism.

What is needed is a change in underlying systems. As it is difficult to educate private investors in investment techniques and provide the necessary market infrastructure in a short period, their indirect participation in the securities market through institutional investors of their choice, while acquiescing in the policy for the protection of investors pursued under the assumption that the investor is ignorant, should not be barred. However, it is important to take measures not to put private investors wishing to participate directly in the market at a disadvantage.

Conclusions

Steps must be taken to encourage investors to develop the ability to make informed and selective choice of investments at their own risk, and at the same time, it is necessary for other participant groups to spur them along such a line.

To start with, securities companies must change their approach to investors in such a way as to encourage them to make discriminating choice of investments. More specifically, securities companies must exercise due care to offer investments that are most suited to achieving the investment objectives of their customers and match their resources available for such investment.

The same is true of the rules adopted by self-regulatory organisations and regulators. In describing the Tokyo market, foreign market watchers often use the words 'rig' and 'manipulate'. What these words imply is the repugnance for deliberate distortion of the market mechanism. To ensure unhindered functioning of the market, there is no alternative to overhauling the market system itself.

The key to achieving a real reform of the system lies in accepting diversity. By its very nature, diversity of choice – diversity of investment motives, investment periods, and expectations – is an assurance of the formation of efficient and fair prices. When seen in this light, the lack of diversity of choice and uniformity in Japan's financial market has long reigned over investment behaviour. In order for the financial markets of Japan to become active internationally, allowing their participants diversity of choice is of critical importance.

In this context, the accord between the United States and Japan in January 1995 may become another milestone, like the recommendations by the Yen/Dollar Committee in 1984, for the reform of the Japanese financial markets. It aims to open up the asset management business in Japan and raise the level of transparency in policy formation. But its impact is yet to be seen.

Index